New forms of work organisation

New forms
of work organisation
1

Denmark, Norway and Sweden
France
Federal Republic of Germany
United Kingdom
United States

International Labour Office   Geneva

ISBN 92-2-101991-8 (limp cover)
ISBN 92-2-102005-3 (hard cover)

First published 1979

Printed by Icobulle, 1630 Bulle, Switzerland

79 006586

PREFACE

The creation of jobs that correspond to human needs and aspirations is a complex task, but one that must be faced in the modern world as an increasingly educated and younger workforce demands better jobs. Good jobs have many features, including adequate pay, job security, and a safe, healthy and pleasant working environment. Some aspects of such jobs also relate to the content of the work itself: they allow self-expression, learning and communication; they involve the workers in the definition of their work; and they offer a good future. These characteristics of good jobs are closely related to the way in which work is organised. Long a management prerogative, directed essentially by concern for efficiency, the organisation of work is now perceived in many quarters as offering significant opportunities for making work more human as well as more productive. On the basis of a variety of experiences in different countries, a consensus has emerged that more emphasis should be placed on the organisation of work as a key aspect of working conditions.

Over the past few years, numerous experiments have been made with new forms of work organisation, in some cases to test or apply the results of experience already acquired in that field. The experiments have confirmed that scientific and technical methodology is now so sophisticated and diversified that any particular goods or services can be produced in a variety of ways. Numerous publications bear witness to the relevance and range of these experiments and the feasibility of applying new methods of work organisation at most stages of production. To evaluate the results of these experiments, as well as their cost and benefits for employers and workers and their repercussions on conditions of work, a systematic study of new forms of work organisation was included in the programme of the International Labour Office for 1976-77. The study was carried out in three stages:

(a) an analysis of national experience on the basis of a common research design adopted at the outset;[1]

(b) the subsequent preparation of a series of national monographs along the lines suggested in the research design, plus a general assessment of the economic costs and benefits of work re-structuring; and

(c) a comparative study giving an over-all view of the findings and conclusions of the national monographs, supplemented by guidelines for the comparative analysis of national experience with regard to new forms of work organisation.

The work undertaken on this project fits naturally into the programme of the International Labour Organisation which, since its founding in 1919, has had a direct interest in making work more human. In 1976 it launched the International Programme for the Improvement of Working Conditions and Environment (PIACT) with the goal of reinvigorating its activities in this field.[2] Under this new programme, the organisation of work is a key area of research and action.

Previous work undertaken by the ILO is relevant to the present project. For example, a symposium on workers' participation in decisions within undertakings, held in Oslo in 1974, considered in some detail the question of workers' participation in the organisation of their work at the shop-floor level.[3] A major study and seminar on the effects of group production methods on the humanisation of work were carried out in co-operation with the International Centre for Advanced Technical and Vocational Training.[4] The *International Labour Review* has published a series of articles related to the organisation of work, covering technical analyses, case studies, national policies and institutional frameworks and the views of trade unions.[5]

Thus the publication of this volume is the latest development in a recent series of activities launched by the International Labour Office with regard to improvements in the organisation of work. In this field the Office has been actively assisted under sub-contract by the International Institute for Labour Studies. First, the Institute has prepared an annotated bibliography which covers material that has been published on the topic in many countries.[6] Concurrently, the Office and the Institute commissioned the series of national monographs of which the present volume contains the first instalment. They relate to Denmark, Norway and Sweden, France, the Federal Republic of Germany, the United Kingdom and the United States. The second volume is to contain the papers concerning Italy, the German Democratic Republic, the USSR and India, together with a study of the economic costs and benefits of the new forms of work organisation. Most of the papers describe the situation as it was towards the end of 1976, though the introductory sections on national conditions have been to some extent updated.

This work has laid the foundation for future ILO activities concerning work organisation and job content. These activities include a closer study of specific problems of work organisation as it affects different sectors of the economy, and the preparation of material to encourage the adoption and effective use of better forms of work organisation. In this connection, increasing attention will be paid to the effects of automation, and to how it could improve jobs. Within the framework of the PIACT programme, it is proposed to make the International Labour Office a clearing-house of information on the quality of working life. The Office hopes in particular to promote the use of a carefully developed universal model for case studies on new forms of work organisation, and to make available the resulting studies.

This project is still in its preliminary stage. In accordance with the plan outlined above, the Office is now publishing two volumes of national monographs before carrying out the comparative study.

It will be seen that some of the papers have been prepared by independent research workers, and others by specialists attached to official bodies. Although a common outline was developed before the monographs were written, they are very different indeed not only in their arrangement but in their treatment of the subject of the organisation of work and its relationship to national political, social and economic institutions. The views put forward may be challenged, from different points of view, in government, business, union or academic circles. Without necessarily endorsing the opinions expressed in the monographs, the Office has deemed it worth-while to publish these papers in order to show how different research workers and specialists attached to official bodies see the subject in different countries.

There is much to be learnt about new forms of work organisation from the national monographs presented in this volume: the trend toward increased adoption in different contexts, the difficulties and complexities involved, the potential for success, and also the considerable differences in national approaches and experience. It is hoped that this information, together with the other activities described above, will contribute to the growing endeavour in many countries to improve working life.

Notes

[1] The design was prepared by a consultant, Mr. Henri Douard, of the Institut d'études et de développement "Entreprise et Personnel" (Paris).

[2] See Jean de Givry: "The ILO and the quality of working life: A new international programme: PIACT", in *International Labour Review* (Geneva, ILO), May-June 1978, pp. 261-271.

[3] ILO: *Workers' participation in decisions within undertakings,* Summary of discussions of a symposium on workers' participation in decisions within undertakings (Oslo, 20-30 August 1974), Labour-Management Relations Series, No. 48 (Geneva, 1976).

[4] J. L. Burbidge: *Final report on a study of the effects of group production methods on the humanisation of work,* . . . prepared at the completion of a study executed under contract to the International Labour Office by the International Centre for Advanced Technical and Vocational Training (Turin, International Centre for Advanced Technical and Vocational Training, 1975); and J. L. Burbidge (ed.): *Proceedings.* Seminar on the effects of group production methods on the humanisation of work (Turin, International Centre for Advanced Technical and Vocational Training, 1976).

[5] The following articles are included in this series:
Bluestone, I. "Creating a new world of work", Jan.-Feb. 1977, pp. 1-10.
Carpentier, J. "Organisational techniques and the humanisation of work", Aug. 1974, pp. 93-116.
Davis, L. E. "Enhancing the quality of working life: Developments in the United States", July-Aug. 1977, pp. 53-65.
Delamotte, Y. "Working conditions and government policy: Some western European approaches", Sep.-Oct. 1976, pp. 139-154.
Engelen-Kefer, U. "Humanisation of work in the Federal Republic of Germany: A labour-oriented approach", Mar.-Apr. 1976, pp. 227-241.
Gustavsen, B. "A legislative approach to job reform in Norway", May-June 1977, pp. 263-276.
Johnston, R. "Pay and job satisfaction: A survey of some research findings", May 1975, pp. 441-449.

Roustang, G. "Why study working conditions via job satisfaction? A plea for direct analysis", May-June 1977, pp. 277-291.

Tchobanian, R. "Trade unions and the humanisation of work", Mar. 1975, pp. 199-217.

Thurman, J. E. "Job satisfaction: An international overview", Nov.-Dec. 1977, pp. 249-267.

Wnuk-Lipiński, E. "Job satisfaction and the quality of working life: The Polish experience", Jan.-Feb. 1977, pp. 53-64.

Yoshida, K. and Torihara, M. "Redesigning jobs for a better quality of working life: The case of the Tokyo Gas Co.", Sep.-Oct. 1977, pp. 139-151.

[6] See ILO: *Bibliography on major aspects of the humanisation of work and the quality of working life* (Geneva, 2nd ed., 1978).

CONTENTS

INTRODUCTION

Most of this introduction is devoted to outlining the main trends in work organisation since the beginning of the century. It should be noted that work organisation is not the only factor that distinguishes an economic undertaking; in other words, the emphasis on work organisation in these pages and in the study as a whole does not imply that there is not multiple interaction between organisation, technology, economic efficiency, human factors, conditions of work and the social and cultural setting. All these factors are either implicitly or explicitly taken into account in this volume even though organisation problems constitute the focus of inquiry.

SCIENTIFIC MANAGEMENT

An understanding of new forms of work organisation presupposes an identification of traditional or earlier forms. The traditional form of organisation of work since the beginnings of industrialisation has been known as "scientific management" from the title of a book by F. W. Taylor (and hence also as "Taylorism"). Its most distinctive feature is a clear-cut distinction between the planning (and organisation) of tasks and their execution; this reflects the fact that at the time there seemed to be very few people in industry who could have performed both functions well and simultaneously. Specialisation is another essential principle connected with the complex organisation of production. Under this system the "atomisation" that might otherwise result is warded off by the existence of a large management staff at various levels. At the lowest operative level, specialisation leads to the fragmentation of tasks and of the craft skills on which production formerly depended. Another major element of the system—of which it is in fact both a cause and a result—is the principle of measurement and norms: the individual worker is hemmed in by quantitative accounting of the unit times required for task performance, which further accentuates the characteristics of the system.

The economic and productive goals of scientific management are quite well known. However, it may be worth identifying the psychological assumptions on which it rests. In the nineteenth century scientific management was justified by a certain conception of the worker and of working-class psychology. At that time few skilled workers were employed in factories. Most of the craftsmen were opposed to mass production, and their power was undermined by recruiting workers with more rudimentary aspirations who had often been forced to leave the land. In brief, under this system the operative is regarded as a person of a very low intellectual and educational level, a waster with an innate tendency towards low output, needing regular pacing to overcome habitual apathy, and requiring close supervision, but capable of positive motivation through payment by results. The development of motivational research makes it easier to understand now why such an obviously crude conception was not altogether fanciful and enabled industry to operate without major mishaps.

On the economic plane, scientific management can be given credit for bringing about a sizeable increase in productive efficiency. From the First World War to well after the Second, work organisation was marked by measurement, by efficiency engineering, by a tremendous effort to cut down waste, reduce stocks and simplify layout, by time and motion study and by a careful study of work and process flow and of balanced flow-line production. Although there is now a tendency to give the individual worker more leeway, it is generally held that such measures as careful preparation, evaluation, rationalisation, and a concern for savings at all levels are of permanent value in keeping costs down and reducing waste.

HUMAN RELATIONS

The psychological profile attributed to the typical worker under the scientific management system soon gave rise to organised resistance, and the need to develop human relations appeared as a corrective to the Taylorian image of a human robot. The "human relations" school emerged after the First World War and grew by leaps and bounds in the 1930s and 1940s. It fought for recognition of man's emotional needs, a denial of which in fact opens the door to breakdowns in the productive process. In employment it is possible to identify a need—

(a) for communication and self-expression, which are largely eliminated by the assembly line and all other fragmented production systems;

(b) for some degree of security (occupational safety and job security); and

(c) for recognition.

Industry then developed sensitivity training programmes in human relations for management, but without restricting the pursuance of scientific management, which was still regarded as the only method really applicable in the industrial field.

SOCIO-TECHNICAL SYSTEMS

New developments have succeeded each other at a rapid pace over the past 15 years or so and have led to the introduction of new forms of organisation. Whereas hitherto the advocates of higher productivity and of the workers' interests had been thinking along lines that never met, they now began to stress common needs. Management has reviewed the situation and come to the conclusion that the major problem is not merely how to maintain or increase output but how to ensure rapid adaptation of the production system to changes in market demand. Traditional forms of work organisation cannot keep up with rapid change. For example, fragmentation of tasks in the interests of efficiency has sometimes turned out to be very expensive when allowance is made for breaks in the work flow which occur even in the best balanced production system. Even a minor divergence from quality or quantity targets affects the outcome, and final cost estimates rarely cover the cost of remedial action. The third and most decisive finding relates to the workforce. The workers are now better protected than they used to be from unemployment, and are often called upon to perform particular tasks that do not correspond to their level of education. Under the influence also of the society in which they live, they lose their devotion to work; in fact in many branches of industry the work they are asked to do no longer makes sense to them at all. Many sectors of management then plead for new forms of work organisation, and it is with their support that social scientists have succeeded in imposing the theory of socio-technical systems, i.e. the notion that any form of work organisation should be based on adjustment between the workers' needs as social beings and the technique of production used, both of these interacting factors being also subject to independent variation. It can be held that progress is always achieved by bringing together factors that had previously been viewed in isolation; and thus the systematic establishment of a connection between the operations workers perform and their psychology marks a step forward in our knowledge of man at work. Humane, moral or psychological considerations on their own had been powerless to achieve a humanisation of work that is now regarded as essential in view of economic requirements and in order to avoid the penalty of a withdrawal of labour.

As already stated, this is only one of a number of approaches. It can be safely said, however, that without it automation, progress made in adapting machines to the operators' requirements, occupational safety and new systems of hours of work fail to ensure that the workers will be not merely on the job but playing their part to the full.

The new forms of organisation are based on a new conception of man at work. In this connection five characteristics of new forms of work organisation can be distinguished:

(1) They recognise that there is a close link between human nature and human work, and interaction between the development of individuals and the development of their work. The aspiration to learn new skills and put them to use is not just an effect of education and training but a direct result of undertaking work at all. Work without initiative destroys initiative, and initiative will be fatal if the work does not provide for it. Workers must therefore be provided with work of increasing complexity as and when they look for it.

(2) New forms of work organisation are centred on informal groups that grow up spontaneously. On close observation, it will be found that a formal organisation of work in accordance with the requirements of scientific management

co-exists with an informal organisation that gives expression to human needs and thanks to which the system works. The work is better suited to the worker, and vice-versa, if the patterns of formal and informal co-operation coincide, but that cannot always be ensured.

(3) It is recognised that the worker's personality and the worker's job should each form a coherent whole. To segment the worker's role by task fragmentation and extreme specialisation is to forget that the individual's personality is and must be a coherent whole, and that the individual cannot show initiative and assume responsibility where tasks are artificially fragmented. This is an argument for consolidated job assignments providing opportunities to perform a variety of functions at various levels.

(4) It is recognised that commitment to work requires a knowledge of its results ("feedback"). Scientific management deprives the workers of the possibility of identifying a product as theirs since they do not know exactly where their work leads and precisely what its results will be. The continual lack of fulfilment in fragmented tasks leads to fatigue and a variety of disorders. Feedback should therefore be ensured by including control tasks in the job. Man has a natural urge to complete a job, as is evident from the pathological states that arise when it cannot be done.

(5) It is necessary to meet the requirements of sociability. As social beings, men and women need to function in a "peer group". If they are too much on their own or too strictly supervised, it is more difficult for them to express themselves or exercise self-control. Work in groups is most conducive to high output.

THE ORGANISATIONAL AND SOCIAL ENVIRONMENT

A number of other aspects of the worker's organisational and social environment are also very relevant to new forms of work organisation.

First, such new arrangements affect jobs at all levels of the undertaking. Many changes apply not only to operatives but also to craftsmen, technicians and supervisors. For senior and middle management, the changes take the form of delegation of authority, decentralisation, and management by objectives. Any reorganisation bears most heavily on foremen, on supervisors, and on technicians with similar functions connected with process work, maintenance or monitoring. Their responsibilities are transferred to workers at a lower level, and half the difficulties of reorganisation are due to this deprivation of previous supervisory roles. An attempt is generally made to create new supervisory and technical posts either with new training functions or with highly specialised technical assignments.

Secondly, there is a definite and very obvious link between new forms of work organisation and the development of technology. Job content cannot be the same in the petrochemical industry, in the mass production of cars and in aircraft manufacture with its small production runs. However, it would be a mistake to claim that technology rigidly determines the form of work organisation; in fact no such claim was put forward even in the days when the traditional organisation of work in industry was accepted as a matter of course. The possible disappearance of assembly lines today clinches the argument. The novelty in the new approach lies above all in the fact that the desirable forms of work organisation are now borne in mind at a very early stage, when equipment and plant are being designed. Automation is a case in point. The design of machines and their inter-relation are now influenced by ergonomics and a desire to eliminate tedious or wearisome tasks and ensure a layout that will be meaningful for the team or individual on the job. Current thinking about electronic data-processing equipment reflects these concerns.

There are also repercussions on industrial relations, which are the subject of much investigation. The national monographs show quite clearly that at first the trade unions giving priority to the traditional aims of better working conditions opposed the introduction of new forms of work organisation suggested by management and social scientists. Without denying that the new arrangements may lead to some objective improvements provided that they are not accompanied by a deliberate and marked increase in workload, the unions nevertheless often denounce such solutions as constituting a manipulation of labour opinion with a view to winning the workers over to the management point of view.

Thus the details of work organisation are less important than the way changes are introduced, and above all whether the workers themselves can play a part in their introduction. The direct participation of the workers in the process of change is a fundamental question that is continually being raised in collective bargaining. This is a major issue. Change itself is the underlying theme of this study. It may be desired or sometimes rejected by management; because of the difficulties to which it gives rise, it will sometimes be rejected by the workers concerned and their representatives; and it raises all sorts of problems of method on which light needs to be shed.

METHODS

The foregoing is a brief survey of major trends. As will be seen from the national monographs in this volume, those trends can be reflected or expressed through a variety of concepts such as job enlargement, which may be "horizontal" (variety of tasks) or "vertical" (degree to which job holders control the planning and execution of their job and participate in the setting of organisation policies); or job enrichment, a form of job enlargement with emphasis on the "vertical" component. The changes often consist in the inclusion in a job of tasks previously located either upstream or downstream of that particular job in the flow of production. These new tasks, while directly connected with production proper, may relate to the preparation or ordering of supplies; monitoring the quantity and quality of output and making any necessary adjustments; the despatch of the finished product; some immediate maintenance work; and certain adjustments to the equipment. From another angle, it can be said that wherever possible, jobs are enlarged by merging tasks previously performed by different workers at neighbouring work stations. Thus a re-designed job may cover the production of an entire assembly or sub-assembly, and the job cycle time may increase from a few seconds or minutes to a quarter of an hour, half an hour or longer. For monitoring jobs in process industries, it is often not particularly difficult to add a variety of maintenance, adjustment, cleaning and administrative functions. In office work a job can be centred on the files or accounts of particular customers or groups of customers. Where no other possibilities exist, job rotation can permit the exercise of a variety of skills in different functions. Tasks can also be re-assigned to semi-autonomous groups of varying sizes (usually between 3 and 20 workers) whose members organise the work themselves. Group organisation, which has been the subject of much study and is referred to in some of the monographs, constitutes an interesting application of industrial psychology.

Some parts of the monographs themselves are perhaps best read in that light. It must be realised that there are no objective studies of this matter: some are sponsored by management, some by labour; and social scientists, when they approach the subject, are sometimes criticised for being obsessed with the alienation of the workers, for failing to take account of over-riding social and economic requirements and of the real strength of organised management and labour, and for being somewhat optimistic about the possibilities of reform. The authors of the national monographs were accordingly asked to draw facts and opinions from a wide variety of sources and to check the objectives and results of the field experiments to which they referred. It should be emphasised that the funds available for this work were not sufficient to finance special new experiments in the field, and that the authors consequently had to rely on examples of experiments that had already taken place and if possible been reported.

DENMARK, NORWAY AND SWEDEN

DENMARK, NORWAY AND SWEDEN

Peter Dundelach and Nils Mortensen*

In spite of the existence of a common framework of institutions for industrial democracy in the three Scandinavian countries dealt with in this paper—Denmark, Norway and Sweden—the extent and types of experiments with new forms of work organisation vary from country to country. A tentative explanation of the different character of experimentation in the three countries may be sought in the fact that there are important differences in their economic structure.

NATIONAL CONDITIONS

Pattern of industrialisation

The varying availability of natural resources in Denmark, Norway and Sweden had a marked influence on the start of industrialisation, the form it took and the rate at which it proceeded, as well as on the different economic structures that now exist in the countries in question. Apart from the soil, which provides the basis for agriculture and the production of certain goods for which earth and stone are the raw materials, Denmark has virtually no natural resources. Norway has huge water resources for hydro-electric energy, as well as some metallic minerals and timber, which are, however, more difficult to exploit than in Sweden because they are located in remote areas at higher altitudes. Sweden has large forests within easy reach for lumber, paper and pulp production, a rich supply of high quality ores, and some hydro-electric potential, although not to the same extent as Norway. Norway is very mountainous and has relatively little land that can be cultivated, whereas the southern and middle parts of Sweden contain extensive tracts of arable land. Table 1 shows that this difference in natural resources still plays a significant role.

* Institute of Political Science, University of Aarhus. This paper was written with the assistance of many people and institutions who provided much essential information. The authors wish to express their special thanks to the employers' associations, the confederations of trade unions and the co-operation boards in Denmark, Norway and Sweden; Mr. Truls Frogner, of the secretariat of the Nordic Council of Ministers, Oslo; Mr. Jan Balstad, of the Norwegian Iron and Metal Workers' Union; the Institute for Industrial Social Research, Technical University of Trondheim; the Work Research Institutes, Oslo; Mr. Per Sørensen, of the School of Economics and Business Administration, Aarhus; Mr. Alf Andersson, of the Ministry of Industry of Sweden; AB Volvo, Kalmarverken; and Mr. Niels Ole Vonsild, Plant Manager, Bang and Olufsen, Struer.

Table 1. Difference in utilisation of natural resources between Denmark, Norway and Sweden, 1974

Country	Arable land (100 ha.)	Production forests (100 ha.)	Production of iron ore ('000 tons)[1]	Percentage of energy consumption supplied by hydraulic power
Denmark	2 660	472	4	0.0
Norway	793	6 482	2 584	63.5
Sweden	3 026	23 473	22 071	32.3

[1] 1973.

Source: Nordic Council: *Yearbook of Nordic Statistics, 1975* (Stockholm, 1976).

A possible explanation for the late industrialisation of Norway and Sweden may be that it was made possible only by the technological advances that occurred around 1895 in the transmission of electric power, which permitted the large-scale utilisation of their water resources.[1] An additional explanation is that the iron ore deposits in northern Sweden are not easily accessible and could not be exploited without a well developed transport system.

In the early nineteenth century Denmark has reached quite a high level of economic development with rather well developed urban handicraft occupations, and had the highest standard of living in Scandinavia.[2] By comparison with the great importance of agriculture, industry was on a small scale, and produced mainly for the home market. The balance had none the less tipped towards industry by the end of the 1960s, as shown in table 2.

All things considered, Sweden seems to have had its most rapid early economic development, with the largest transformation in the distribution of the

Table 2. Economic development in Denmark, 1938-68

Item	1938	1958	1968
Percentage of the population[1] employed in—			
industry	25	26	24
agriculture	28	19	15
services	7	14	19
Percentage of gross national product provided by—			
industry	15	19	19
agriculture	17	14	7
public services	7	10	15
Percentage of exports provided by—			
industry	24	39	62
agriculture	71	50	27

[1] For the years 1940, 1960 and 1970.

Sources: Erik Ib Schmidt: *Dansk økonomisk politik. Tidens problemer og deres baggrund* (Copenhagen, Fremad, 1971), tables 2, 9; Danmarks Statistik, Statistik Tabelvaerk 1977: II, *Folke- og boligtaellingen 1970*, C. 3: Hele befolkningens erhvervsfordeling (Copenhagen, 1977).

labour force, between 1870 and 1915.[3] Already by 1910 some 32 per cent of the labour force was employed in manufacture and handicrafts (as compared with 28 per cent in Denmark and 25 per cent in Norway). Sweden was affected by the depression of the 1930s at a comparatively late date, and recovered quickly. The country's neutrality during the Second World War was a further favourable factor. The result was what has been described as the fastest and most balanced economic growth not merely in Scandinavia but in the whole capitalist West.[4] It is estimated that the Swedish income per head overtook the Danish around 1940.[5] Since 1960 Sweden has had a slightly slower economic growth than Norway and Denmark.

In Norway industrialisation started later than in Sweden. Between 1905 and 1920 wood products and chemicals for industrial and agricultural use (nitrogen, calcium carbide and saltpetre) were produced with the help of inexpensive domestic power resources and foreign capital. In the 1920s and the 1930s growth fluctuated much more in Norway than in Sweden. Norway was more affected by the Second World War than Denmark and, of course, Sweden. Since the war, however, Norway has had the fastest growth rate of the Scandinavian countries in terms of gross national product per head of population. Since the nineteenth century Norway has had a large merchant fleet, in contrast to those of Denmark and Sweden. As early as 1870, at a time when domestic transport was still undeveloped, 28 per cent of the economically active Norwegian population were employed in transport.[6] Another remarkable aspect of Norwegian industrialisation is the low degree of urbanisation. This is mainly due to the fact that most of the early Norwegian industries consisted of single-plant enterprises in isolated locations.

Table 3 shows that the degree of concentration in manufacturing is highest in Sweden and lowest in Norway. There are very few statistics on the subject of concentration of ownership. There is some evidence that the relative position of Norway and Denmark changes if one uses employment in the five largest concerns as a measure of concentration. In 1967-68 the five largest concerns had 198,400 workers in Sweden, 33,700 in Norway and 26,350 in Denmark,[7] which is approximately 32 per cent of the Swedish, 10 per cent of the Norwegian and 6 per cent of the Danish labour force in manufacturing industry (in establishments with over 10 workers employed). There are also other indications of the outstanding degree of economic concentration in Sweden. In 1970 the ten largest concerns in Sweden were responsible for a third of all Swedish exports, while in 1970 the ten largest Danish exporters accounted for only 15 per cent of Danish industrial exports.[8]

Social and political development

In Denmark, Norway and Sweden the late but rapid development of an industrial and post-industrial economy was accompanied by the emergence of modern parliamentary democracy and the Welfare State. There have been considerable improvements in the standard of living, the educational level of the population and other social indicators. On the other hand social and cultural ties have been dissolved and life has been segmented into separate spheres of work, education,

Table 3. Degree of concentration in the manufacturing industries in Denmark, Norway and Sweden, 1973

A. Distribution of establishments according to size of workforce

No. of workers	Percentage of establishments		
	Denmark	Norway	Sweden[1]
10 – 49	69	72	70
50 – 99	15	14	14
100 – 199	9	8	8
200 +	7	6	8
	100	100	100
No. of establishments	*5 547*	*5 259*	*7 590*

B. Distribution of manufacturing labour force according to size of establishments

Size of establishment (in terms of number of workers)	Percentage of labour force		
	Denmark	Norway	Sweden[1]
10 – 49	21	25	20
50 – 99	14	15	13
100 – 199	16	17	14
200 +	49	43	53
	100	100	100

[1] Groupings: 11 – 20, 21 – 50, etc.
Source: Nordic Council: *Yearbook of Nordic Statistics, 1975* (Stockholm), p. 101.

family and politics. The workers are in a dependent work situation, with little influence on their working conditions: for many workers in the industrial as well as in the services sector this often means highly routinised jobs with high health risks.

The frequently conflicting policies of capital and labour have not been reflected in political turbulence. Since about 1930 the three countries have mainly had Social Democratic governments—Sweden uninterruptedly from 1929 to 1976. This is in part due to the fact that the working class in each of the three countries is comparatively united in a single party and does not have the strong religious and ideological allegiances that have split the working class in many other European countries. The three social democratic parties have traditionally had some differences in outlook. In 1922 it was noted that of the labour movements in the three countries, the Norwegian was most radical and the Danish most moderate, the Swedish labour movement coming somewhere in between. An obvious sign of the radicalism of the Norwegian party is to be found in the fact that it was a member of the Comintern from 1919 to 1923. This could be explained by a very fast rate of industrialisation between 1905 and 1920,[9] but it is difficult to prove that industrialisation proceeded faster in Norway than in Sweden during the period in question.[10] The moderation shown by the Danish party can be explained by the small scale of industry in the early days of the labour movement, the dominance of skilled workers in the first unions and the rather late and slow coming of industrialisation in Denmark. In all three countries the Social Democratic Party and the unions, together with the co-operative societies, are regarded as three dependent elements in the labour movement. Thus there is a considerable integration between the Social Democratic Party and the unions. This integration is even formalised, since in Sweden and Norway the members of the federation of trade unions are collectively members of the Social Democratic Party. In Denmark there is an overlap in the membership of the executive of the federation and of the Party.

In all three countries the general political and economic interests of industry are mainly taken care of by the interest organisations—the employers' associations and the industry societies. Whereas the social democratic parties and the unions are integral parts of the labour movement, there is no such direct relationship between the employers and a political party. The liberal nature of the opposition to the social democratic parties in Denmark and Norway may be due to the small scale of Danish—and to a lesser extent Norwegian—industry, and to the preponderance of medium-sized farming, and in Norway of typical small-scale farming.

In recent decades the national employers' and workers' organisations have been increasingly involved in government and central administration: members of the organisations have increasingly become members of government committees, and the organisations are often deeply involved in most phases of the decision-making process. On the one hand the organisations try to influence labour market policy and general economic policy, and on the other hand the government and administration are dependent on the organisations for statistical and other information. The attempts to establish an incomes policy over the last decade have especially led to increasing co-operation between the organisations and the government and administration.

Recent economic and employment trends

The 1920s can be characterised as having been a period of economic liberalism in Scandinavia. The economic depression of the 1930s, however, brought so much regulation and government activity that the decade can be regarded as having marked the first phase of a planned economy.[11] The involvement of the State and the expansion of the public sector have increased considerably since the Second World War, after which labour market policy also became a matter of public concern. In Denmark, Norway and Sweden the greatest public influence on the economy is exerted through subsidised consumption for welfare purposes. Denmark has virtually no public production apart from public utilities. In Norway and Sweden the State has economic interests or ownership in a number of manufacturing companies and in mining. The amount of public production in Sweden rose from an estimated 15 per cent of total output in 1950 to 20-25 per cent in the early 1970s.[12] In Norway the rapid development of oil extraction in the 1970s probably involved an increase in public ownership too.

Employment problems in the three countries since the Second World War have included immigration, regional adjustment and unemployment. During the

1950s and 1960s Sweden had quite a high immigration rate. Immigration to Sweden between 1960 and 1969—more than half of which came from Finland—accounted for one-third of Sweden's increase in population. Between about 1945 and 1960 Denmark and Norway had a small net emigration, and between 1960 and 1969 a net immigration, although not on the same scale as in Sweden. The result is that by the mid-1970s Sweden had quite a large number of foreign workers, whereas Denmark, and especially Norway, had a very small number of foreign workers by comparison with other developed Western European countries. In 1973 Norway imposed a ban on the immigration of foreign workers.[13] By 1 January 1975 Denmark had 25,273, Norway 7,839 and Sweden 58,507 foreign workers from Mediterranean and Middle Eastern countries (Morocco, Portugal, Spain, Italy, Yugoslavia, Greece, Turkey and Pakistan). To these figures one should add 183,000 Finnish residents in Sweden.[14]

In Sweden the Government has formulated a so-called "active labour market policy". The elements of this policy are first to improve the mobility of the workers by education and by economic support for migrants and commuters and secondly to influence the location of enterprises by various financial measures. This is combined with a policy of regional development. Both Sweden and Norway have a low population density. The increased concentration of economic activity has been accompanied by regional problems. In view of Denmark's very fast economic development from 1958 onward, with great shifts between agriculture and industry, the Danish labour market can be said to have developed quite smoothly. The unions especially have advocated a labour market policy like the Swedish one. As a matter of fact only a small amount has been spent under the Danish labour market policy: in 1972 the proportion of central government expenditure used to implement labour market policy (minus the part used for unemployment relief) was approximately 1 per cent in Denmark, as compared with about 7 per cent in Sweden.[15] The corresponding figure for Norway is 1 per cent.[16]

Since 1974 the growth of unemployment, initially in Denmark, has put most other labour market problems in the shade. Table 4 shows the unemployment rate in the three countries up to 1975. Of the three Denmark has unquestionably had the highest unemployment almost ever since the Second World War; only between 1960 and 1973 did the Danish figures approached those for Sweden and Norway. The difference was very marked between 1946 and 1960, and again from 1974 onward. In the 1950s, and again from 1974 onward, many Danes moved to Sweden to get work. Since 1974 Norway has also received unemployed Danes. There has been a common labour market in the Nordic countries since the beginning of the 1950s, and it has continued even since Denmark joined the European Economic Community in 1973.

The general economic depression following the energy crisis has hit Denmark especially hard. Besides the increase in unemployment, new investment has fallen off and foreign debts have increased considerably. The Government has tried to counter this by a general policy of economic restriction combined with incomes policy. In general the situation for many Danish firms has been one of relative stagnation. Maybe this is not the best climate for starting new experiments with

Table 4. Unemployment rate[1] in Denmark, Norway and Sweden, 1946-75

Years	Denmark	Norway	Sweden
1946-50	9.2	2.9	2.7
1951-55	9.8	2.8	2.4
1956-60	8.0	2.9	1.9
1961-65	3.4	2.1	1.2
1966-70	3.8	1.1	1.7
1971	3.5	0.7	2.0
1972	3.7	0.9	1.9
1973	2.1	0.8	1.9
1974	5.1	0.7	0.8
1975	10.8	1.2	1.3

[1] In these three countries the unemployment rate is based not on the total labour force but on the number of members of unemployment insurance schemes or of trade unions.

Source: 1946-70, Lennart Jörberg and Olle Krantz: "Scandinavia, 1914-1970", Chapter 6 of Carlo M. Cipolla (ed.): *The Fontana economic history of Europe*, Vol. 6: *Contemporary economies* (London, Collins/Fontana Books, 1975), p. 16; *Yearbook of Nordic Statistics, 1975*, op. cit., p. 65.

forms of work organisation, although many permanent changes in production processes have in fact been introduced. The impact of the depression has not been the same in Sweden and Norway. In Sweden the depression was met initially by expansion of stocks, and consequently came later. The rapid growth in the exploitation of the oil resources of the North Sea from the beginning of the 1970s helped to cushion the impact of the depression in the latter country.

General system of industrial relations

The three countries have elaborate and complex systems for the regulation of industrial conflict. Both employers and workers are very organised: 80 to 90 per cent of the industrial wage earners are members of a union; the figures are somewhat lower for salaried employees. In each country the workers are organised in a single organisation, the confederation of trade unions, known as the LO (in Sweden the salaried employees are organised in the TCO, but that organisation co-operates closely with the LO). Practically all the unions are members of the LO, and there are no competing confederations apart from a small syndicalist one in Sweden which does not have much influence. With regard to the employers' organisations it is the expert opinion of Galenson[17] that employers in the three countries "have united for the purpose of collective bargaining to a degree unmatched elsewhere". The organisations are highly centralised and bureaucratised. Employers' organisations especially have large and highly educated staffs. The staff employed has grown rapidly in the last decade owing to the increasing consultation between the organisations and the government.

The most important difference between the three LOs is that the Danish unions are organised on a craft basis, whereas those in Norway and Sweden are industry-based. One reason for this is that in Denmark the guilds, and later on the journeymen's organisations, were highly developed before industrialisation, whereas there were much fewer guilds in Norway and Sweden because of a much smaller degree of urbanisation. Another reason lies in the small scale of Danish industry, or rather, since the average Norwegian plant is smaller than the average Danish one, in the relative lack of larger enterprises. Another difference is the higher degree of centralisation of the Norwegian and Swedish unions. One important indicator of this difference is that in Norway and Sweden the cóntrol over strike funds lies with the national confederations, but in Denmark with the individual national trade unions. Another indicator is that in Denmark the general agreements must be confirmed by the members by ballot, which is not the case in Norway and Sweden. A plausible explanation of the different degrees of centralisation is to be found in the Danish craft basis of organisation as compared with the Norwegian and Swedish industry basis.

In each country the national employers' and workers' organisations have entered into national "general agreements", that is agreements that are applicable to all members of the signatory organisations. Such agreements were introduced in Denmark in 1899, in Norway in 1935 and in Sweden in 1938.[18] Other Norwegian and Swedish arrangements established at the beginning of the century contained many elements also found in the general agreements. For example, a conciliation and arbitration agreement between the two national organisations was concluded in Norway at the beginning of the century. The general agreements have in fact been revised several times since their first formulation, but the general principles have remained the same, at least until very recently. In each of the three countries the main agreement was formulated at the end of a period of intense class conflict resulting in a large number of lockouts and strikes. In the case of Norway and Sweden a labour government hinted that legislation might be used to settle labour disputes. Instead the organisations reached the general agreements and concurred in the view that the government should not interfere in the regulation of industrial relations. The most important elements in the general agreements are as follows:

(a) the organisations recognise the right of both employers and workers to organise freely;

(b) an agreement concluded by one of these central organisations is binding on its subordinate organisations;

(c) where a collective agreement is in force, no labour disputes shall occur; and

(d) the employer has the right to manage and to distribute work.

Other essential elements in the systems of industrial relations are the following:

(1) Centralised collective bargaining between the central organisations. All agreements expire simultaneously, as do the specific agreements on conditions of work and wages that are negotiated separately by the member organisations.

(2) An industrial court (established in Denmark in 1910, Norway in 1915 and Sweden in 1928), most of the judges being representatives of the central organisations; the industrial courts are the final instance of appeal.

(3) Arbitration institutions both at the local level, for disputes in single enterprises, and at the national level, where arbitration is an important element in the collective bargaining between the central organisations.

Table 5.   Average annual number of work stoppages[1] in Denmark, Norway and Sweden, 1965-74

Period	Denmark	Norway	Sweden
1965-69	29.2	6.2	19.8
1970-74	96.4	11.8	104.6

[1] Virtually all work stoppages are strikes.
Source: *Yearbook of Nordic Statistics, 1975*, op. cit., table 41.

As a consequence of the agreements and the rules mentioned above, legitimate open conflict is virtually restricted to the periods when the general agreements expire. Another result is the absence of disputes concerning the workers' right to organise.

The high developed institutionalisation of industrial conflict has been accompanied by a low number of work stoppages. While Denmark had the lowest rate and Norway the highest among the three countries before the Second World War,[19] the picture had reversed after the war, Denmark apparently having the highest rate and Norway the lowest.[20] However, in all three countries the number of strikes has increased since 1965, as table 5 shows. Institutions for the regulation of industrial conflict apparently do not entirely prevent strikes, but instead make the strikes that occur illegitimate: a considerable number of the recorded strikes are contrary to collective agreements. It is remarkable that the number of strikes should have increased simultaneously with the development of institutions for industrial democracy and experiments with new forms of work organisation.

The highly centralised structure of the two central employers' and workers' organisations in each country has had a number of consequences. It is an advantage for the employers' organisation to have a workers' organisation with a sound structure very similar to its own as its opponent; and it may be an advantage for labour to be able to secure more uniform rates of wages and other conditions of work than it would have secured through agreements reached by various individual unions. Finally, in times of crisis—in wartime and during economic recessions—it has been very useful for the governments to have institutionalised industrial relations systems to put through incomes policy measures.

Democratisation of the workplace

Since the Second World War important changes have taken place in terms of institutions for enabling workers to exert some influence in the undertaking, and there has been a trend towards so-called "democratisation of the workplace". A distinction can be drawn between representative (or indirect) and direct forms of influence: representative influence is acquired when people are elected by their fellows as their representatives on some council, committee or board where the representatives will try to influence or take decisions in the interests of the group they represent; direct influence is influence in terms of autonomy, responsibility, or possibility for discretion in a certain job. In the three countries dealt with in this paper, representative institutions within the undertaking have provided a framework for experiments with more direct influence.

An important and widespread representative institution is the system of shop stewards, which was provided for in collective agreements shortly after the turn of the century. Shop stewards have retained their position as the primary medium of co-operation at the workplace in the three countries. An extract from the Norwegian general agreement of 1974 (section 6) gives an inkling of the shop stewards' tasks:

Together with the employers and persons representing the undertaking in its dealings with the workers, it is the shop stewards' duty to do their best to maintain peaceful and effective co-operation at the place of work. . . . The shop stewards have the right to take up and seek to settle amicably any grievance of the individual worker against the undertaking, or of the undertaking against the individual worker. . . . Like the employer, the shop stewards shall see to it that the obligations of the parties under the collective agreement, the factory regulations and the Workers' Protection Act are observed to the extent that these duties are not particularly vested in other institutions. It is therefore inconsistent with the duties of the employers and the shop stewards to instigate or participate in unlawful conflict.

Under the influence of the political situation in Europe and under pressure from the radical Norwegian labour movement, legislation on worker representation in management was passed in Norway as early as 1920.[21] Under the terms of the Act the workers were entitled to form a committee *(Arbejderutvalg)* which could discuss a rather limited number of matters. The employer was to inform the committee before major changes and the committee could make a statement on the matter.[22] The Act did not have much influence, but was not repealed until 1962. Similar institutions were discussed by government commissions in Denmark and Sweden in the early 1920s, but without the passing of any relevant legislation.[23]

Collective agreements on "co-operation committees"[24] were concluded between 1945 and 1947, first in Norway, then in Sweden, and later in Denmark. The setting up of co-operation committees was part of the programme of the Norwegian Government in exile during the German occupation of Norway in the Second World War, and a joint declaration on the subject was put out by the political parties in 1945;[25] however, the co-operation committees were not established by law but under collective agreements, admittedly reached under political pressure. In Sweden and Denmark the labour movement took the main initiative.[26] The relevant agreements have been revised several times, but the basic principles relating to the co-operation committees have remained the same. The committees have an equal number of management and worker members. Their functions are consultative only. The Danish co-operation committee agreement of 1947 may be used as an example: according to that agreement the committees' terms of reference cover—

(a) the promotion of the efficiency and quality of production;

(b) discussion of measures for rationalisation, alterations, and adjustments of the production process;

(c) endeavours to achieve the best possible conditions for workers through vocational training, etc.;

Table 6. Distribution of Danish, Norwegian and Swedish co-operation committees according to annual frequency of meetings
(Percentages)

No. of meetings per year	Norway, 1950-60	Sweden, 1959	Denmark 1956	1968
0	18	7	15	0
1 – 3	47	31	55	38
4 +	35	62	30	62
All frequencies	100	100	100	100

Source: Arnold Havelin and Sverre Lysgaard: "Bruken av produksjonsutvalg i norske bedrifter", in *Tidsskrift for Samfunnsforskning*, 1964, No. 1, pp. 30-55, as cited in Poul Vidriksen: *Debatten om industrielt demokrati i Norge* (Copenhagen, Arbejdsministeriet, 1969), p. 37; Samarbejdsnaevnet: *De fire første samarbejdsforsøg* (Copenhagen, 1972), p. 18.

(d) discussion of welfare measures, safety, health and security of job tenure; and

(e) promotion of the interests of workers in the running of the enterprise by means of information on employment, investment, production and financial conditions.

When there is agreement, and when it is in accordance with collective agreements, the following matters may also be discussed:

(f) the setting-up, effect and application of principles of wage systems designed to promote productivity; and

(g) the establishment of funds for educational and welfare purposes.

A central point in the general agreement is, as mentioned, the unions' acceptance of the right of management, and the co-operation committee agreements may thus be seen as implying a limitation, however moderate, of the power of the employer to manage and distribute work. From the late 1940s to the present there has been a large increase in the number of co-operation committees. In Denmark they increased from 471 in 1948 to 595 in 1957 and about 650 in 1970, covering about 80 per cent of commercial and industrial enterprises. In Sweden the number of such committees rose from 500 in 1947 to 3,737 in 1959.[27] In all three countries the committees tend to be established in larger rather than in smaller enterprises.[28]

A Norwegian survey carried out in 1950 showed that the worker representatives on the committees are of the opinion, to a higher extent than the ordinary workers, that workers and management have common interests and that the committees function well.[29] Similar findings were made years later in Denmark, where surveys show[30] that the subjects most frequently discussed in 1968 were economic and employment conditions, the manufacturing process, measures to promote efficiency and labour relations policies (in privately owned firms). In general the workers are sceptical about the importance of the committees. The workers' representatives on the co-operation committees, however, appreciate the importance of the committees much more. Thus a barrier is created between workers and their representatives. Worker involvement in questions regarding co-operation committees is generally weak; "one consequence of this barrier could be that the workers to an increasing extent would view the members of the co-operation committees as identical with the management rather than with the workers".[31]

Parallel to the development of co-operation committees, "co-operation boards"[32] have been established at the national level, by agreement among the central organisations. In Denmark the Co-operation Board was established in 1947, but the agreement was revised in 1964, when a secretariat taking care of day-to-day business and servicing the Board was set up. In Sweden a specialised board for co-operation committees was not established until 1966; before 1966 national co-ordination was achieved through another body, the Labour Market Board (*Arbeitsmarknadsnämden,* established in 1938) which, however, had many other functions. In Norway a national body for co-ordination of the local co-operation committees was established in 1945. In 1966 it was reorganised and strengthened and a secretariat was established. The co-operation boards consist of an equal number of persons representing the employers' associations and the unions. The boards operate within the fields of information, training, and research for the promotion of local co-operation. They have prepared various kinds of information material and organised courses and conferences.

The trend towards industrial democracy

Industrial democracy was an issue after the First World War, but was rather unimportant during the 1930s and the Second World War. The debate then intensified and resulted in the agreements on co-operation committees. The issue came to a head again in the 1960s, when a number of central organisations issued reports on their attitudes toward industrial democracy. The Swedish and Norwegian LOs issued their reports in 1961, and the Danish LO in 1967. The confederations of trade unions stress that co-operation committees should be given more influence or that representative bodies should be established with a more important position in the decision-making process of the company, while the employers' associations stress the functions and responsibilities of owners and management. It is on the issue of equality between labour and capital versus the primacy of capital that the debate on industrial democracy in the three countries has taken place.

Apparently the most far-reaching proposals have been made by Norwegian labour. A committee set up jointly by the Norwegian Workers' Party and the Norwegian Confederation of Trade Unions (the *Aspengrenkommiteen*) proposed in particular the establishment of industrial councils in all larger enterprises, with functions that should be not merely consultative but similar to those of a general meeting of shareholders. In fact some industrial councils were set up in Norway as a result of legislation passed in 1965 to establish a more developed form of representative influence in the small number of State-owned businesses. In Sweden the main themes of the debate have been how much authority the co-operation committees should have, whether industrial democracy was a matter for legislation or for collective agreement, and the question of workers' shares. In Denmark—as in Norway and Sweden—the main point made by the confederation of trade unions has been that representative institutions should be developed; but in Denmark the proposals and demands for extended industrial democracy have had a somewhat lower priority than the proposals relating to economic democracy, i.e. the establishment of central funds financed by shares of company profits and administered by the confederation. The Danish employers—like the employers in Sweden and Norway—have expressed scepticism with regard to the notion of representative democracy in industry, and laid emphasis on forms of direct influence, namely more responsibility for individual workers and the introduction of systems of workers' shares or profit sharing.

In conclusion it can be said that a general agreement on the desirability of a higher degree of industrial democracy is emerging, but while the labour side has tried to find ways of giving greater weight to the workers' interests the employers' side has tried to achieve a stronger attachment of the workers to their firms and a commitment to their goals. The divergent views have increasingly been reconciled in agreement on the principle of the dual aim of the undertaking: productivity and satisfaction. There have of course been internal disagreements both on the labour side and among the employers. The confederations of trade unions have been accused by the Left of following a strategy of class co-operation, while the employers' associations have come up against individual employers' scepticism regarding the new type of "participation management" which the associations have promoted.

Worker representation on company boards does not seem to have been the major objective of either party; however, laws on worker representation at the board level were passed in the three countries between 1970 and 1973. (In contrast to the other measures of industrial democracy dealt with above, worker representation at board level was a matter for legislation, because it required amendment of the Acts regulating joint-stock companies.) The statutory provisions are largely the same in the three countries. They concern joint-stock companies with more than a specified number of workers. Smaller companies can voluntarily offer their workers the same opportunity. The workers may elect two members to the board of the company with the same rights and obligations as other directors. The decision to join the board may be taken by the workers through a poll (in Denmark) or by the local union (in Sweden). The arrangement allows the representatives to follow the decision-making, and may be regarded as ensuring access to information. A current research project in Denmark[33] shows that this arrangement meets with difficulties similar to those of the joint work committees: a gap is found to exist between the workers and their representatives.

A radical change in the system of industrial relations has recently taken place in Sweden. On 1 January 1977 the traditional agreement on the employers' right to direct and allocate work was abolished by legislation,[34] and a number of other rules were introduced instead.[35] These new provisions stress negotiations before any change in management: the Act on participation in decision-making extends the right of unions to collective agreements on decision-making in many areas such as organisation, project development, personnel management and supervision. The parties have a residual right to resort to industrial action if questions concerning participation are not covered by collective agreement. The local trade union enjoys precedence of interpretation in disputes about collective agreements. The employers' primary obligation to negotiate requires that management initiate negotiations with trade unions before making any change in management or supervision of work. The employer is required to provide workers with information on company production plans, economic position and personnel policy. The parties must undertake to maintain industrial peace, and employers may be sued for damages in cases of violation of the rules. On the other hand the local union is required to start negotiations to settle the issue at stake if any wildcat strikes occur. Penalties for breaches of industrial peace have been increased.

In 1973 a new Worker Protection Act was passed in Norway which in some respects limits the employers' right to manage and distribute work. The pace of work must not be controlled by machines or assembly lines: the workers themselves should be able to control the pace of work, and repetitive work should be avoided; the workers should have a reasonable possibility of self-determination. These rules were drawn up in co-operation, in particular, with the consultants of the Work Research Institute in Oslo. The observance of these rules would be tantamount to applying some important principles that underlie experiments with new forms of work organisation. It remains to be seen, however, just how far-reaching will be the practical consequences of the provisions regarding limitation of managerial rights. In Denmark a new Worker Protection Act was passed in 1976 without the provisions of the Norwegian Act, but somewhat influenced by the new ideas concerning psychologically meaningful work. A limitation of managerial rights is implied in the 1973 revision of the Danish General Agreement, which states that the right of the employer to manage and distribute work should be exercised in accordance with the Co-operation Committee Agreement and with the aim of delegating as much authority as possible to individual workers.

Promotion of new forms of work organisation

In the early fifties new elements in the theory of organisation appeared, as various research projects showed a relationship between technological factors and the social, psychological and health conditions of the workers. Both the so-called "socio-technical systems approach" resulting from pioneering research done in British coal mines and the theory of autonomous work groups made an important contribution to the theory underlying the Norwegian experiments with new forms of work organisation. Norway has had a number of very creative and active research workers and research institutions supported by the central employers' and workers' organisations and by individual companies. In 1958 the Institute for Industrial Social Research was established at the Technical University in Trondheim with the help of a donation from a major Norwegian company, A/S Freia (chocolates, etc.), for which Einar Thorsrud, the leading figure in the Norwegian experiments, had formerly been a personnel manager.[36] Most of the researchers from Trondheim later joined the work research institutes in Oslo, where very diversified research on work problems is taking place today. The Co-operation Board has acted as a permanent supervisory council for a Norwegian project known as the LO-NAF Co-operation Project, which started in 1962 under an agreement between the Institute for Industrial Social Reserach, the Norwegian Federation of Trade Unions (LO) and the Norwegian Employers' Association (NAF). This project can in fact be regarded as a collective agreement between the central organisations regarding the terms on which experiments with new forms of work organisation should be made.

In phase A of the LO-NAF Co-operation Project the influence of representative institutions in enterprises was evaluated. Researchers looked into experience with co-operation committees and with other formal means of giving workers representation at the top echelons of companies in Norway and abroad. The conclusion reported in 1964 was that on the whole worker representation at the top level cannot be regarded as an effective means of achieving industrial democracy.[37] Perhaps unexpectedly, the central organisation agreed with this conclusion. Phase B of the project consisted of a number of field experiments, in which the research workers in co-operation with members of the workforce and management representatives tried to develop new forms of organisation which would give the individual possibilities of greater direct participation in the job. The aim of the re-designing process was formulated in six so-called "psychological job demands":

(a) variation and meaning in the job;

(b) continuous learning on the job;

(c) participation in decision-making;

(d) mutual help and support from fellow workers;

(e) meaningful relation between the job and social life outside; and

(f) a desirable future in the job—not only through promotion.

To this the organisations added that the rate of increase of productivity in companies participating in the experiments should be at least equal to the general average in similar companies. Four companies were selected for the field experiments, and the general conclusion reached[38] was that by comparison with traditional forms of work organisation, the experiments had shown that it was possible to create a high degree of personal commitment and opportunity for development of skills and competence by organising the work in autonomous groups.[39]

Only a limited number of experimental projects were accepted as a part of the LO-NAF Co-operation Project. This was unfortunate[40] because it made many people believe that a great deal of specialised assistance was needed. In later years the emphasis of the Norwegian experiments changed, and in the latest experiments stress has been laid on the "action approach" which had been an integral part of the theory of Norwegian experiments from the start. The action approach implies that research workers should not have a fixed preconception of the aim of the redesigning process, but should let workers and other persons involved decide through repeated trial and error. Several companies have been experimenting either on their own or in co-operation with others, and without research assistance. In Norway experiments have also been made outside industry. Under the Co-operation Project experiments have started, for example, in hotels and on ships, which shows that the principles governing experiments in industry can also be applied to other sectors of the economy.

In Sweden the initial phase of experiments with new forms of work organisation was inspired by the first Norwegian field experiments. Early in the 1970s the Swedish Co-operation Board started some systematic projects. These experiments were mainly carried out in State-owned companies, and a special committee *(Företagsdemokratidelegationen)* was established to promote and supervise them. Almost simultaneously, a large number of projects were started through the initiative of individual employers and without any central co-ordination. The title of a book published in 1975 by the Swedish Employers' Confederation, *Job reform in Sweden: Conclusions from 500 shop floor projects*,[41] suggests the rapid spread of experiments. In contrast to the Norwegian Co-operation Board, the Swedish Board *(Utvecklingsrådet för Samarbetsfrågor)*, which was formed in 1966, does not seem to have played a leading role in promoting experiments, except in the state companies. The Council for Personnel Administration *(Personaleadministrative Rådet)* formed by the Swedish Employers' Association financed research projects on work satisfaction and possibilities for more meaningful work situations which to a certain extent have influenced Swedish experimentation. However, in Sweden such experimentation is a decentralised process, initiated by individual employers and supported by the Employers' Association, with less control by the trade unions than in Norway, without a fixed theoretical framework, and with comparatively little research support.

In Denmark the first experiments were the result of a study tour to the United States in 1969. The group included managers and shop stewards from four factories and members of the central organisations. The Co-operation Board made the travel arrangements.[42] Partly because of the study tour to the United States, Danish experimentation has to a large extent been based on North American theories of job enrichment. This applies not so much to the formal experiments with research participation as to informal organisational re-design initiated by individual employers. Through the Danish Employers' Association many top and middle managers have learned the North American theories of motivation and job enrichment, but it is impossible to tell how this has influenced the changes in the organisation of work in the companies. The first four experiments, inspired by the study tour and by Norwegian experience, had varying degrees of success.[43] In 1971, experiments in seven firms were initiated by the central organisations of employers and workers in the metal industry; they formed a committee which was to follow and guide the research, the cost of co-ordination and research being covered by the Danish Productivity Council. The Institute of Organisation and Industrial Sociology of the Copenhagen School of Economics and Business Administration provided reserach workers to monitor the experiments. The experiments were carried out on the shop floor, and were to a very high degree based on the ideas of the workers and foremen involved, the idea being that research workers should proceed on their own. The over-all outcome of the experiments is limited in terms of organisational re-design. The experiments tended to be successful when the companies concerned were already in a process of organisational change.[44]

CASE STUDIES

In this paper two company-conducted changes of work organisation are selected. The first experiments of the Bang and Olufsen company in Denmark were very limited, but the latest development is a change of the entire production process of a plant. The Volvo factory at Kalmar in Sweden is a new large plant which has been designed with the specific purpose of creating semi-autonomous groups. Both Bang and Olufsen and Volvo have used the principles of new forms of work organisation in various plants and departments, but the selected cases are probably the most advanced and best documented ones in the companies concerned. The case reported from Norway is an example of the experiments that were carried out under the auspices of the influential Co-operation Project and assisted by experienced personnel from the work research institutes in Oslo. The Høegh Shipping Company's ship, the Høegh Mistral, is a comparatively recent experiment conducted under the Co-operation Project and provides an example of the diffusion of experiments from manufacturing industry to other sectors.

Bang and Olufsen[45]

The Bang and Olufsen company produces electronic consumer goods at Struer in North Jutland, a part of Denmark which has a relatively high rate of unemployment. Two of the factories are located in other small towns near by. The company is the largest firm in the area, and has a dominant position in the community. It employs about 2,000 people, and is thus one of the major Danish companies. By international standards, however, the company is perhaps the smallest of all the producers of colour television sets in the European Economic Community. An important element in the image of the company is that it manufactures handsome and functional quality products that are somewhat more expensive than others on the market. More than half the output is exported, mainly to other parts of Scandinavia and the Community, a smaller proportion going to the United States. The company is still owned and controlled by the family of the founders of the enterprise.

Bang and Olufsen was one of the four firms whose worker and management representatives went to the United States in 1969 in order to become acquainted with the most recent management research, and which subsequently began to experiment with new forms of work organisation, with mixed results. In 1972 the company encountered serious problems in the production and sale of its television sets. The production of colour sets, which accounts for about half the company's sales, ran into many difficulties. The sets were produced on an assembly line. Five hundred workers produced 200 sets a day with a production cycle of 20 days. Absenteeism was running at 15 per cent and labour turnover amounted to as much as 30 per cent a year. The quality of the products was falling. This fall was particularly damaging because the high price structure could be justified only by a solid reputation for quality. Supervision was increased, with little effect on quality. The type of production was inflexible, which made it difficult to switch rapidly to new models. The factory's wage system contributed to the difficulties: the system of piecework, individual bonuses and group bonuses led to constant conflicts. In August 1973 the company switched from a traditionally made set to a new product derived from a more advanced technology and a reorganisation of the work. The change was made by a small group of managers headed by Niels Ole Vonsild, who had previously been facilities manager at the General Electric capacitator plant at Hudson Falls, New York, and had participated there in a switch to group assembly. Bang and Olufsen also called in an American consulting firm, H. B. Maynard and Co.

The result of the switch was that the assembly line was dismantled. Previously there were from 4 to 17 operators at each assembly line, sitting side by side assembling equally large fractions of the total assembly; the job cycle time was 8-12 minutes and there were no buffers between the individual operators. Under the new system the workforce was split into 34 groups ranging in size from individuals working alone to teams of 10 or 12. The colour set is now built from modules and each group is given the task of completing various sub-assemblies of the set. The modules function independently of each other so that replacement of one module does not involve any re-adjustment of the others. This makes the set easier to service and inspect. Now each group receives ready-made printed circuit boards, with components clipped and bent to match. All components (transistors, resistors, capacitators, etc.) are mounted according to the drop-in method. Nimble-fingered girls can complete the mounting of a circuit board in a short time, since they have a finger feel of where the various components go. Checking is performed by comparison with a standard. When all components have been mounted, the frame with the printed circuit board is put on a conveyor belt. The belt runs by all groups, carrying the boards made by the various groups to a soldering machine, in random order. There each board is first heated with hot air and thereafter briefly dipped into a bath of liquid solder, thus soldering the joints in one operation. After soldering, the board is returned by conveyor belt to the group which mounted it and the soldered joints are visually checked for faults (e.g. short circuits). The board now proceeds to the next member of the group, who performs electrical adjustments. This is done at specially devised stations. Test equipment comprises a colour set, in which the appropriate module is mounted. The new module can easily be checked and adjusted on the set, and any defects can also be corrected at that stage, so that when the board has been approved the group has finished with it. Thus, a complete unit has been produced, ready for use in a colour set. Any defects that may have arisen in the process have been corrected by the group members themselves, who sit so close to each other that the person responsible for an error can be notified quickly.[46] Each group has to put a coded tag on its sub-assembly, so that if a defect arises in the process of production it can be corrected by the group members themselves, and so that the group can be notified if any errors are detected by a consumer or dealer.

The most radical reorganisation was carried out in the cabinet assembly department, where the assembly line gave way to assembly by individuals. Each worker picks up the parts of the television set from the buffer stock, takes them to his place of work and performs the assembly. After this he checks and adjusts the set. The production time is now 24 minutes, with each worker producing 20 sets daily. The operator may work at his own pace from day to day, provided that in the long run he conforms to the general output norms. The wage system has been changed, and conflict accordingly reduced. Every person is paid at a fixed daily rate, but in addition a bonus is calculated on a group basis according to how many sets each group produces. The bonus, however, accounts only for 10-12 per cent of the total wages.

The development of a new type of production was expensive, involving training of the workers and duplication of some tools and equipment. It is estimated that it has cost twice as much to establish the group assembly system as it would have cost to install a new traditional assembly line. Furthermore, the period required to train the workers has increased. However, this may in turn ease future production changes. The change in the system has improved production dramatically. Labour turnover has gone down close to zero. The production cycle is now 5 days, as compared with 20 before. Productivity has increased by 150 per cent. The firm has been able to reduce its labour force by almost 200 workers and one-third of the supervisory staff. Furthermore, the system is much more flexible. In a recession the company can reduce (and actually has reduced) the size of the assembly groups while maintaining the same labour productivity; when sales go up, it is easy to switch back. The company has also been able to cut down its stock. In addition there is a marketing advantage: reporting test results concerning the turntables and other products of Bang and Olufsen, several technical magazines included descriptions of the assembly system. In this way the new form of work organisation may have an even more direct influence on the sales.[47]

On the negative side it may be mentioned that there were initial difficulties, and there were problems in maintaining a stable level of product quality. For some of the workers the new organisation has meant dissolution of the social relationships of the assembly line. The workers do not have the same group relations and solidarity as before. In some groups the workers have become extremely individualistic and fail to help each other.

The success at the colour television plant has induced the company to use the same system for its other products. This is being done in the production of a new high-fidelity turntable, since early 1977. In this case each worker assembles all parts of the turntable, and then tests and packs it. The turntable is also coded with the worker's number so that the worker can be notified of any defects. Training takes eight weeks, and includes instruction in the use of colour slides that show how the turntable is to be produced, step by step. Each worker has a projector at hand and can control its speed (and thereby the pace of work).

The firm has come a long way with these experiments. They have resulted in greater productivity, better quality and a higher level of job satisfaction for the worker.

The Volvo factory at Kalmar[48]

Volvo, the automobile manufacturer, is the largest corporation in Sweden. Besides 20 factories abroad, it has 28 within the country; one of them, at Kalmar, is an outstanding experiment with new forms of management. (The Kalmar factory is not the sole example of team or group assembly in the transport equipment industry in Sweden. Saab-Scania began to use teams for final engine assembly in its Södertälje plant in 1972. In 1974 Volvo opened a tractor plant at Eskilstuna, and more recently a bus plant at Borås, both using team assembly.)

During the 1950s and 1960s production of the Volvo factories had been increasingly systematised. As in other car factories the jobs had been broken down into small standardised and specialised elements in respect of which each worker was expected to carry out only a single function, or at any rate very few. Types of production had been introduced that resulted in a faster flow and a larger output. This type of management also included central planning of production, which was most economically and efficiently carried out in large factories. The traditional principles of technological organisation had important consequences for the workers, the most important being strong dependence on the assembly line and often very short-cycle tasks. In short, types of work had been introduced that are considered tedious among workers with relatively high levels of education.

In the late 1960s and the early 1970s the Volvo factories in Gothenburg experienced serious problems of labour supply. As a result of high turnover, absenteeism and difficulty in recruiting Swedish workers, a growing proportion of jobs in the factories came to be held by foreign workers, who constituted nearly half the workforce on the assembly lines in the Gothenburg factories (by 1973, fewer than 20 per cent of the new workers taken on were Swedish). It was felt that something should be done to reverse the trend, and a group of technicians, supervisors and architects was established at the beginning of the 1970s to try to develop solutions. In 1972 Volvo's board of directors decided to build a new, nontraditional plant, where production started early in 1974. Pehr G. Gyllenhammar, Volvo's managing director, gave the following description of the objective of the new factory: "In Kalmar we intend to build a factory which, without reducing efficiency and the economic result, will make it possible for workers to work in teams, to communicate freely, to vary the speed of work, to identify with the product, to feel responsible for the quality of the product and to be able to influence their work environment." To stabilise the labour force the factory was built in an area of relatively high unemployment.

The Kalmar factory is an assembly plant. Car bodies and frames, as well as other parts, are sent to the factory from other points of manufacture. The plant itself has a rather unusual form. The main building is composed of four hexagons, each with four sides facing outward and two inside the building. Three of the four hexagons are two-storey structures. A general storage centre is in the middle of the building. Bodies are assembled step by step in a loop along the outer side of the upper floor. The engines and gear boxes are assembled in a loop on the ground floor, and then the two lines of production are combined. The total area of the building is 40,000 m². The intention has been to try to establish small factories in a large one. Production is carried out by some 25 teams of assembly workers. Each team has its own entrance, rest room and other facilities. The workers on a team have a relatively large number of operations to carry out, which makes it possible for them to perform longer work cycles and to have more variety in their work.

Close team work has been made possible by breaking down the long assembly line of a traditional car factory. A key element in this solution is Volvo's "assembly carrier", a mobile unit which transports the car that is being manufactured. (There are two different types of assembly carrier, high and low. The low type is used mainly on the upper floor of the factory where car bodies are assembled. The carrier is long and broad enough for a worker to stand on, and this makes work easier. It is also constructed in such a way that it can tilt the body through 90°; thus operations on the underside of the body can be carried out more easily and comfortably. A high assembly carrier is very much like a low one, but is equipped with a lift.) Each carrier has an electric motor and can move in any direction; the speed ranges from 3 to 30 metres per minute. The carrier can stop for periods of varying duration at different places on the production lines. Normally it is directed by a computer, following a fixed route through the factory marked out by magnetic cables in the floor, and advancing automatically from one production area to another. When it enters a team's production area it stops in a buffer zone from which it is released when there is room in the work area. A change to semi-automatic driving is possible, in which case the carrier still follows the cable route but stops when the controls are released. It can also change to manual operation, in which case it can be driven in any direction by the operator. On entering the factory the chassis of each car to be produced is given a specific number which remains with it all the way through the production process, and the computer monitors the progress of each new car as it goes through the process. Because the order of the assembly carriers can therefore be changed without disrupting production, the organisation of work is of course much more flexible than with a traditional assembly line.

A team's work can be organised in two different ways. In both cases the work is divided into smaller sections, but the difference is that in the one case the assembly carrier moves between each operation whereas in the other it remains in the same place. The first type may be called line assembly, the principle of which may be demonstrated as in figure 1. The team's assignment is divided into sec-

Figure 1. Line assembly at the Volvo factory at Kalmar

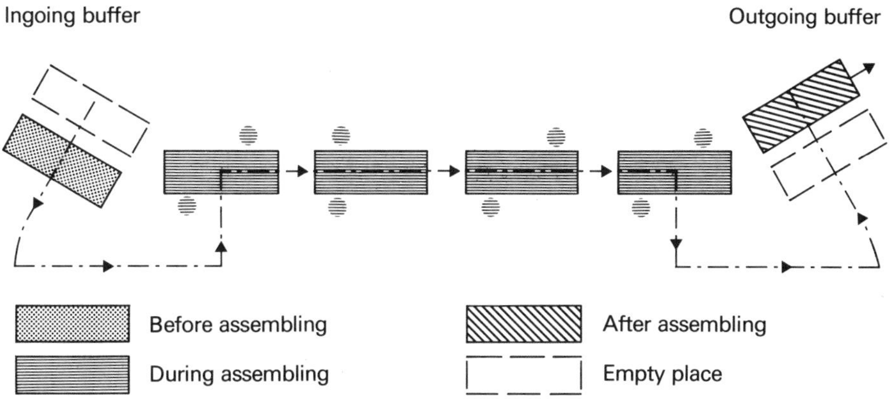

Ingoing buffer

Outgoing buffer

| | Before assembling | | | After assembling |
| | During assembling | | | Empty place |

tions (normally six) and each section is carried out at a separate station. The carrier moves from one station to another. At each station two or three persons work, their work cycle being approximately 5 minutes. Normally the workers can do the work at all six stations, and follow the carrier through the whole line. In this way each worker carries out all the functions allocated to the team and performs a work cycle of 20 to 30 minutes. Three-quarters of the production teams are organised for line assembly. The rest are set up for "dock" assembly. This second type can be illustrated as shown in figure 2. In this case the carrier remains in the same place during the time needed for the job assigned to the team. Two or three people work at each "dock", their work cycle being also of 20 to 30 minutes.

Figure 2. Dock assembly at the Volvo factory at Kalmar

Ingoing buffer   Outgoing buffer

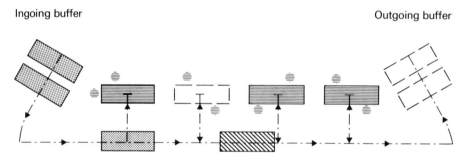

In a survey carried out in 1975,[49] three-quarters of the workers indicated that they had job rotation in their teams. The reason for the change between different types of work is that some types of work are considered to be more difficult or unpleasant than others. The workers on a team try to divide good and bad types of work as fairly as possible. Each team has from 15 to 20 members. In terms of age, sex, and other factors the composition of the teams varies, but teams with a wide age spread are normally regarded as functioning somewhat better. One member of each team is the "instructor", who is often regarded as an informal leader of the team, and is appointed by the management and the union. His job is to instruct new members, receive information on the quality of the team's output, and act as the team's spokesman in relations with supervisors and managers. The results of production control were at first communicated to the team instructor by the computer on a data screen. Owing to some dissatisfaction among the workers with this impersonal procedure, an increasing number of communications are now person-to-person. Besides an opportunity for personal contact, this new system allows a more flexible information flow. Communications of this type give better results, especially in the case of negative information, e.g. a fall in output, or more errors. At present 75 per cent of the production control reports to the teams are oral.

When asked for their opinion, almost all of the workers seem to have found this type of team work very satisfactory. Factors such as solidarity and tolerance among the workers were prominently mentioned. The relative autonomy of the team was also appreciated. The organisation of the system allows the workers to rotate among different types of work in the team and to "over-work" in order to be able to have a break. Whereas the workers are in favour of job rotation, they are opposed to change-overs between teams. It is not easy for a worker to work in another team for a short period: such a change causes inter-personal problems, and it makes work harder for the old as well as the new team. The solution to this difficulty has been to establish a group of workers with no special job who can take the place of workers in a number of teams in case of illness or the like. These workers are trained in various operations. The size of the group is computed in relation to average absenteeism.

It is not easy to evaluate a totally new type of factory. However, the following list of points is helpful:

(1) The investment in the Kalmar factory was estimated to be about 10 per cent higher than in a traditional plant.

(2) The efficiency of assembly is approximately the same as in a traditional factory.

(3) There are fewer supervisors at the Kalmar factory because teams carry out many of the traditional supervisory functions, such as introduction of new workers and dealing with reports on the volume and quality of output.

(4) The assembly carrier makes production more flexible. This means that it is less expensive to change to a new product (i.e. a new car model).

(5) There is somewhat less absenteeism at the Kalmar factory than at Volvo's similar factory at Torslanda. Among assembly workers at the Kalmar factory absenteeism was 14 per cent during the first half of 1976, as compared with 19 per cent at the traditional factory.

(6) Labour turnover is also lower at Kalmar. In the first half of 1976 turnover was 16 per cent at Kalmar and 21 per cent at Torslanda.

(7) The 20 workers who have worked both at a traditional factory and at Kalmar state that they are more satisfied with working conditions at Kalmar.

It is very difficult to compare the Kalmar factory with a traditional factory. As indicated at the beginning of this case study, Volvo was in a difficult situation, with severe problems of labour supply which would not have been solved by building a traditional factory: in a society where workers demand better working conditions with more varied work and greater control of the work situation, Volvo had to establish a factory based on new principles. New technology and establishment in a new labour market have helped to make the Kalmar factory as efficient as a traditional factory. It can be asserted, however, that a new factory built according to traditional principles in a highly industrialised local labour market would have been much less efficient at the start, and especially later.

The Høegh Mistral[50]

In the 10 or 15 years to 1975, economic, technological and social conditions in the maritime industry underwent rapid change. The considerable increase in world trade affected ship design in two ways: ships became both more specialised and more mechanised. In 1960 some 57 per cent of the Norwegian mercantile marine consisted of ordinary line and tramp ships. The number of these has diminished, while the number of special-purpose ships (bulk and ore carriers, container ships, tankers, gas carriers, etc.) has increased.[51] Because of the large share of capital investment in the total expenditure pattern of shipping companies, there has been a powerful impetus to reduce the length of stay in harbours considerably. Mechanisation or automation affected the engine, navigation, and methods of loading and unloading. At the same time the shipping companies tended to enter into long-term contracts for the carriage of oil, cars, and other freight in respect of which receipts are relatively fixed.[52]

On the manpower side, shipping has been affected by rising educational levels. According to Rogne, "changes in the Norwegian comprehensive school system from the seventh to the ninth year of schooling, and a broadening of opportunities for secondary schooling also in rural districts, have decreased the size of the group from which seamen traditionally have been recruited (boys aged 15-16) from 30,000 a year to 3,000".[53] In contrast to the usual situation in industries ashore, however, seafarers have a very rigid career system. The careers of a deck officer and an engineer officer are sharply differentiated, and in the Norwegian merchant navy they include a comparatively long period as ordinary seaman or donkeyman respectively. At the same time, and again in contrast to the situation ashore, the rules for the number and types of officers and crew are highly inflexible for certain ships owing to safety standards set by national authorities. Hence reductions or other changes in manning require not only agreement with the organisations directly concerned but also exemptions from or changes in the manning rules officially laid down. Another relevant pecularity of the maritime industry is its traditional employment practices. It is usual on board Norwegian ships engaged in overseas trade that the crew and junior officers do not stay with the same ship for several years; instead they sign on a certain ship for a trip of perhaps five or seven months, and after a couple of months' break they join another ship. However, this does not usually mean a switch to another shipping company. As a final but not least important feature of the organisational pattern of ships, the fact must be stressed that the officers and crew not only work on the ship, but spend their leisure time there too, and can be said in a sense to be on call around the clock.

In spite of changing economic, technological and labour force conditions, the organisational pattern of ships is formalised to an unusually high degree, for reasons that lie partly in the inflexible manning rules, the rapid personnel turnover in individual ships and long traditions. Figure 3 shows a pattern that is found in many types of ship. Usually an organisation chart expresses the ideal or planned, but seldom fulfilled, pattern of authority and communication; but in the case of ships the chart is an almost perfect reflection of the actual organisation pattern. Personnel are sharply divided into a deck hierarchy and an engine hierarchy, with the mess and cabin personnel forming a less important group. Another aspect of the formalised structure is that communication takes place almost exclusively from the top down. This is literally true: officers are on the bridge or in offices in the superstructure while the crew are on the deck or below; the telephones in the crew quarters are one-way phones which it is only possible to call to, not from.

Figure 3.   Traditional organisational pattern on board Norwegian ships

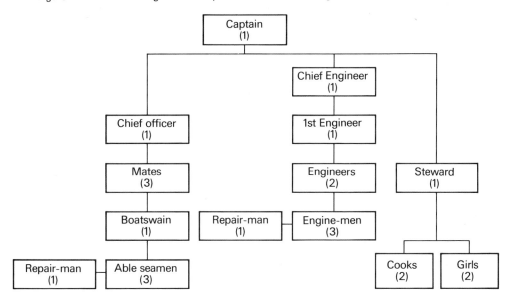

The differentiation of status according to work role is clearly supported by differentiated sleeping, eating and leisure facilities. Officers' cabins are located on upper decks, while the crew's quarters are located below the main deck. Within these two groups the accommodation is differentiated: the captain often has his own dayroom as well as a cabin, and the chief engineer usually has better accommodation than the chief officer, who again has better accommodation than the junior officers. Officers and crew have separate messes and dayrooms, and often the senior officers even have their own mess separate from the mess of the junior officers. The standard of the accommodation is, of course, also highly differentiated.

In 1966 the Norwegian Shipping Employers' Association, individual shipping companies and personnel federations applied to the research workers engaged in the LO-NAF Co-operation Project with a view to having research carried out regarding possibilities of new forms of organisation in ships and the possibilities of improving recruitment and training. Exploratory research pointed to the following three problems in connection with organisational experiments in ships:[54]

(1) The high turnover of personnel on individual ships seemed to preclude the stability of employment that is necessary for co-operation on organisational changes.

(2) The different methods of working of different ships in a variety of trades would probably make it impossible to continue to abide by the traditional organisational pattern and the inflexible manning rules.

33

(3) Social life on board seemed firmly locked in by traditions and by physical barriers. Changes in that respect were important to support new forms of work organisation.

In 1969 the research workers entered into a contract with Leif Høegh and Company, a major Norwegian shipping company which had been among those most interested in new forms of work organisation. (It has the legal status of a limited company and is involved in many types of international shipping. Most of its ships are engaged in overseas trade, and only exceptionally do they call at Norwegian ports; despite this, officers and crew are mainly recruited in Norway.) The project was supported by the Norwegian Co-operation Board, and a special contact group consisting of the Shipping Employers' Association, the personnel federations concerned and representatives of the authorities was formed. In addition a special project committee was set up within the Leif Høegh Company.

Experiments with new forms of work organisation have to date been carried out in four different ships of the Høegh Company. This is a report on the first and most far-reaching experiment, concerning the Høegh Mistral. The experiments were based on the three principles of the Co-operation Project: the theory of socio-technical systems, the six psychological job demands and the idea of an action research project.

The Høegh Mistral is a medium-sized bulk/car carrier with a total crew of 26, including officers. The ship has a periodically unmanned engine-room, i.e. the engine is watch-free at night. The design of the organisational experiment was planned before the launching from the shipyard, and it was therefore possible to choose a captain and other officers who would be interested in the experiment. By the end of 1969 the project team (the captain, the chief officer, the chief engineer, a representative of the shipping company and sometimes a research worker from the work research institutes) planned to carry out the following changes:

(1) *Introduction of increased autonomy for senior officers on board* in relation to the shipping company. This meant that the officers would have greater control over the ship's budget, and that the number of reports from the ship to the company in Oslo would be considerably reduced.

(2) *Integration of the deck and engine-room crews,* i.e. the creation of a combined job of seaman and engine-man. This was to be achieved through initial training of the seamen in the engine-room and of the engine-men on deck. This combination of the crew was also to be helped by the third proposed innovation.

(3) *A new system for planning day-to-day work.* A planning committee would be established consisting of the captain, the chief officer, the chief engineer and the boatswain as permanent members, the steward if need be and two members of the crew in rotation. Before a monthly planning meeting the chief engineer and the chief officer would produce lists of jobs to be done in the next month. At the monthly meeting each of those jobs would be given a priority rating. On the basis of that rating the chief officer and the chief engineer would each night divide the crew between them according to the jobs to be done, and the jobs would be recorded on a "work board".

(4) *Changes in the pay system.* The traditional system of overtime pay would be overhauled: a system of fixed overtime pay according to the average overtime on board similar ships in the company would be substituted for the old system whereby each seafarer received pay according to actual overtime worked. Another change was the introduction of delayed wage payments related to shore leave. The purpose of this was to motivate the crew to come back to the ship after their holidays.

(5) *Introduction of a common dayroom for officers and crew* in order to eliminate some of the status problems on board ship.

On the first voyage of the Høegh Mistral, which started in February 1970, a number of problems arose. The crew and a number the officers had doubts regarding the motives of the company in making the experiment. More specifically, many were concerned about the consequences the system of fixed overtime pay would have. Traditionally overtime had often provided a welcome opportunity to earn extra pay, and this had been achieved partly by slowing down the work pace on ordinary watches. Many feared that the captain and chief officers would misuse the new system by ordering more overtime than would be paid for. As time went on, however, the system of fixed overtime pay proved satisfactory in the opinion of most of the crew, and did not give rise to major trouble on board.

The senior officers were satisfied with the new system of budgeting and reporting; they considered that the new system made their work more interesting, and that they had gained new insights into the economic aspects of ship operation; and they felt more responsible.

It is fair to say that the EO-system with watch-free periods and the fact that the engine was new and did not need much control and repair were the main reasons for some of the most difficult problems which arose. First, it meant that the combined deck and engine-room crew worked most of the time on deck. In the beginning some of the former engine-men had some doubts whether deck work would be satisfying or not. They felt that the usual engine work was of a higher level and more demanding, and that deck work, which consists mostly of painting and cleaning, was dull. However, the principal operation to be carried out on the new engine was painting and cleaning, just as on deck, and the crew, including former engine-men, preferred to paint and clean in the open air rather than in the noisy and less pleasant engine-room. Secondly, the small amount of engine control required also meant that the engineers were able to take on more manual work such as small repair jobs. This strengthened the tendency for the crew to work most of the time on deck. In consequence the balance between deck and engine-room shifted in favour of the deck. The chief engineer was involved in work planning in the above-mentioned planning committee. However, the day-to-day organisation of work in the engine-room, which had formerly been one of the main duties of the first engineer, was now somewhat reduced, and he expressed much dissatisfaction with the new system. This led the chief engineer to play a more passive role in the planning, and the result was that the chief officer was increasingly identified as the only important person involved in the day-to-day organisation of work, and he was accused of acting as if he "owned" the whole crew.[55]

Controversies about the respective roles of the officers became the main problem on the first voyage of the Høegh Mistral. Another major problem arose in connection with the organisation of work on deck. The existence of the "work board", on which the crew could see whether they were to work on deck or in the engine-room the next day, and which jobs there were, meant that they began to feel more independent in their work; to a certain, though still limited, extent they could plan their own work, and they increasingly felt that the control and supervision of the chief officer were unnecessary and annoying: "On a rationalised ship it is idiotic to have a man who just stands and watches—that's back to the old style", said one of the seamen.[56] After initial scepticism the crew gradually accepted the combined seaman's and engine-man's job, and were eventually very satisfied with it. However, the promises that former seamen would have opportunities of engine training were not fulfilled because the engine ran so well. In addition the combined jobs caused problems for crew members who needed a specified amount of deck or engine-room experience in order to be admitted to the deck or engineer officers' schools.

In spite of the various problems at work, both officers and crew were satisfied with the common dayroom, and felt that crew-officer relations had become more relaxed. The common dayroom had eliminated some of the increasing problems of social contact, caused by the gradual reduction of crew numbers in recent years. However, problems created by the traditional high level of status differentiation on board ship had not been eliminated. This could be seen at the joint meetings on the progress of the experiment, where communications were strictly one-way: the captain did most of the talking. The crew and junior officers felt that everything had been decided in advance and the captain was disappointed with what he regarded as a very low degree of participation and interest, but nobody could help it.

At the end of the first trip the experiment looked like an almost complete failure. Nine people left the ship, seven because of the experiment, and seven more were planning to leave. However, the experiment was to be consolidated at a later stage. In the engine-room the junior engineers had felt that they did too much manual work, that the planning committee allocated too few crew to the engine-room, and that the crew tried to avoid engine-room work. These problems were solved by the permanent assignment of two cadets and one member of the crew to the engine-room, and by giving up the fixed overtime pay which had reduced the willingness of the crew to take on overtime work in the engine-room. The problem of the reduced role of the first engineer was solved by arranging for the chief engineer to consult the first engineer before planning meetings, by a less specific recording of engine-room jobs on the "work board", and by the fact that three persons were now permanently available for jobs in the engine-room. These solutions to the organisational problems in the engine-room were, in fact, a return to the pre-experimental situation. On later trips, however, some further changes were made. The highly automated engine which requires little supervision and repair has enabled the Høegh Mistral to navigate without a repair-man in the engine-room. The repair jobs are done by the junior engineers and by the permanent engine crew.

During the second and third trips the chief officer reduced the amount of supervision of the crew working on deck. Because of a work accident the boatswain had to leave the ship. This was a great relief for the crew, not because of any personal feelings towards the boatswain but because the crew to an increasing extent had begun to organise their own work. The work planning system and the "work board" had made the job of the boatswain redundant. When it was not possible to do a planned job because of bad weather, the crew found another one by studying the programme for the month or by doing jobs not yet included in the programme but which they had noticed themselves as needing to be done. Jobs formerly done by the boatswain, for instance cleaning and mending of tools, were done by the crew.

The results of the experiment after the first two years can be assessed as follows in terms of the five initial goals:

(1) The increased autonomy of the senior officers in relation to the shipping company has been a success both in the view of the senior officers and for the company. The budget performance of the Høegh Mistral was over the average for the company as a whole.

(2) All things considered the introduction of a combined seaman's and engineman's job may be judged a failure. It was not possible to give the former seamen the technical engine-room training that had been planned. Although training programmes were tried out they had not lasted long, partly because there was comparatively little work to be done and the training could therefore not be done "on the job", partly because the engineers were not interested in playing their parts in the artificially created training situations.

(3) The new work planning system ultimately proved efficient, but this result was achieved partly by special arrangements regarding the role of the first engineer (e.g. consultation between the chief engineer and the first engineer). The research workers hesitated to formulate a conclusion which is more evident to an outside observer: it seems that the role of a first engineer is superfluous and that his work planning duties could be done by the chief engineer; in fact this was done initially. The consequences of the new planning system for the crew were of a previously unforeseen magnitude. According to the project plan one purpose of the new system was to create a more autonomous work situation for the crew. This happened to a considerably greater extent than planned. The introduction of variety, autonomy and responsibility in the seamen's job was evaluated as the main achievement of the experiment by the crew themselves, by the officers and by the research workers.

(4) The system of fixed overtime pay functioned for nearly half a year, and statistics showed that everybody apart from the chief officer and the junior engineers had gained from the system. However, the system was abolished because a new collective agreement was awaited. When it came, the overtime

provisions were rather favourable (in terms of individual overtime pay), so nobody tried to have the fixed system re-established.

(5) The common dayroom proved a success, although the officers had to give up former privileges regarding possibilities of buying alcoholic beverages.

The over-all result of the experiment is difficult to assess in terms of productivity. However, the experiment seemed to show that quite a considerable reduction in the number of officers and crew was possible. The boatswain and the engine-room repair-man had been made redundant. Two-and-a-half years after the start of the experiment, the captain and chief engineer proposed that the ship's complement should be reduced to a total of 19 when at sea, and supplemented when the ship was in harbour. However, the contact group (with representatives from the unions and other personnel organisations) hesitated to approve this proposal. The experiment proved successful in giving the crew and the three most senior officers more autonomy at work. The work situation of the junior officers was not changed, and the role of the first engineer became rather less autonomous. As for over-all work satisfaction there are two main indicators. First, stability of employment on board the Høegh Mistral is reported to be quite high. Whereas a high personnel turnover is usually almost a part of the system of employment at sea, many members of the crew of the Høegh Mistral wanted to return to the ship after their holidays. This does not apply to the same degree to the junior officers, because to them experience with different types of ships is important for their careers. Secondly, the research workers have interviewed persons who had signed on when the work was already organised along the new lines. New crew members are impressed by the autonomy of deck work and by the relaxed relations between crew and officers at work and in the common dayroom.

Experiments similar to those on the Høegh Mistral have been carried out on board three other ships. On the Høegh Multina (a liquid-gas carrier) experiments have been adapted from the experience of the Høegh Mistral (the planning system, the autonomy of work on deck, the common dayroom). Experiments have also been focused on the relations between the work roles of deck and engine officers. The project has been based on the theory of matrix organisation. In order to avoid a high degree of rigid specialisation of officers in modern technologically advanced ships an attempt has been made to let the deck officers share the engine watches and the engineers share in some of the navigation jobs. This solution was based on a more diversified training of both deck officers and engineers. The experiment was partly successful, but the two categories could not be integrated to the degree intended. The Høegh Shipping Company has tried to apply to the Høegh Mallard and the Høegh Merit the experience acquired on the Høegh Mistral, but apart from a common mess and a common dayroom there is not much to point at that is not found on any conventional vessel.[57] However, successful experiments have been carried out on board the M.S. Balao of Torvald Klaveness Shipping Company, Oslo. Problems regarding the integration of deck and engine-room work were solved.[58]

GENERAL CONCLUSIONS

Most of the experiments with new forms of organisation of work in Scandinavia appear to be conducted in Sweden, and the fewest in Denmark. The most satisfactory explanation of the different diffusion of new forms of work organisation in the three countries covered in this paper is their different economic structures. For example, in terms of degree of economic concentration (measured by average plant size and financial commitment) Sweden clearly comes first, while Norway has the lowest average degree of concentration. In Norway the work research institutes and the LO-NAF Co-operation Project have provided efficient institutional backing for a number of carefully designed experiments that have afforded considerable inspiration to other innovators in Norway and Sweden. However, the Norwegian experiments cannot be compared to some of the Swedish experiments with regard to technological redesign. This picture is supported by a recent comparative investigation of automation in the three countries: "A continuous improvement of machinery has taken place, and in Sweden automation is a rather widespread feature whereas it is of a more concentrated nature in Norway and not yet of much importance in Denmark".[59] The industrial relations systems and the institutions of industrial democracy are roughly similar in the three countries, but this has not produced similar patterns regarding new forms of work organisation.

As regards the involvement of individual enterprises or companies, Gulowsen[60] reports systematic investigation of 13 experiments that were part of the LO-NAF Co-operation Project in Norway. He tried to arrive at general conclusions regarding the prerequisites for the success of such experiments, and related the amount of success (in terms of more influence for the workers and better opportunities for the development of skills and competence) to the following nine variables:

(a) the amount of autonomy or influence before the experiment;

(b) the amount of skill in the job before the experiment;

(c) safety and health risks;

(d) high or low personnel turnover;

(e) competence and efficiency in management;

(f) project competence on the part of the research workers;

(g) the amount of support from top management;

(h) the strength of the local unions; and

(i) the strength of social ties among the workers when away from work.

It is not possible to reproduce all the results of Gulowsen's detailed analysis in this paper. His general conclusion is that with low scores on all of the variables the prospects for an experiment are very bad. Two factors coincide with the success of all the experiments—low personnel turnover *(d)* and strength of social ties outside work *(i)*. Low safety and health risks *(c)* are a feature of the successful experiments, and also of some of the less successful. Successful experiments are also distinguished by good relations between the departmental management *(e)* and the research workers *(f)*. The development of the projects also depends on active support from the management of the company as a whole *(g)*; without such support only unimportant and short-term changes are possible. However, successful experiments do not seem to attract support from top management; in fact on certain projects the opposite would seem to be true.[61] Gulowsen's explanation is that top management views an experiment as providing a possible solution for a short-term problem, and loses interest once that problem is solved. Regarding the unions *(h)*, Gulowsen's conclusion is that the existence of strong, active unions contributes very positively to the success of the experiments.

It must be said that Gulowsen's conclusions are in terms of what is sometimes called "the micro-situation" of the "social actors" in the experiments. He did not include the influence of technology because the types of technology involved were so different that he could not establish a satisfactory common scale of measurement for them. Regarding the labour market, he makes the point that when the 13 experiments were carried out there was very little unemployment. However, one of the experiments reported in the present paper (Bang and Olufsen) was carried out in a context of high unemployment. The experience of the Høegh Mistral and of the Volvo factory at Kalmar seems to support the conclusion that scarcity of labour in the labour specific labour market of an enterprise is often an important reason for experimenting. The purpose is often to reduce turnover and to attract qualified labour, and this is often achieved by the experiments through better working conditions, job enrichment and participation.

Regarding productivity, a balanced conclusion from the 13 Norwegian experiments and from the others reported on in the present paper would seem to be that productivity is seldom reduced, except perhaps during a short initial period. On the contrary there are examples of high increases in productivity (e.g. Bang and Olufsen). In other cases the amount of increase in productivity is difficult to assess, and in yet other cases an increase can be inferred from the fact that it has been possible to reduce the number of workers employed. Through some experiments it was possible to halt falls in product quality and sales. Other cases seem to point to the conclusion that it is possible to improve adjustment to changing market conditions through the introduction of a more flexible work organisation. From the employers' point of view, therefore, experiments with new forms of work organisation often seem to have a number of benefits: increased productivity, lower personnel turnover and better adjustment to changing technology or market conditions. To secure some of these benefits, however, it may in some cases (e.g. Volvo, Bang and Olufsen) be necessary to make rather expensive new technological investments.

From the workers' point of view the conclusion must be twofold. On the one hand a more satisfying work situation is often obtained, but the amount of job enrichment or participation is often exaggerated: all things considered the amount of increased variety, autonomy and participation is often marginal, although it may be a change at a very critical point of the scale, as in the case of a change from repetitive jobs without autonomy to jobs with at least some variety and autonomy. On the other hand, these new forms of organisation seldom created more jobs; on the contrary they often reduced the number of personnel required. This is important where unemployment is high, as it was in Denmark. In fact, this has raised doubts on the part of the unions and other personnel organisations regarding the value of some of the experiments. Nor do experiments with new forms of work organisation promote the workers' involvement in union matters: in fact some of the workers who participated in experiments felt that unions at whatever level might be a hindrance to the progress of an experiment. Finally, it is difficult to assess to what degree the increase in productivity which regularly follows from new forms of work organisation is reflected in increased wages.

Notes

[1] Walter Galenson: "Scandinavia", in W. Galenson (ed.): *Comparative labor movements* (New York, Russell and Russell, 1952), p. 105.

[2] Lennart Jörberg and Olle Krantz: "Scandinavia, 1914-1970", Ch. 6 of Carlo M. Cipolla (ed.): *The Fontana economic history of Europe,* Vol. 6: *Contemporary economies* (London, Collins/Fontana Books, 1975), p. 7.

[3] ibid.; also William M. Lafferty: *Economic development and the response of labour in Scandinavia* (Oslo-Bergen-Tromsø, Universitetsforlaget, 1971), p. 53.

[4] Assar Lindbeck: *Swedish economic policy* (London, Macmillan, 1975), pp. 1-2.

[5] Jörberg and Krantz, loc. cit.

[6] Lafferty, op. cit., p. 44.

[7] Ingemar Lindblad, Krister Wahlbäck and Claes Wiklund: *Politik i Norden* (Stockholm, Aldus-Bonniers, 1972), p. 32.

[8] Jörberg and Krantz, op. cit., p. 61; Handelsministeriet: *Perspektivplan-redegørelse 1972-1987,* Bilag III: *Byerhvervene* (Copenhagen, 1974), p. 64.

[9] Galenson, op. cit.

[10] Lafferty, op. cit.

[11] Jörberg and Krantz, op. cit., p. 63.

[12] Lindbeck, op. cit., p. 8.

[13] Norges Offentlige Utredninger (NOU): *Immigrations politik* (Oslo, 1973), p. 17.

[14] Nordic Council: *Yearbook of Nordic Statistics, 1975* (Stockholm, 1976), p. 37.

[15] Stig Kuhlmann: *Danske arbejdsmarkedsforhold 1974* (Copenhagen, Arbejdsministeriet, Økonomisk-statistik konsulent, 1974); Arbetsmarknadsdepartementet: *Att utvärdera arbetsmarknadspolitik,* Statens offentliga utredningar 1974: 29 (Stockholm, 1974).

[16] *Nasjonalbudsjettet 1975,* St. medl. nr. 1, 1974-75 (Oslo).

[17] Galenson, op. cit., p. 134.

[18] Fairly recent versions of these agreements (in English translation) are reproduced in ILO: *Basic agreements and joint statements on labour-management relations,* Labour-Management Relations Series, No. 38 (Geneva, 1971), pp. 28-32, 119-150 and 168-186.

[19] Galenson, op. cit., p. 141.

[20] Nordic Council: *Yearbook of Nordic Statistics, 1975,* op. cit., p. 66.

[21] Poul Vidriksen: *Debatten om industrielt demokrati i Norge* (Copenhagen, Arbejdsministeriet, 1969), pp. 10-11.

[22] G. Wiesener: *Midlertidig lov om arbeider-utvalg i industrielle bedrifter m.v. a 23. juli 1920 med anmerkninger og henvisninger* (Kristiania, Steenske Forlag, 1920); A. Molin and R. Sohlman: *Studier rörande industriell demokrati i Norge, England, Tjeckoslovakien och Österrike,* Statens offentliga utredningar 1925: 30 (Stockholm, 1925).

[23] Erik Orth: *Demokrati på arbejdspladsen—debatten i Sverige* (Copenhagen, Arbejdsministeriet, 1969), p. 10.

[24] *Samarbejdsudvalg* in Denmark, *Produktionsutvalg* in Norway, *Företagsnämud* in Sweden.

[25] Vidriksen, op. cit., pp. 12 and 46.

[26] Orth, op. cit., pp. 18-19.

[27] ibid., p. 22.

[28] Vidriksen, op. cit., p. 37; Erik Orth: *Participation in management: A Danish approach* (mimeographed), p. 20.

[29] Harriet Gullvåg (Holter): *Posisjon og innstillinger hos industriarbeidere, Nordisk Psykologi,* monografi nr. 6 (Oslo, 1955).

[30] Sten Martini Jørgensen: *Kommunale samarbejdsudvalg,* Socialforskningsinstituttets publikationer 50 (Copenhagen, Teknisk Forlag, 1971); K. Tolderlund: *Samarbejdsudvalgsundersøgelsen 1968* (Samarbejdsnaevnet, Dansk Arbejdsgiverforening and LO Landsorganisationen i Danmark, 1972).

[31] Martini Jørgensen, op. cit., pp. 149 ff.

[32] *Samarbejdsnaevnet* in Denmark, *Samarbeidsrådet* in Norway, *Utvecklingsrådet för samarbetsfrågor* in Sweden.

[33] Ann Westenholz: *Lønmodtagerrepraesentation i aktieselskabsbestyrelser,* Foreløbig rapport om erfaringer fra de første par år efter lovens ikrafttraeden. Nyt fra samfundsvidenskaberne (Copenhagen, 1976).

[34] English translation in the ILO *Legislative Series,* 1976—Swe. 1.

[35] Edmund Dahlström: "Efficiency, satisfaction and democracy at work: Conceptions of industrial relations in post-war Sweden", in *Acta Sociologica,* No. 1, 1977, pp. 25-53.

[36] Arnulf Kolstad: "Samarbeidsprosjektet—LO/NAF", in *Kontrast,* Nos. 4-5, 1970, pp. 2-13.

[37] Einar Thorsrud and Fred Emery: *Industrielt demokrati. Representasjon på styreplan i bedrifterne?* (Oslo, Universitetsforlaget, 1964), p. 11.

[38] idem: *Mot en ny bedriftsorganisasjon* (Oslo, Tanum, 1969).

[39] Øyvind Skard: *Organizational change and job design,* A manual of the Co-operation Council LO-NAF (Oslo, 1976).

[40] Einar Thorsrud: *Democracy at work and perspectives on the quality of working life in Scandinavia* (Oslo, Work Research Institutes, 1976; mimeographed).

[41] Swedish Employers' Confederation (SAF): *Job reform in Sweden. Conclusions from 500 shop floor projects* (Stockholm, 1975).

[42] Sekretariatet for Danmarks Erhvervsfond: *Motivation* (Copenhagen, 1970).

[43] Samarbejdsnaevnet: *De fire første samarbejdsforsøg* (Copenhagen, 1972).

[44] Flemming Agersnap, Finn Junge, Ann Westenholz, Palle Møldrup and Lisbeth Brinch: "Danish experiments with new forms of cooperation on the shopfloor", in *Personnel Review,* No. 3, 1974, pp. 34-50.

[45] The description is based on the following sources: DASF: *Motivation og selvstyrende grupper* (Copenhagen, 1971), and background papers for the seminar which was the point of departure for the writing of the pamphlet; Sekretariatet for Danmarks Erhvervsfond: *Motivation,* op. cit.; Bang and Olufsen: *Samarbejde og ledelse,* Rapport om 1 års forsøgsvirksomhed hos Bang og Olufsen A/S (Skive, 1972); Samarbejdsnaevnet: *De fire første samarbejdsforsøg,* op. cit.; Søren Grundtvig Sørensen and Herluf Trolle: *Montage af TV-Kabinetter på B and O, Struer* (Copenhagen, Teknologisk Institut, 1977; mimeographed) and various articles from periodicals, especially *Business Week* (New York), 8 Dec. 1975 and *Financial Times* (London), 12 Sep. 1975. In addition discussions were held with the plant manager, Mr. Niels Ole Vonsild.

[46] From an information sheet issued by the company.

[47] The Norwegian producer of television sets, Tandberg, has done the same: advertisements in newspapers have mentioned the autonomous group organisation of the company.

[48] This section is based on Stefan Agurén, Reine Hanssen and K. G. Karlsson: *The Volvo Kalmar plant: The impact of new design on work organization* (Stockholm, The Rationalization Council SAF-LO, 1976); Jon Gulowsen: *Arbeidervilkår. Et tilbageblikk på Samarbeidsprosjektet LO-NAF* (Oslo, Tanum-Norli, 1975); Rolf Lindholm and Jan-Peder Norstedt: *Volvo rapporten* (Stockholm, Svenska Arbetsgivareföreningen, 1975); *Volvo Pressinformation* (Gothenburg, 1974; mimeographed).

[49] Agurén et al, op. cit.

[50] This account is based on Jacques Roggema and Einar Thorsrud: *Et skip i utvikling: Høegh Mistral-projektet* (Oslo, Johan Grundt Tanum Forlag, 1974); Jacques Roggema and Nils Kristian Hammarstrøm: *Nye organisasjonsformer til sjøs: Høegh Multina-forsøget* (Oslo, Tanum-Norli, 1975); Karl Rogne: "Redesigning the design process: Superstructures of ships", in *Applied*

ergonomics, 1964, 5.4, pp. 213-218; Ragnar Johansen: *Changes in work planning increase ship-board democracy: The first 3 years of experience from M/S Balao,* Work Research Institutes, AI-DOC. 47/1976 (Oslo, 1976).

[51] Roggema and Hammerstrøm, op. cit., pp. 25-26.

[52] Roggema and Thorsrud, op. cit., p. 16.

[53] Rogne, op. cit., p. 214.

[54] Roggema and Thorsrud, op. cit., p. 14.

[55] ibid., p. 59.

[56] ibid., p. 72.

[57] Roggema and Hammarstrøm, op. cit., p. 133.

[58] Johansen, op. cit.

[59] Reinhard Lund: "The Scandinavian countries", in Albert A. Blum (ed.): *Contemporary developments in industrial relations* (Westport, Connecticut, Greenwood Press).

[60] Gulowsen, op. cit.

[61] ibid., p. 82.

FRANCE

FRANCE
Yves Delamotte*

NATIONAL CONDITIONS

Distinctive features of the student riots and other happenings of May 1968 in France were a challenge to the legitimacy of established institutions and a tidal wave of critical analysis. Both these features naturally affected the exercise of management authority and the condition of the workers. However, conditions of work in industry, especially for unskilled or semi-skilled workers on assembly lines, came to the attention of the public through the strikes that took place in 1971. In 1971 and 1972 the problem of semi-skilled work on assembly lines was widely discussed and became a focal point of social concern.

The serious human consequences of a certain kind of organisation of production, of fragmented tasks, had of course already been denounced by philosophers like Simone Weil and sociologists like Georges Friedmann. In his works the latter had analysed the Hawthorne studies[1] and the experiments carried out by the human relations schools;[2] he had even referred to the possibility of job enlargement. However, another 15 years were to elapse before these problems took on a national political dimension as it became clear that for a variety of reasons (such as changes in the national outlook and in the educational level of the population) the workers were becoming increasingly restless under prevailing conditions, especially on the assembly line.

The sources and manifestations of that restlesness will not be dealt with in the present paper; they were the subject of a number of percipient remarks in the report of the Director-General of the International Labour Office to the 1975 Session of the International Labour Conference,[3] and it is significant that the same economic and social factors should have produced the same effects in all the industrialised countries. What does merit attention is the action taken to deal with the problem by the various parties concerned; and because original solutions can emerge in individual countries there is a justification for publishing national monographs such as the present one on France.

In France measures concerning work organisation have never been put forward as a panacea: other matters such as hours of work, occupational safety

---

* Conservatoire national des arts et métiers, Paris. Formerly director of the National Agency for the Improvement of Working Conditions (ANACT).

and security of employment or the physical environment have also been regarded as very important. It is therefore advisable to begin by distinguishing the various phases and aspects of the over-all endeavour to improve conditions of work on the part of the public authorities, individual employers, employers' organisations and the trade unions.

The question of the unskilled or semi-skilled worker emerged in 1971 as a major social problem worthy of management concern. A working party of the main French employers' organisation, the Conseil national du patronat français (CNPF), had produced a report on the subject by the end of that year. The matter was further discussed at the national conference of that organisation held in Marseilles in October 1972. A national body entitled "Entreprise et progrès" (Management and Progress), which is essentially a discussion group for the more progressive firms, and is concerned with pursuing ideas and not with the defence of employers' interests, had produced in May of that year, in preparation for the above-mentioned conference, a document[4] which was based on a survey of the opinions of chief executives. The document put forward various proposals for incorporation in future CNPF policy, and suggested, in particular, that it should become a CNPF objective to do away with assembly-line work in the sense of work divided into repetitive fragmented tasks of very short duration, performed at an unchanging pace imposed by an external authority. It was proposed that concerted action along those lines should be taken throughout the European Economic Community.

The trade union reaction to all this was rather muted. In February 1972, however, the Confédération Générale du Travail (CGT) made public its own proposals for the improvement of conditions of work. On 22 February the Minister of Labour, Mr. Fontanet, appeared in a television debate on conditions of work with the General Secretary of the Confédération Française Démocratique du Travail (CFDT), Mr. Edmond Maire. This showed that the Government, too, was now aware of the urgency of the problem.[5]

The importance now attached by the Government to the improvement of conditions of work was shown by its drafting of an Act of Parliament concerning the improvement of conditions of work, which was adopted on 27 December 1973.[6] The Act governs the machinery and subject-matter of consultations on conditions of work between heads of undertakings and the workers' representatives on works committees: it provides in particular that works committees must be consulted before new work structuring methods are introduced. The Act also established a National Agency for the Improvement of Working Conditions.

The Act contains no substantive provisions requiring employers to observe specified norms or to make any necessary adjustments in their existing practice. This is in striking contrast with the Workplaces Ordinance, 1975, of the Federal Republic of Germany. The discretion shown by the authorities when drafting the French legislation can be attributed to the fact that in March 1973 national talks covering the whole economy were held between the CNPF and the most representative national trade union organisations.[7] Rules and standards could be expected to emerge from the talks, and the Government refrained from including in the Bill any measure dealing with the substance of the issues at stake, so as to allow the talks to proceed unhindered and to give them every chance of producing worth-while results. The Government can almost be said to have laid a wager on the fruitfulness of collective bargaining. It was quite a gamble, as time was to show. First of all, the talks proceeded very slowly, and reached a conclusion only in March 1975, i.e. two years after they had begun. Above all, the 1975 agreement contains statements of principles and intentions rather than binding rules. This aspect of the agreement was denounced by the two organisations most representative of industrial workers (the CGT and the CFDT), which did not sign.

A few examples taken from the agreement give a better understanding of its scope and its limitations. Under the first heading, dealing with work organisation, there are first a number of general indications concerning labour standards. The volume of work, the number of operations to be performed, the number of machines to be operated must correspond to a normal effort. The workforce must be sufficiently numerous to avoid any excessive overwork resulting in particular from the need to carry on the work of workers who may be away. A technical assessment may be made by an outside expert if there is a disagreement about workload. Article 5 provides that it is desirable to achieve job enlargement with longer job cycles. Job enrichment and the formation of teams with some degree of autonomy are mentioned as interesting possibilities. Such work restructuring should be carried out in accordance with the principles laid down at the beginning of the agreement with regard to standards and workload. In addition wage rates and grading should take account of the increases in skill that may result from job enrichment and enlargement.

These provisions give explicit expression to the value attached by French management to work re-structuring and new forms of work organisation. It is also recognised that action along those lines may affect grading and wage rates. Both the CGT and the CFDT would have liked these parts of the agreement to be more specific and to include more formal commitments. The CGT, for example, would have liked to see recognition of the following principles: re-structuring of work should not lead to an increase in workload; it must be accompanied by a considerable vocational training effort, and it must lead to higher qualifications, reflected in grading and earnings.

The same description can be made of the other parts of the agreement, which also contain statements of principles and intentions. For example, it is said to be desirable to try out and introduce flexible working hours and to restrict shift working; and to be desirable to do away with payment by results, or at any rate to reduce its relative importance, for example by incorporating the piece-work element in basic rates. The CGT and the CFDT would have liked to substitute more binding and specific provisions, especially with regard to all aspects of shift work.

Having been concluded for the economy as a whole, the agreement was admittedly bound to be of a very general character, and its value was bound to lie in the recognition by management of the existence of certain problems and of the lines along which they would have to be solved. In addition, it was only an outline agreement, and as such understood to be only the first stage in a bargaining process that was to be extended at a later stage to individual industries. Those further negotiations began shortly afterwards, and by the beginning of October 1976 they covered the cement, furniture, brick and tile, insurance, chemical, building, public works, fireproof materials, banking, textile, food and petroleum industries, while discussions were continuing in some 30 other industries.

The extent of the agreements reached varies from industry to industry. In some cases the agreement merely amends some provisions of the national collective agreement that already existed in the industry concerned. For example, the agreement on conditions of work in the insurance industry contains provisions on the reduction of hours of work for pregnant women and on short-term holidays with pay for workers with dependants. In other cases, the agreements introduce innovations in respect of important points that have a closer bearing on conditions of work. In the chemical industry, for instance, it is provided that the share of investment set aside for the improvement of conditions of work shall be a separate entry in each firm's budget. Various provisions relate to workers on continuous or semi-continuous processes. If they have been employed on continuous processes for five years, they shall be granted priority of employment on non-continuous work, and shall on transfer receive an indemnity of a declining amount, for a period of one year. Workers on semi-continuous processes shall be entitled to one day of compensatory rest every six months. Additional holidays are specified for workers nearing retiring age. Other provisions increase, subject to certain conditions, the hours credited to shop stewards and trade union delegates when workers on continuous or semi-continuous processes account for 15 per cent or more of the total workforce. However, this agreement was not signed by the CGT and the CFDT.

These industry agreements generally do not deal with work organisation, no doubt because the employers' organisations regard the provisions of the main agreement as sufficient. However, the agreement concluded in the petroleum industry provides that experiments with job enrichment and autonomous group working shall be made after consultation with the works committee.

It seems that while some of the agreements constituted a step forward on important points like shift work, most of them only introduced minor changes stemming logically from the application of an existing industry agreement, or did no more than reproduce the gist of the main agreement.

The legislation and agreements just described originated in 1973. In May 1974 Mr. Giscard d'Estaing was elected President of the Republic, and on his initiative social thought and policy began to revolve around two main subjects, namely reform of the undertaking and the upgrading of manual labour.

On the first subject a committee was set up under the chairmanship of a former Government minister, Mr. Sudreau. After consulting many managers, experts and trade unionists, the committee submitted its report to the President in February 1975, and it was then immediately published.[8] The report contains numerous proposals relating to a variety of aspects of the undertaking. The improvement of conditions of work receives a good deal of attention, being treated as a present-day necessity. It is pointed out that such an improvement is not just a matter of accident prevention and better physical facilities; it must also involve giving the workers a greater variety of more skilled tasks and a greater measure of responsibility, semi-autonomous group working being mentioned as an interesting avenue to be explored. It is suggested that all workers should have the right to express their views on the content of their jobs and on their conditions of work. In this respect the report argues from the positive results of a few trials made in undertakings where the workers in a particular shop hold regular meetings with their immediate supervisors to discuss what changes may need to be made to the working environment or the organisation of work. In the report, management is encouraged to draw on these experiments. All these suggestions lead up to the central theme of the upgrading of manual labour. The committee found that the position of manual workers in France was inferior, both financially and in terms of social status, to that of manual workers in other industrialised countries. Upgrading is therefore required both through management and through the Government.

Economic trends were not conducive to the rapid implementation of the various proposals made in the report, and by October 1976 it was in relation to the upgrading of manual labour that the most progress had been made. Since January 1976 a Secretary of State for manual workers had been assisting the Minister of Labour. An Act has been adopted whereby manual workers who have been in certain kinds of employment (continuous working, assembly-line working, furnaces, construction sites) for five years shall be entitled to retirement pensions at the full rate at the age of 60 instead of 65. Under another Act, workers doing overtime were entitled to compensatory rest on full pay in addition to the usual overtime pay. The improvement of conditions of work is one of the essential components of this upgrading policy. Others are action in relation to pay (special provisions of the anti-inflation plan to promote collective bargaining when it relates to the wages of manual workers) and an endeavour to influence public opinion (poster campaigns have reminded the nation of the extent of its debt to manual workers). The Secretary of State has repeatedly urged public and private undertakings to go in for work re-structuring. The financial resources of the National Agency for the Improvement of Working Conditions (ANACT), which were modest in 1975, were much increased, to 8 million francs in the 1976 budget, and a special Fund for the Improvement of Working Conditions (FACT) has been set up.

ANACT, established under the Act of 1973, is a public agency supervised by the Ministry of Labour and having a tripartite governing body comprising representatives of employers, of the most representative national trade union confederations and of various government departments, in addition to a number of experts. Its essential purpose is to collect and disseminate information on all aspects of conditions of work, for use by management and trade unions. It publishes material and holds meetings on a great variety of subjects such as industrial architecture, consequences of certain technical developments, shift work, flexible working hours and trends in conditions of work. It provides technical assistance and teaching aids for training bodies, which are increasingly showing an interest in conditions of work. Above all, it helps undertakings of various kinds to carry out experiments (i.e. launch pilot projects), and evaluates the experiments with a view to helping other undertakings to take similar action.

The limitations of ANACT derive from the fact that it can only inform, train and try to convince; it has no power to compel. Nor can it grant financial aid (though it does meet part of the cost of the preliminary surveys required for a pilot project, the rest being paid for by the undertaking). However, in 1976 the Government set up the Fund for the Improvement of Working Conditions, which amounted to 24 million francs for that year. The Fund is in fact one entry in the budget of the Department of Labour, and the aid is granted by the Minister on the technical advice of ANACT. To qualify for aid, projects must meet certain requirements (comprehensiveness, novelty, possibilities of diffusion), and ANACT is responsible for drawing lessons from all projects receiving aid from the Fund and for publicising them among the largest possible number of undertakings, thus justifying the use of public funds. On the average, financial aid may not exceed 15 per cent of the investment. An undertaking receiving aid must commit itself to allowing the Department and ANACT to monitor the experiment, and to providing any information ANACT may require for the purposes of analysis and publicity. This freedom of access is the necessary counterpart of the aid supplied. It should be noted in conclusion that the opinion of the works committee regarding a proposed project must accompany the undertaking's application to the Department of Labour.

A number of undertakings made trial runs with work re-structuring before the public authorities and the employers' and workers' organisations entered the field. In 1975-76 ANACT tried to build up an over-all picture[9] of what they had achieved. The information collected related to 60 establishments belonging to 49 undertakings (certainly more undertakings had been engaged in such activities, but some of them were not covered by the survey or did not choose to respond to the request for information). In the 60 establishments covered, the experiments began before 1971 in 10 cases, and after that year in 50. The biggest number in any one year (22) started in 1973. There was job rotation in 14 undertakings, job enlargement in 10, job enrichment in 15, group working in 43. The last of these features appears to have aroused the most interest, and the ANACT analysis related chiefly to those 43 experiments, of which 24 had been carried out in the electrical engineering industry. Group working had been introduced for a widely varying proportion of the production workers in the establishments concerned, the average being 18 per cent. The reasons given for making the experiments were two:

(a) need to motivate the workers, to make their work more interesting, to improve labour-management relations; and

(b) search for a more flexible system of production.

On the whole, most of the undertakings put forward social reasons, but those where there were long assembly lines also mentioned the technical drawbacks of that kind of production. Few undertakings referred explicitly to increased output as an objective in making the change.

The survey also covered the nature of the changes made. Various arrangements had been tried out in assembly work. Groups had been formed by considerably shortening assembly lines, by cutting them up, or by setting up sub-assembly stations off the line. In a few cases the assembly line had been completely abolished and a group formed instead to assemble the whole product. In machining, group working had sometimes required the relocation of the machines. In most cases the manufacturing process had not been altered and the change related to the functions and responsibilities of the operatives, which had been enlarged and collectivised.

The results of the experiments were described as positive in psychological and social terms. It was reported that the workers directly involved were satisfied[10] and did not wish to revert to the previous work structures. In this connection it should be noted that they were mostly young people, often selected from among those volunteering to take part in experiments. Absenteeism generally fell off slightly, but the reduction was attributed more to flexible working hours, where they had been introduced, than to changes in the organisation of the work itself. In general the management seemed to regard the experiments as providing means of coping with the dislocation caused by absences rather than of checking absenteeism itself. A higher level of skill was reported from all undertakings, in most cases associated with regrading of the multi-skilled.

On the economic and technical plane, almost all of the undertakings reported a fall in the number of rejects and an improvement in quality. Labour productivity was on the increase in most of the establishments (a quarter of the total) that agreed to supply information in that respect. Other gains mentioned were enhanced ability to meet deadlines, a diminution of work in progress and greater flexibility of the production system, which was better suited to the growing differentiation of products. The cost of the changes was often reported to have been high. It was higher when the new organisation called for the design of new jobs, with special equipment (e.g. an assembly station), than when all that was involved was the division of succeeding sections of an assembly line. Even in the latter cases, however, allowance had to be made for the space required for buffer stocks, training centres and often costs resulting from upgrading. There were of course countervailing advantages, such as higher job satisfaction, improvements in quality and falls in absenteeism. These advantages, however, were not as irreversible as the increase in costs, which was permanent. Establishments were extremely cautious in reporting recorded falls in absenteeism ("Will it last?"). These factors may account for the fact that even when management acknowledged a balance of advantage accruing from a change, many experiments none the less remained limited to a fraction of the workforce, even in the particular departments where they had taken place. It was also pointed out that a considerable proportion of the workers prefer the traditional system and that the extension of group working to an entire shop would require a considerable enlargement of the premises, especially if new assembly stations were to be set up. In fact the only changes described as being of interest to the entire workforce were either of limited cost (especially when not calling for new equipment) or involving a new approach to management and a redistribution of responsibilities rather than a search for new forms of organisation of industrial operations.

Besides changes introduced in individual undertakings, action taken by some employers' organisations also deserves a mention. The big Union des industries métallurgiques et minières (UIMM) has set up a service which publishes and gives wide circulation to monographs dealing with experiments, and has organised discussion groups or information sessions for management on recent developments in work organisation. The UIMM also launched "research teams" on the improvement of conditions of work[11]: the workers in a particular shop hold a meeting once or twice a month with the shop foreman to discuss conditions of work and decide on action to be taken, often with funds made available beforehand by the management. An improvement in conditions of work then appears to be the positive outcome of discussions among the workers, who have been called upon to state their views on job content and conditions of work.

The ANACT survey yielded no specific information on the way in which organisational change was introduced and on trade union reactions. At the level of the undertaking, such reactions seem to vary. The most frequent reaction is "wait and see": the union is above all unwilling to be involved and to be regarded as sponsoring or approving the change. At the national level the big trade union confederations have had to take a stand on experiments with new forms of work organisation. The attitude of the CGT-FO is probably much the same as that of the trade unions in the Federal Republic of Germany or in Sweden. More attention will therefore be devoted to the views of the CFDT and the CGT, which in any event represent the majority of industrial workers.

For the CFDT, better conditions of work constitute an objective of long standing. It wants an improvement in physical conditions as distinct from the grant of bonuses or allowances. The improvement should be sought through simultaneous action in different fields—hours of work (especially by reducing them, particularly for shift work), safety and the physical environment, forms of remuneration (elimination of payment by results), work organisation and job content, and status and authority in the undertaking. It can be brought about only by continuous pressure on management, for these changes are expensive and are not necessarily advantageous in terms of the prevailing economic orthodoxy (which leads for example to the extension of shift work in order to compensate for costly investments in plant). Employers also exert their power through the usual scientific management measures designed to perpetuate the isolation, passivity and subordination of the workers. Accordingly, when employers claim to be moving away from scientific management a problem arises, and a counter-strategy is required. The many reports and other documents produced by the CFDT appear to share the following main themes. First, it is right to challenge scientific management, and there can be no question of defending the traditional forms of organisation of work, whose degrading and otherwise harmful effects were denounced years ago. Accordingly, management-sponsored changes in the organisation of work must not be systematically resisted. However, they will be acceptable only if they are introduced in a specified manner and subject to definite guarantees—a relaxation of the constraints on the workforce (pace of work, workload), enhanced safety at work, more skilled employment. The unions must not be left out in the cold or neutralised, and there must be no risks of competition among the workers themselves (one of the CFDT's reasons for not signing the main agreement of 1975 was that under the heading of "organisation of work" the

CNPF draft recommended the gradual substitution of collective bonuses for individual payment by results).[12] In addition these changes must be part of a general programme covering all aspects of conditions of work. More fundamentally, these organisational changes must lead to a recognition that workers have a right to express themselves through their work. This means not that they should be free to convey their wishes or suggestions to the employer or the management, who would be free in turn to take whatever action they saw fit, but that the workers should be able to impose changes on the basis of their own experience of work situations. The union should assist, without substituting itself for the workers, in the systematic utilisation of that experience. This process will tend to eliminate the Taylorian distinction between those who plan the work and those who carry it out: the workers will ultimately be able to exercise a certain amount of collective power in this field. In that perspective of workers' management, the organisation of work in semi-autonomous groups is advantageous.

Like the CFDT, the CGT does not *a priori* reject work re-structuring when it is designed to reduce the unpleasantness and monotony of the work and to promote the identification of the workers' aptitudes and the development of their skills. But there must be an insistence on safeguards to accompany such changes: there must be no reduction in the numbers employed, and no increase in workload or stepping up of the pace of work; the workers must be given prospects of upgrading and higher pay under a comprehensive training and upgrading scheme, especially for the unskilled. This policy had already been decided in connection with the national talks that took place from 1973 to 1975. The definition of the above-mentioned safeguards has not been followed by the establishment of a specific list of claims for the guidance of unions faced with experiments in individual undertakings. Like the CFDT, the CGT has no intention of issuing directions which might not be followed. It is therefore stated to be for workers and militants on the spot to take a suitable stand, but of course without themselves ever appearing to sponsor or give formal approval to a change.

These decisions of principle by the CGT are accompanied by an increasing determination to discover what lies behind employers' moves to introduce new forms of work organisation, and by an endeavour to ascertain how changes in organisation are received by the workers and what the consequences are in terms of workload, job content, grading and remuneration. A painstaking review by the workers themselves would appear likely to be more fruitful than systematic and hasty denunciation. First, it will provide the foundation for the elaboration of specific claims in the light of experience. If, for example, the workers' responsibilities increase, a claim can be put forward for a higher grade and higher pay. Above all, this kind of review will make it easier to distinguish what part of the changes reflect a management initiative and what part is apparently dictated by technological change. If the experiments are only manoeuvres on the employers' part they are bound to be bogged down in the contradictions of class collaboration; on the other hand if they reflect technical requirements, they will probably spread. This desire to make a thorough investigation of changes in work organisation does not imply that the CGT is blind to the intentions of employers taking this course. In every case labour productivity rises, and the employer is bound to gain by the change: the objective remains the same—the maximum output in the minimum time. The CGT considers that only radical changes affecting the ownership of the means of production can provide a genuine solution to the problems with which management claims to be concerned in this context. It was decided that pending such changes, members of the Confederation should endeavour to learn more, so as to acquire a better understanding of what was behind the employers' moves and to be in a better position to decide what action might be called for.

CASE STUDIES

Electrical kitchen appliances

This experiment was made in a plant belonging to a firm which is itself part of a larger group that employs 8,400 people in about 20 plants and is the leading manufacturer of small household electrical appliances. Most of the firm's share capital is still in the hands of descendants of the man who founded the firm in 1857. It manufactures pressure cookers, deep-frying machines, electric coffee pots, grills, electric-powered knives, toasters, ice-cream mixers and yoghurt machines in three plants, located respectively in the Vosges and Pyrene mountains and in Burgundy. In all three plants a policy of active improvement of conditions of work has been adopted at the suggestion of the general management of the firm, and a number of experiments have been launched. The experiment covered in this case study took place in the Burgundian plant.

The products manufactured at that plant are pressure cookers (1.6 million a year), deep-frying machines (500,000) and electric coffee pots (160,000). For all these products the sequence of operations is as follows: cutting, stamping, finishing, assembly and packing. In July 1976 the plant had 1,200 employees. This figure includes 200 employees (mostly commercial travellers) for the marketing department of the firm as a whole. The manufacturing department comprised over 700 people, of whom about 520 were employed on production work. Apart from a management staff of 6, 13 supervisors and some office and technical staff, the latter figure comprised 166 workers employed on presses, 53 on polishing and 280 (mostly women) on assembly work. The experiment was concerned with the assembly of deep-friers, for which the firm holds 70 per cent of a steadily growing market. In 1973 the assembly line for the stainless steel deep-friers was 50 m long, and about 60 people were employed on it. The job cycle time ranged from 12.6 to 75.6 seconds. At each work station the tasks were very fragmented, no part being screwed in place by the worker who fitted it.

The project was started for welfare and psychological reasons: it was desired to give the personnel more interest in their work by altering the fragmented work system, and thus to meet modern requirements. Financial and efficiency considerations and objectives also played a part: by breaking up the assembly line, it was hoped to make the organisation more flexible and to enable it to cope more quickly and productively with increasing demand for a widening range of models. It was also desired if not to reduce absenteeism, at least to attenuate its effects on output.

Early in June 1973 the organisation and methods service and the manufacturing department held a joint meeting at the management's request, and it was decided in principle to stage an experiment, but only after assembly-line workers had been interviewed. Such interviews were carried out by members of the organisation and methods service. It was found that 63 per cent of the workers would prefer a shorter line, and that 75 per cent were in favour of completing an entire assembly or sub-assembly. These indications strengthened the management's intention of breaking up the assembly line and constituting work cells with enlarged jobs. The project was worked out in more detail by the organisation and methods service and the technical and manufacturing departments. It was decided that the work group should consist of eight persons, each with definite tasks to perform. The cost of the experiment was estimated, and members of the group were selected among volunteers, care being taken not to include over-achievers, since their inclusion would distort the results and make it impossible to draw useful conclusions from the experiment.

The group started work early in January 1974. From January till the end of March was hard going: in January there were signs of irritation, and some tension within the group; early in February, after the group had held a meeting, some assignments were altered; on 22 February the experiment seemed to be a failure, the atmosphere was strained and output was very low. What saved the experiment was the decision, taken at the end of February, to add another worker (bringing the size of the group to nine workers) to perform certain preparatory tasks; a review of assignments was also undertaken by the technical services. By the end of March the group seemed to have settled down and output was up to the planned level.

The change had been designed by the technical services without worker participation. Subsequently the group members' reactions led those services to accept or think up further changes. Thus the experiment was initially a trial for the organisation and methods staff. They found it hard to accept complaints about choices they had made, and which they believed to be the best. They felt that the changes requested by the group members were a challenge to their functions and knowledge, and that if they agreed to the changes they would in a sense be failing to perform their appointed task. However, they gradually gave in. Simultaneously the management decided to break up the organisation and methods service into a central office and units in individual shops, reporting to the head of the manufacturing department: thus the job designers were brought back to the shop floor and into closer contact with the production process.

By October 1976 there were three groups of nine workers each. The work was done in five stages. Job No. 1 is held by a man; it calls for some physical effort, since there are a large number of deep-friers to lift and move about. On the original line the main tasks assigned to this job (assembly and fitting of the thermostat and the heating element, check for leaks) were distributed among five different people. This man also does all the heavy work for the group. All the other jobs are held by women, each job consisting of the merger of some ten previously separate operations. Job No. 2 (two women) deals with assembly. Job No. 3 (two women) involves the fitting of a few parts, but most of these workers' time is spent cleaning the inside and checking the electrical fittings. Besides more fitting and (external) cleaning, job No. 4 (two women) involves further checks and packaging. Job No. 5 involves the making of the lid. It should be noted that on most jobs checking alternates with assembly work. The assembly line is now 17 m long, and job cycle times have been increased to as long as 3 minutes. It will be said that such data are typical of assembly-line operation; but clearly the new line with 9 workers is very different from the previous one with 60. The group members' only obligation is to produce a specified number of deep-friers per day. Members are free to rotate jobs as suits them best. By forming buffer stocks, all group members can become to some extent autonomous. As a worker told the author of this paper, "We do as we like here."

It should be noted that this change in work organisation was not accompanied by re-gradings, since the management considers that the change, while providing job enlargement, does not call for a rise in the level of skill. In another part of the shop the operators of heavy or complex machines have also been made responsible for adjustments and repairs; that job enrichment was reflected in higher grading. The new grade, which was at first peculiar to this particular undertaking, has since become one of the steps in the ladder provided for in a national grading agreement for the industry. It is noteworthy that this establishment of a new grade meets the objective of upgrading labour, and provided the trade unions with an opportunity to lodge a claim for similar benefits for other categories. It should also be noted that this was the subject on which the unions spoke up most strongly.

The observed results of the introduction of shorter assembly lines and merged tasks can be evaluated only by reference to the results achieved on assembly lines of the traditional type. In 1976 assembly work was carried on simultaneously on three lines manned by nine workers each and two lines manned by about 30 workers each, the line remaining in 1973 having been cut into two. Interesting information was collected between 1 June and 29 July 1976 by a student in industrial psychology who interviewed people working on the two kinds of line. Apart from one or two workers who did not care, all the workers in the nine-person groups were unwilling to return to the longer line. Their attitude to their work was summed up in the statement that it was "hard work, but interesting": "hard" because only one work station had a seat; at all the others the workers had to remain standing, because if they sat down they were not conveniently placed and were constantly having to get up and fetch the next deep-frier; "interesting" because more things were assembled, the workers changed jobs every day and after a few days they were acquainted with all the operations involved in putting together a deep-frier. It was also said to be interesting because there was more freedom; if a sufficient stock of completed items could be built up to pass on to the next worker, it was possible to have a break of 10 to 15 minutes. The work was also more responsible: "If someone makes a bloomer on the big assembly line, you'll never find the person who did it, whereas there are only four of us on each side."

Working in small groups was also appreciated. A few workers were rejected by a group, but once a group had settled down, it was felt that it was "fine to be working together like this in small groups . . . we can always give each other a hand . . . we are more relaxed". These replies confirm a remark that was over-heard: "It is tiring here, but pleasant, because we get on well together." The inter-viewer also noted that people on short lines were more talkative than those on the longer lines, and that what was said was more coherent, as though the subject had been given some thought. People working on the longer line (of 30 workers) were interviewed also. The interviewer's general impression was that while sorry that their work was not as interesting as group work, the workers on the longer line intended to make the best of the work they had, which was not as tiring as the other.

The management naturally compared the financial and technical results achieved with the different work structures. Output was calculated by dividing the target time for the production of various items by the time actually spent. Com-parisons between the various systems revealed that the highest output was achieved on the shortest assembly lines. Between 2 January and 19 February 1975, in particular, output on the short line increased by 9.3 per cent over output on a traditional line with fragmented tasks. This increase enabled a number of workers to be released for preparatory work. The results in terms of output are such that other effects are of somewhat minor importance. Quality does not seem to have been affected by the change. As for absenteeism, the management doubts whether a change in job content can have much effect, when most of the workers are women ("a woman will always stay away if she has a sick child at home"). It is thought more sensible to try to reduce the effects of absenteeism rather than absenteeism itself. Clearly with the new arrangements the absence of one worker can be overcome to some extent: another member of the group will do the work of two; group output will fall, but production will not be disorganised.

From its assessment of the project the management has drawn certain lessons for the future. One of the first conclusions reached was that organisation and methods staff should not be given sole responsibility for designing new jobs and a new work structure. The jobs designed by such staff had been rejected, and the existing job designs were the outcome of specific demands by the workers and of a process akin to negotiation. The organisation and methods people had initially reacted badly to the criticism, but they had later come to accept it and had learnt to talk things over. The changes in the posting of organisation and methods staff had contributed to a better understanding between job designers and job holders.

Secondly, the reduction in the length of the assembly line involved increased costs. First the equipment had to be re-arranged. Some very expensive items are less intensively used on a short line than on a longer one. Air-driven screwdrivers, for example, can be located at two points on a long assembly line; at each of these two points it will be adjusted to the kind of screws fitted, and it will be fully used. On a shorter line, a worker may have to fix two kinds of screws; she will therefore need two power screwdrivers; moreover for the same output, two work stations will need to be so equipped; so that in the end there will have to be four machines of this type, and none of them will be in continuous use. Secondly, there is the question of floor area. The assembly line operating in 1973 took up 465 m^2, whereas the short line with group working takes up 140 m^2. If the whole shop went over to group working, the floor area occupied would total 956 m², of which some would be taken up by buffer stocks. Admittedly such calculations were not regarded as convincing by the management, which was in favour of comparing the cost per job, and considered that the changing nature of products would also have to be taken into account. The executives in charge of the establishment did not feel that cost was a decisive factor. Noting that the new structure had led to an increase in output estimated at 15 per cent, they regarded that finding as sufficient, and argued that if experiments showed a profit they should be followed up, for reasons for efficiency, backed up by the need to introduce into the production system a degree of flexibility corresponding to the growing range of models. Thus the reason that had justified the original experiment was still valid in respect of its extension. Since there were 150 variations in the models of pressure cookers in production, short lines were to be used for them too.

This support on efficiency grounds was accompanied by a number of reservations. A work structure suited to one product might not be suited to another. Group working was particularly suitable when a product was made up of clearly separate sub-assemblies which a worker could subsequently assemble into a finished product. The deep-frier was not ideal in this respect, since it consisted essentially of one big item onto which various parts were added as it moved on. In future the design of the product itself would have to take account of group working requirements, and all products should be made up of separate sub-assemblies put together at the end of the process. Another reservation relates to the workforce. This kind of work structure involves certain requirements, since there is a certain physical and mental strain involved. Part of the workforce (older workers, pregnant women, invalids, the less able) would always be unable to bear these new conditions of work. These workers should be given a possibility of other employment, particularly on preparatory work. Even for the others, it would be unrealistic to contemplate an undue lengthening of job cycle times, which would impose too heavy a mental strain. For electric coffee pots, the cycle time was about 6 minutes, and that seemed to be the highest acceptable figure. In another of the firm's establishments and for another product, a cycle time of 10 minutes had been tried and abandoned.

Re-bored automobile engines

The undertaking to which this case study relates is a big automobile manufacturer which has always played a pioneering role in matters of workers' welfare. The particular establishment where the experiment was carried out is in the Paris area and has 1,200 workers. It is engaged in—

(a) the manufacture of wire and springs (400 employees);

(b) the production of mechanical parts, tubes and bars for suspensions and for transmission and steering gear (220 employees), as well as the manufacture of plastic roofs (25 employees); and

(c) the re-boring and refitting of second-hand engines (270 employees, half of them foreign).

The experiment took place in the latter department. Of the total of 270 persons employed, production workers account for a little over 200. There is a head foreman, three other foremen, seven charge hands, two technicians, nine toolsetters, 24 testers and 20 storekeepers.

Worn engines that come in are first taken apart and cleaned. Some 30 workers are employed on this work. Once cleaned, the parts are sent to the machining shop, where they are examined by testers. Some parts are discarded, while others are machined to new specifications. About a hundred production workers do this work individually with machine tools. The third phase consists in re-assembly and testing of the engines; about 80 workers are employed on this.

Engines are taken apart by workers on enriched jobs. This process is not carried out on an assembly line by workers on fragmented tasks with very short cycle times; instead, each engine is taken apart by one worker, at his own work station and at a pace determined by him.

Assembly is carried out on a traditional assembly line in one part of the shop and on "enriched" jobs in another. On the traditional line there are 40-odd workers, including those working on sub-assemblies such as pumps and crankshafts. After they are assembled, the engines move on to a testing bench where some 15 workers are employed. There are some 30 workers on enriched jobs, some of them making sub-assemblies while others do preparatory work for the fitters, who work in two shifts, assembling entire engines and doing the testing themselves. It is in respect of assembly that the greatest change has been introduced.

The principle is that each worker re-assembles and tests an entire engine. In one part of the shop workers do the preparatory work, putting together sub-assemblies (that being a first example of job enrichment) and placing the ten main engine components (cylinder head, liners, etc.) on special brackets on a cradle hung from a conveyor. On each side of every cradle (which is two-sided and can be rotated), there is an engine block and a parts grid. The cradles move along a main transfer line, from which they are switched into a siding, where the fitter deals with them in groups of four. After assembling the four engines on one side, he rotates the cradles and assembles the four engines that were on the other side. The main components to be fitted are in each case available on the grid fitted to the cradle. Minor parts are laid out in order on a movable chariot within easy reach. Power screwdrivers hang from the transfer line. The same part is fitted to the four engines in succession and screwed into place.

Whereas on the assembly line the cycle time is 1.10 minutes, a fitter assembling an entire engine has 25 minutes, so that for eight engines a fitter is given 3 hours and 20 minutes. An assembly team consists of three workers; two are always assembling while the third tests the engines already assembled. On the average, 20 engines are produced per man-day. Hours of work are from 6 a.m. to 2.46 p.m. and from 2.31 to 11.17 p.m. Each of the two teams always works the same hours; there is no shift rotation.

In addition to the assembly unit proper there is a training unit with only two persons (the instructor, who works on two engines, and next to him the trainee with another two).

After assembly and bench testing, one engine in 120 is taken apart again for inspection. Any faults are traced to the appropriate phase of the work and a display board in the workshop gives the results, indicating departures from the specified norm.

The experiment began towards the end of 1973. The general management had made up their minds to take advantage of a proposed transfer of the re-boring department to look into a new form of work organisation. The plant management believed that in this particular case improved conditions of work might be compatible with economic efficiency.

The system just described was not introduced immediately. A fitter employed on the traditional assembly line was first asked to assemble an engine entirely on his own. The equipment used was fairly simple, and he took 42 minutes to do it. At a second stage a group of 16 workers was chosen from among the adjusters and multi-skilled workers. They were given special training with a view to the assembly of entire engines. Their time ranged from 39 to 67 minutes. At the third stage a work station was equipped for the simultaneous assembly of four engines, with a workforce of eight persons working in shifts. Assembly time then fell to 28 minutes. It was at the end of this stage that assembly and bench testing were combined. The workers were given technical training, while the shop foreman managed to convince them that the objective of 20 engines a day was within reach.

The attitudes of the workers' delegates and the trade union representatives showed that they did not want to appear to be either for against the experiment. While acknowledging the value of any alternative to assembly-line working, they dwelt on the productivity angle, and pointed out that management did not stand to lose by the change. The circumspect trade union reaction can also be attributed to the influence of the shop foreman and the fact that in this small plant trade union representatives had very close links with the workers and were well informed of their reactions (positive, as will be seen later). Throughout the exploratory phase, the personnel as a whole was also very reserved. A worker-priest employed in the plant gave his impressions as follows: "The men are waiting before making up their minds. It is too early yet. They tend to be mistrustful, believing that they are going to be swindled again."[13]

It is by no means certain that the workers now holding the enriched assembly jobs share that belief. They state that they have no desire to go back to a traditional assembly line. No attempt was made to interview them methodically, but an examination of some changes in the conditions suggests that they probably have some reason to be pleased. They have been upgraded from operatives to tradesmen.[14] They earn a little more than on a traditional assembly line (180 per cent of the basic wage instead of 170); in November 1976 that made a difference of about 200 francs a month for a 40-hour week.

From the psychological point of view, it should be noted that the work was more varied, since assembly work alternated with testing. Even within a six-day cycle, there is some variation in the way the workers spend their time from day to day. Since entire engines are assembled, their operation is now understood; something of potential use in everyday life has been learnt in the three-week training course. Even more important, no doubt, is the fact that the workers have a degree of freedom in the performance of their tasks. Eight engines have to be assembled every 3 hours 20 minutes, and the components have to be assembled in a certain order. But during the period in question nobody tells the workers what to do, since they know perfectly well. On a traditional line the supervisors are giving orders, on the fullest authority, from the very beginning of the day's work, as they find substitutes for workers who are absent and re-allocate work for individuals; with the new system, on the other hand, the supervisors no longer intervene directly in the organisation of the work; relations with supervisors have accordingly improved. Not only is the worker no longer liable to outside interference but he can also build up a buffer stock of cradles between the preparatory work and assembly, as well as between assembly and testing, and thus arrange to have some latitude in the way he organises his time, provided he achieves the prescribed output by the end of the day's work.

As regards physical conditions of work the existing shop is antiquated, dimly lit and cluttered. However, the work stations have been designed to reduce fatigue and the amount of movement required. The engines can be tipped up in the cradle in the interests of easy handling. However, the question of workload has been raised, especially by the trade union representatives. An attempt was made to measure the effort involved objectively by electrocardiogram, and it was found that the number of heartbeats remained within acceptable limits. In view of the small number of workers involved in the experiment (30-odd if those on preparatory work are included), the absenteeism figures cannot be significant.

From the technical and economic points of view, it must first be noted that under the new system an engine is assembled in 25 minutes, whereas 38 minutes are required on a traditional assembly line. Clearly the new system is markedly more productive. (It may be noted also that the output norms under the new system are fixed by the management on the basis of traditional time and motion study. The management has never contemplated negotiating in this respect.) Another advantage lies in the enhanced flexibility of the production system. Demand for the product is subject to fluctuations due to factors such as the oil crisis and the imposition of speed limits by the public authorities, and also falls off in the winter owing to climatic conditions. The level of output is therefore variable and hard to predict. Moreover there are numerous different engine types (64, plus 120 different specifications subject to change), partly because the engines sent in for re-boring belong to different generations of models. On the traditional assembly line this factor leads to constant adjustments. With the new system, on the other hand, output can easily be increased by adding a new team of three men (producing 40 more engines), or reduced by not finding substitutes for any absentees. The variety of models can also be accommodated more easily by allocating engines to particular teams according to type. It is doubtless these advantages, in addition to the improvement in the workers' conditions, which account for the plant manager's enthusiastic conversion to the new system.

The experiment just described covered only a small number of workers, and an observer might therefore be tempted to underestimate its importance. However, after this initial trial run and assessment it is now clear that the system is a good one and could be extended to the whole assembly operation, the traditional assembly line being then abolished. Such an extension could not be carried out in the existing shop, but was to take place in a new building which was being planned.[15] The new workshop was to be much bigger than the existing one, and the working environment was to be considerably improved. There was a considerable accident hazard in the existing shop because of the excessive amount of equipment in a limited area, with consequential reduction of the amount of space for personnel movement. That hazard would be reduced, and the positions for work on the cradles would be improved. The building of the new shop would therefore demonstrate the desire of the general management of the firm, and of the plant management, to design and carry out a comprehensive project for the improvement of conditions of work. The project would call for considerable expenditure on plant and equipment. Although increases in productivity are expected, they will depend on an increase in demand, which is not certain. In any event, productivity gains will never make up for more than a small fraction of the investment. The project has been adopted not to increase profits but to improve conditions of work, because the management regards that as being necessary for the future of the firm.

Aluminium tubes[16]

The programme to be described was introduced in an undertaking belonging to a firm which is part of one of the larger French industrial conglomerates, and which is partly concerned with the fabrication of aluminium, from the processing of bauxite to the manufacture of aluminium packaging. The firm produces four kinds of hollow packaging—tins (especially for preserved foods), aerosol containers, caps for clamping over bottle stoppers, and tubes for paints and for pharmaceutical, health and beauty products. In five plants, the firm produces over 500 million of the total of over 650 million tubes used in France each year. It has a workforce of 3,500 people. The general manager is assisted by four functional managers (personnel, finance, accounts, development) and four line managers, one for each product line.

The plant dealt with in this case study produces tubes (100 million a year). Most of them (65 million) were still made of lead in 1976, but it was expected that by 1977 half would be made of aluminium. The plant is in the northern suburbs of Paris. The workforce varied between 260 and 300; 60 per cent were women and 32 per cent were immigrants. There were a few short-term employees. Of the total workforce, 30 were office workers or technicians, 12 were supervisors, 60 skilled tradesmen (35 toolsetters, 25 maintenance workers) and 150 semi-skilled workers (i.e. unskilled workers who had been trained to perform only one or two operations). Of the latter, 120 were engaged in the production of tubes (as distinct from initial processing of ingots, packing, inspection). These 120 workers were employed in three shops, as follows:

No. I shop, called "the old girls' shop", had three assembly lines operating by day;

No. II shop, called "the shift shop", had eight assembly lines operated on a two-shift system; and

No. III shop, called "the beauty shop", had five assembly lines, on day work.

The tubes were produced on short four-person lines. In the first operation (extrusion) aluminium slugs went through a press and acquired a tube shape. The tube then moved on to an automatic lathe where it was cut to the proper length, trimmed of the rough edges left by the press, and threaded (the opening being threaded to receive a cap at a later stage). The tube was then lacquered in blue or white preparatory to printing. After the tube had passed through a drier, the text was printed on the lacquer base, after which a cap was fitted (as well as a ring if the tube was to be sold sealed) and the tubes packed for despatch.

The machines were aligned over a length of about 15 m, and there were several parallel and more or less identical production lines in each shop. At the head of a line, a press and lathe operator introduced the slugs into an automatic press and supervised the operation of the press and the lathe. At the next work station the painter operator saw to the thickness, density and regularity of the film of varnish and made sure it was dry. The third work station had a printing machine, generally operated by a woman, who with her right hand took the tubes arriving by overhead conveyor from the previous work station and placed them on a belt feeding the printing machine, while with her left hand she retrieved the tubes emerging from the printing machine and put them back on the conveyor. The last work station was occupied by a packer, who fed in the necessary number of cardboard boxes as well as of the caps and rings required for capping. She kept an eye on the quality of the finished product and counted the tubes in order to fill customers' orders. She put the tubes in the cartons and then placed the cartons on pallets for despatch.

The production process was an automated, high-speed one (on a new line the rate of output was 120 tubes a minute and manual transfer to the printer belt feed was eliminated). At the first station the work comprised feeding and supervising a machine; at the second it was chiefly a matter of supervision. The third station (printing) was the only one where continual manual operation was required; it called for considerable dexterity, which could be acquired only after several weeks of practice, and failure to keep up the pace at that station would hold up the whole line of machines and operatives.[17] Under this system the technical arrangements were a given quantity. The sponsors of the experiment made it clear from the first that no change in the manufacturing process could be considered.

It was after the events of May 1968 referred to at the beginning of this paper that the general management gave consideration, in 1971, to doing something about the position of the unskilled workers. At that time the attention of French managers had been drawn to Herzberg's work and job enrichment. Although initial thinking was along those lines, it became apparent that these concepts did not provide a solution. (Herzberg preserves the Taylorian distinction between those who plan and those who execute, and stresses the direct nexus between the man and the job.) Instead of imposing on the workers changes supposed to make them happy, it was thought that they should be given a possibility of making up their own minds as to what was needed. This approach rested on the conviction that improvements in the situation of unskilled workers could be brought about more particularly by improving social relations within the undertaking.

The tube plant was chosen as the location for the experiment, and recourse was had to a firm of engineering consultants which had already been employed by the undertaking and which was known to advocate negotiating changes with the workers or their representatives instead of imposing them. The contract was signed in July 1972, and at the end of August a new manager was appointed who had taken part in the preliminary consultations at the head office.

A few subjects were put forward for consideration: improvement of conditions of work, retraining of the personnel, extension of responsibilities, changes in the pay system. It was also suggested that discussions should take place in groups of 10 or 12 people, without supervisors but in the presence of a discussion leader made available by the consultants. The groups' proposals were to be sent forward to a joint committee chaired by the plant manager and consisting of six persons appointed by the management and six by the personnel representatives. The committee would assess the proposals in relation to proclaimed objectives, and would be free to refuse, accept or alter them.

At the end of 1972 all the proposals, whether of substance or of method, were communicated to the works committee, the workers' delegates and the entire workforce (on notice boards). The unions represented on the works committee were mostly affiliated to the CGT. They raised a few preliminary issues concerning employment and remuneration. The management undertook to take increased productivity into account in setting rates of pay, and gave an assurance that the project would have no repercussions on employment. A third issue related to the remuneration of the workers attending the group meetings: it was decided that the matter would be discussed at the group meetings themselves. Early in 1973 the personnel representatives announced that they were not opposed to the experiment, and the joint committee was set up.

The committee in question was first called upon to choose the shop where the experiment should take place. In this respect it endorsed the managers' proposal, and chose "the beauty shop", where between 35 and 38 workers (a foreman, 10 skilled toolsetters and between 25 and 27 semi-skilled workers) were employed on the manufacture of tubes for beauty products. The manager now regrets that choice; he feels it would have been more consonant with the spirit of the project to leave the matter to the joint committee, and that his proposal did not take sufficient account (as will be seen later) of a whole number of factors that emerged at a later stage, when it was proposed to extend the experiment to other shops.

Three groups of 12 to 15 workers each were formed. As agreed, the first item to be discussed was the remuneration of the participants; this was complicated by the fact that there were output and no-waste bonuses in addition to base pay. After much hesitation, the groups suggested the grant of a uniform bonus at a rate equal to average bonus earnings in the plant. The joint committee accepted this suggestion. It may be noted that at this stage group members felt that they were in a traditional collective bargaining situation, with differences of outlook, whereas the manager was trying to promote a joint examination of the matter, outside the usual framework of claims and negotiation. It was decided that each group should meet for half a day each week, and this they did until June 1973.

The subjects put to the group for consideration related essentially to the organisation of work, and it was stated at the outset that there could be no questioning the suitability of the existing manufacturing processes. A subject that came to the fore almost immediately was product quality. It may be thought surprising that this subject, only remotely connected with the improvement of conditions of work, should have been discussed. A comment[18] by the consultant who was acting as unofficial discussion leader is very enlightening in this regard: "For the operatives, the subject of conditions of work did not just cover heat and noise. Conditions of work were conditions in which good work could be done. They said they knew that they were in the factory to be sweated, but at least they could be given the necessary resources—good machines, competent toolsetters, proper equipment." This desire to work in better conditions (in view of the object of their work rather than the existing physical environment) was particularly marked because the tubes manufactured in the shop in question were intended for difficult customers (famous perfumers). The workers felt that the quality of the product was not always up to the customers' expectations, and also that the supervisor was chiefly concerned with achieving output targets, and prevented them from concerning themselves with this matter. In stressing the importance of quality, therefore, the workers were in a sense asserting themselves in relation to the foreman, and perhaps even claiming a certain power.

Group members asked to see the letters of complaint from customers. Then they decided, with the agreement of the joint committee, to carry out a systematic analysis of the defects that might be found in the tubes and to draw up an exhaustive list giving their nature, causes and frequency. This took up a few months, with the assistance of the supervisors when required. The list ran to 110 pages and distinguished over 400 defects; it was completed in May 1973. Over 5,700 hours had been devoted to the meetings. The groups (and the shop committee that will be described subsequently) then wondered how they could avoid the defects listed. In view of the rate of output, there could be no question of checking each tube. To determine what proportion of the tubes should be checked, the groups called on a statistician made available by the consultant. She produced a learned work with findings that were mathematically sound but struck the groups as completely unrealistic (she advocated a check on 800 tubes every half-hour).

The workers pointed out that since the defects arose out of deterioration of the equipment, as soon as one defective tube was produced all those produced subsequently were bound to be defective too. It was therefore not necessary to check 800 tubes, but simply a number of tubes equal to the number of machines operating simultaneously. (In the case of the printing machines there were two blankets per machine, operating alternately; consequently if two consecutive tubes were examined the state of the two blankets could be checked.) The groups then decided to draw up clear instruction on the checks to be made at each work station. For the press and lathe station, for example, eight categories of defects were distinguished, and consequently eight checks were made every half-hour on a batch of 11 tubes (or on only two of them for some defects). The results were given on an inspection sheet filled in by the operator, the checks being carried out at the work station by the operators themselves: as a natural consequence of the involvement of the operators themselves in the detection of faults and the drawing up of the list, the idea had very quickly emerged, with the encouragement of the joint committee, that instead of creating a supplementary inspection job the work should be done by the operators themselves, whose jobs would thus be enriched.

This grant to the operators of the possibility of checking the results of their own work was bound to lead to a determination of the decisions to be taken by the operators when defects were found. The workers took the view that in such a case an operator should be entitled to stop the line. Only foremen had the right to do this, but the joint committee considered the matter and expressed the view that this right was a logical corollary of the operators' new inspection responsibilities. Accordingly the joint committee endorsed the proposal, and later the inspection instructions for each work station included a last column listing after each check the decisions that could be taken, i.e. either allow the line to move on or stop it and call in a toolsetter to make the necessary adjustment. Thus a power which had traditionally been exercised by foremen alone came to be shared with all the machine operators.

An idea that emerged in the groups at a very early stage was the notion that quality control would be facilitated if the operators had advance knowledge of incoming orders and could organise their work accordingly. With the encouragement of the joint committee this led to consideration of collective management of the workshop, and a few changes in its management did in fact take place. It is unnecessary to describe here the different arrangements that were successively considered and the difficulties that arose. The scheme ultimately adopted by the joint committee was to set up a shop co-ordination committee. It first met in June 1973, and subsequently superseded the groups, whose many meetings were becoming tedious and which no longer met regularly after that date. The shop committee consisted of nine persons (unskilled, toolsetters and the foremen). It was decided that a third of its membership should be renewed every three months, so that all the shop's workforce would serve on it, and that it should meet twice a month.

The shop committe had its ups and downs over the next 12 months, but it managed to draw up the instructions for inspection after the list of defects had been issued in September. Early in 1974 it seemed to be moribund: a few group meetings were held, and even some general meetings of the whole workforce. Then the committee revived, the consultant who had been away for some time returned, and it was decided to set up specialised subcommittees. After that, the committee and its subcommittees met regularly. The three subcommittees' dealt respectively with programming, quality and objectives, as described below:

(1) The programming subcommittee, consisting of toolsetters, is in touch with the programming unit and is informed in advance of the production proposed for the month, whereas previously even the foremen received the programme only two or three days beforehand. The members of the subcommittee now discuss the scheduling of orders with the programming unit, in the light of the specific kind of product involved.

(2) The quality subcommittee works on the returns from the inspection carried out by the operators. It can thus identify the parts of the line where the reject

rate is highest and consider remedial action with the assistance of a specialist from the inspection unit. Most of the members of this subcommittee are machine operators.

(3) The terms of reference of the objectives subcommittee are to make proposals to the production engineer concerning output targets for the coming month. It obtain returns on the previous month's output, the number of orders processed in the previous month and the number to be met in the coming month and the names of the customers, and on that basis it sets a target which is communicated to the production manager. It is reported that there had been only one case of disagreement, and that it was the manager who gave way.

This structure, with a shop co-ordination committee and three specialised subcommittees, was still in existence in 1976.

Simultaneously with the establishment of this new work structure, the management made changes in respect of training, remuneration and hours of work. By 1976 there were 80 workers receiving either induction training or multi-skilled training to enable them to rotate jobs. Remuneration was considered by the joint committee, which met 17 times in that connection. The operators' jobs were analysed, evaluated in relation to four criteria (knowledge, practical skill, workload, autonomy), and divided into five classes (from 1 to 5), there being four other classes (6 to 9) for operators who were more or less multi-skilled. The earlier bonuses, which were affected by operational changes, were abolished. The inclusion of inspection functions in the operators' jobs was accompanied by a small rise in their remuneration. As regards hours, operators wishing to stay away from work for personal reasons were allowed to do so on condition that they made up for it by remaining at work during meetings of the shop committee or its subcommittees.

It would seem natural to include in a survey of the results of this experiment an account of its effects on members of the workforce who were not in the beauty shop. The inspection unit was obviously most affected. Besides a supervisor, it used to comprise eight (unskilled) inspectors, whose task consisted in moving down the line, removing a few tubes, and stopping the line if one of them was defective. This operation would become pointless if the inspection was to be made directly by the operators. A way out of the difficulty was sought through the quality subcommittee of the shop committee, with the help of a statistician and in close touch with the inspectors themselves, who felt they had better take part in the meetings rather than let things take their course without them. It was agreed that the inspectors should concentrate on more elaborate statistical checks on sample tubes obtained from the end of the production lines. Previously they had been able to assess the work of the operators and stop their machines. They were now deprived of that authority, but their checks were now based on stricter criteria and they had learnt to draw useful lessons from the checks for production purposes (they had asked to be trained in the preparation of charts).

From the point of view of psychological satisfaction, interesting information was collected by Annie Borseix,[19] who interviewed nine people in the shop (the foreman, two skilled tradesmen and six unskilled workers) at the end of 1974. On the whole the changes had been favourably received. People were glad to know (thanks to the programming subcommittee) what work was coming up and thus to have knowledge previously reserved for management. The fact that they could discuss output targets gave them an incentive to achieve the target output, and some of the operators interviewed said they were pleased when targets were exceeded. Inspection by the operators themselves reduced the reject rate: "One can be sure one is doing good work."

Relations with the foreman were also good. He was regarded as being there to get the best out of people without bossing them. "He doesn't give orders, but he asks for things so nicely that we do them just the same." This state of affairs was of course partly due to the personality of the foreman, a former toolsetter who had already been the recognised leader in the shop before the management endorsed the workers' choice and made him foreman. However, as Annie Borseix pointed out, this relationship was probably due even more to the changes made in work organisation and to the fact that foremen's decisions now seemed to be more the outcome of discussions in the shop committee or its subcommittees than individual decisions. As for relations among the workers, interviews revealed a better mutual understanding and more solidarity. It was thought that in the event of a strike there would be more solidarity in that shop than in others. Annie Borseix commented[20] that for the moment solidarity in the workshop was productive: it helped to ensure that the shop's commitments were fulfilled, to reach set output targets and to meet quality standards. On the other hand there was nothing to indicate that it might not serve other purposes in other circumstances.

While the outcome of the interviews was on the whole favourable, the fact remained that some discontent was expressed also. Physical conditions of work were regarded as bad ("in summer the heat is something awful"). The greater involvement in the attainment of targets and the pursuit of quality made workers more sensitive to certain unexpected difficulties (for example, a delay before a toolsetter came in response to a request) and to the state of the machines. The new work situation therefore gave rise to mixed feelings, even though they were on the whole predominantly favourable, and it is understandable that Annie Borseix should have deliberately refrained from giving any verdict in regard to such a simple concept as "satisfaction".

In economic terms, it will be noted that output, which had amounted to 1.58 million tubes (monthly average) in 1972, had fallen to 1.2 million in 1973 and 1,142,000 in 1974. In 1975 it rose again to 1,238,000, and was expected to be 1,575,000 for 1976. These results could, of course, have led to a cessation of the experiment if the plant manager had not been supported at the highest level within the firm, and even within the group of firms as a whole. If a balance sheet were to be drawn up one would see on the debit side the not inconsiderable consultant's fees, the time paid for but not worked (spent in meetings) and the loss of output, and on the credit side a reduction of labour turnover and absenteeism (by 2 per cent), a reduction in the orders returned by dissatisfied customers and a fall in the proportion of rejects at the production stage. Another element, on which it is impossible to put a price tag, is the fact that there had been no strike since March 1972. The calculations made on the basis of the factors for which figures could be produced showed that over the 1973-75 period the costs of the new organisation of work were twice as high as its benefits. However, forecasts for 1976-77 indicated that there would be a considerable reduction in costs (because the consultant was no longer needed, and because the effect of meetings on output had been diminished). An increase in benefits was also foreseen, so that for 1976-77 benefits were expected to exceed costs considerably, and for the 1973-77 period as a whole a balance was likely to be struck. Four years to write off such an investment was not long, as the plant manager said.

To his mind, the experiment should not be limited to the beauty shop; that had been a pilot project. In the shift shop a system was gradually introduced that was similar to the on-line inspection in the beauty shop, but by the end of 1976 the extension of the system to the old girls' shop had not been a success, though they had decided to form new discussion groups. In that shop group meetings had been held, with the assistance of the same consultant, from July to November 1973. Whereas in the beauty shop product quality had been selected almost at once as the theme of the meetings, the old girls' groups announced at the end of November that they refused to consider job enrichment or multi-skill operation (proposed by the manager) and would discuss only the physical constraints of the work. For a whole month the groups catalogued the various unpleasant features (smells, noise, dirty flooring) common to the entire shop or peculiar to certain jobs. This was not in conformity with the rules originally laid down to define in general terms what should be discussed. The manager was unable to overcome this refusal to engage in the experiment. He accounted for the old girls' attitude by their feeling of superiority to other, newer shops whose workforce consisted of persons who had not fitted in well in their own shop. They could not bear the thought that they might have something to learn from the beauty shop, since they firmly believed that they were perfectly acquainted with every aspect of their work. Annie Borseix noted[21] that the old girls' refusal could be interpreted as a defensive reaction against a slur on their professional conscience. If they had agreed to change their methods of work and engage in systematic quality control, they would have been admitting that their work over the previous 20 or 30 years had been rather bad. Things might have turned out differently if the old girls' shop had been chosen for the pilot scheme. (As already indicated, the manager now regrets his initial choice.) However, there is no guarantee that the workers would in that event have spontaneously opted for quality control. Such disappointments seem inherent in this kind of experiment.

GENERAL CONCLUSIONS

In conclusion, the three cases will be reviewed jointly, from the point of view of the design and implementation of the projects, their results and their implications for the future.

Design and implementation of projects

The first two cases concerned assembly work. In the manufacture of deep-friers, a long assembly line had been considerably shortened (from 60 to 9 workers), and it had thus been possible to form a group in which all the members formed a team. The project had been designed by the manufacturing department and the organisation and methods specialists, without worker participation. However, at the implementation stage some resistance became apparent and it was found necessary to talk the matter over with all concerned and accept certain modifications.

In the second experiment the project had not initially been precisely defined. The management had been feeling its way towards the general objective of enabling each worker to put together an entire engine. Little by little, by hit-or-miss methods and with the assistance of the participants in the initial trial runs, the solution ultimately adopted was found. The invention and refinement of a technical aid (the cradles) marked a turning-point.

The technical background of the third case was very different. Aluminium tubes were mass-produced by a sequence of machine operations. The management regarded this technical process as not being open to change, so that in this experiment, unlike the other two, the production technique would not be altered, and any changes would be sought by changes in functions and in social relations. The workers employed in the workshop were asked to think up desirable changes. Initially the management had no particular project in mind, merely a belief that the workers should once more be able to exercise some initiative. Of course there were risks involved: there was no guarantee that the workers asked to express their views would do so along lines acceptable to the plant management; the "old girls'" reactions were to show that the risk was not imaginary. To reduce the risks the management stated that the technical production process was not open to discussion. A joint committee was set up under the manager's chairmanship, and was to have the right to refuse to accept any suggestions made if they seemed to be contrary to the general aims of the project as initially laid down. An external consultant assisted the management at each stage of the project and followed the group discussions.

To sum up, in the first case the project, while providing for change, was designed in the usual manner by organisation and methods staff. Difficulties of application unexpectedly made it necessary to practically negotiate with the workers directly concerned. In the second case the project was worked out by stages with the assistance of the workers concerned. In the third case the workers were encouraged to take the initiative, and the distinctive feature of that project was not a change in the organisation of work so much as the freedom given to the workers and the initial innovation regarding the distribution of functions.

By definition and of necessity, it was in this third case that the workers were best informed at the outset of the nature of the forthcoming experiment. It was also in this case that the workers' representatives were most directly associated with the experiment, through the joint committee.

Results

The economic results confirm the general findings of the National Agency for the Improvement of Working Conditions (ANACT), at any rate as regards assembly work. The drawbacks of long assembly lines are well known; a more flexible system of production is better suited to the growing variety of models and to fluctuations in demand. Accordingly, labour productivity increased, though there was no improvement in the quality of the deep-friers. On the other hand a rise in labour productivity is not necessarily accompanied by increased profitability; this point will be referred to again in connection with the extension of the experiments.

From the psychological point of view, it seems that the workers concerned were pleased with the changes and did not wish to return to the old ways, which struck them as now quite out of date. This also was a finding of the ANACT survey. However, the elements of the workers' satisfaction differ from case to case.

In the first case the operator's task had become a little more varied than on a long line, but cycle times were still quite short and the experiment could be summed up as consisting of job enrichment. What satisfaction did exist was often due to the feeling of belonging to a group: it was a matter of affective environment at work.

In the second case each worker assembled his engine and tested it. The change in job design was much greater than in the former case, and this time satisfaction seemed to be much more closely linked to work performance and to the feeling of autonomy that can be associated with a long-term task. A period of preliminary training had been required, and it had been necessary to increase remuneration. On the other hand the feeling of belonging to a group must have been less marked, since individual assignments were not complementary but identical.

In the third case the work itself was no doubt enriched by the inclusion of inspection among the tasks of the on-line operators. Multi-skilling was encouraged, and higher remuneration was payable to workers able to rotate jobs. However, the most welcome change was the closer participation in the operation of the workshop as a whole. In this third case there was participation in programming and in the organisation of work, in distinction to the other two cases, in which the workers were mere agents. Only in "the beauty shop" was there any discussion of output targets.

In all three cases relations with supervisors improved. They no longer intervened at every stage, but were called upon in case of need.

The favourable psychological results do not imply an unqualified improvement in the workers' welfare. In all three cases the workload was not reduced. Output targets remained high, even in the beauty shop, where they were a subject of discussion so that the workers made them their own. The workers assembling the deep-friers mentioned how tiring their work was. In the engine shop electrocardiograms had to be made to convince the workers that their feeling of working harder was purely subjective. Trade union vigilance in this respect is therefore understandable, as is the fact that the unions view with some apprehension the competition in meeting output targets which may be a consequence of group working.

Extension of experiments

The experiments considered in the present paper involved only a fraction of the workforce (27 persons out of 87 for deep-friers, about 30 out of 270 for automobile engines) or only one of a number of shops (the beauty shop). The difficulties that arose in the third case when the management tried to extend the experiment to the whole plant have already been described. Such difficulties are inherent in the method chosen, which cannot guarantee that the groups called upon to express their views will spontaneously take the right line.

In the first case (deep-friers) the management had decided to extend the arrangement to the manufacture of other products, while respecting the freedom of choice of workers who might wish to continue working under the old system. The cost of the extension would not appear to be an obstacle to a move which is clearly justified by the results achieved by the groups in terms of labour productivity. This relatively limited experiment seems assured of a bright future.

In the second case it would be possible to apply the new system more widely only in a new workshop which was planned, and the financial management was assessing the profitability of the whole operation of building new plant, with new equipment and the new work stations. In its view the operation would not be a financially sound one unless a high level of production and demand was achieved.

It is therefore by no means self-evident that new forms of work organisation are bound to spread by virtue of some peculiar advantage of such innovations. Influential decision-makers can oppose their extension on grounds of profitability. Among the workers there seems to be no pressure to extend to all of them the systems tried out by a few. There is therefore a danger that the experiments will remain isolated cases, or in other words that they will continue in being, but as experiments only. They may also be brought to an end, thus revealing their tentative character. It is striking that the boldest of the experiments described in this paper should also have been the one with the most uncertain future. It had remained in being thanks to a good consultant and the manager's insistence, but what would happen when the consultant left and the manager was promoted?

The experimental approach of most firms has its attractions and appears sensible: a system is given a trial run before being possibly applied to the whole workforce. However, problems arise owing to the change of scale: for example, it may be found that it would have been better to start in a different shop (as in the third case) or that the supervisory role has to be completely re-assessed, particularly with regard to recruitment and prospects. In fact the whole managerial and supervisory structure was affected by the proposed changes. Current experiments are ventures that provide an insight into all the difficulties inherent in organisational change. To be followed up on a wider scale, experiments should be part and parcel of an over-all approach to the re-organisation of undertakings, and a reflection of a general attitude to progress.

Notes

[1] Carried out by Mayo, Roethlisberger and Dickinson at the Hawthorne plant of Western Electric in Chicago in the late 1920s. It was found that various successive changes in working conditions, for better or for worse, all led to an increase in output. This was subsequently attributed to "the Hawthorne effect": the workers apparently worked hard largely because they felt that they were participating in something new and special.

[2] See Introduction, p. 6.

[3] ILO: *Making work more human: Working conditions and environment,* Report of the Director-General, International Labour Conference, 60th Session (Geneva, 1975), pp. 5-8 and 46-50.

[4] *Dix propositions pour l'orientation future du CNPF.*

[5] See *Recherches en vue d'une organisation plus humaine du travail industriel,* rapport établi, à la demande de M. Joseph Fontanet, ministre du Travail, de l'Emploi et de la Population, par M. Yves Delamotte, directeur du Centre de formation des inspecteurs du travail et de la main-d'œuvre, mars 1972 (Paris, La Documentation française, 1972). This report contains no specific action proposals but describes a few experiments made in France, Italy and the Scandinavian countries, with a brief analysis of the problems that arose; it concentrates on job enrichment and semi-autonomous group working.

[6] ILO: *Legislative Series,* 1973—Fr. 2. An analysis of the Act by the author of the present paper will be found on pp. 146-147 of "Working conditions and government policy: Some western European approaches", in *International Labour Review,* Sep.-Oct. 1976.

[7] Confédération générale du travail (CGT), Confédération française démocratique du travail (CFDT), Force ouvrière (FO), Confédération française des travailleurs chrétiens (CFTC), Confédération générale des cadres (CGC).

[8] *Rapport du Comité d'étude pour la réforme de l'entreprise, présidé par Pierre Sudreau,* rapport remis au Président de la République et au Premier ministre le vendredi 7 février 1975 (Paris, La Documentation française, 1975).

[9] Through a questionnaire, supplemented in some cases by interviews. The results of the survey were published in the ANACT newsletter (No. 7), Sep. 1976.

[10] Information in this respect was supplied by the correspondents of the Agency, who were very often chiefs of personnel or production managers; in this broad-scale inquiry it had not been possible to question the workers concerned themselves.

[11] Equipes de recherche d'amélioration des conditions de travail (ERACT).

[12] Paradoxically, there is little reason for workers to compete with each other when individual incentive schemes are used. On the other hand, group incentive systems can lead to pressure on the slow members of the group.

[13] "Un atelier d'OS. Témoignage", in *Projet* (Paris, CERAS), No. 84, Apr. 1974, pp. 394 ff.

[14] From "agent de production" to "agent professionnel".

[15] It was expected to qualify for a subsidy from the Fund for the Improvement of Working Conditions.

[16] This section is largely based on a remarkable work by Annie Borseix and Daniel Chave: *Réorganisation du travail et dynamique des conflits* (Paris, Conservatoire national des arts et métiers, Laboratoire de sociologie du travail et des relations professionnelles, 1975).

[17] The machines were serviced and repaired by toolsetters who were skilled workers.

[18] See Borseix and Chave, op. cit., p. 71.

[19] Borseix and Chave, op. cit.

[20] ibid., p. 210.

[21] ibid., p. 229.

FEDERAL REPUBLIC OF GERMANY

FEDERAL REPUBLIC OF GERMANY
Wolfgang H. Staehle*

NATIONAL CONDITIONS

Statutory framework

In the Federal Republic of Germany wages and working conditions are supposed to be entirely determined through collective bargaining between the representatives of workers and employers, under the principle of so-called bargaining autonomy.[1] However, the State exerts indirect influence on the negotiating process through various aspects of economic and social legislation and proposals for concerted action, voluntary restraint and so on. At the insistence of the trade unions and the Social Democratic Party, statutory provisions were laid down at a very early date in respect of labour-management relations,[2] the remuneration and welfare of the workers[3] and co-management[4] within undertakings. For many decades the three parties thus directly or indirectly involved in industrial relations have shown special interest and concern for industrial safety and for improving general working conditions. In recent years questions related to newer forms of work organisation have come into the spotlight.

The emergence of new forms of work organisation is in fact facilitated by the statutory provisions for co-management[5] and through bodies such as works meetings, works councils, finance committees, supervisory boards and boards of management with labour representation that exist at the level of the undertaking.[6] A landmark in this connection is the new Act of 1972 concerning the organisation of the undertaking.[7] Although worker representatives had participation rights in various fields under the provisions previously in force, the works council's rights to information and consultation have now been extended to job

* Technische Hochschule, Darmstadt. The author wishes to acknowledge the valuable assistance he received from Dr. M. Gaitanides and Mr. K. Trebesch, of the Institut für Betriebswirtschaftslehre, Technische Hochschule Darmstadt, in collecting information for the case studies. Special thanks are also due to the following persons who contributed expert knowledge to the development of the case studies and the interpretation of the cases in question: Mr. M. Granel, Volkswagenwerk AG, Salzgitter; Dr. H. Kieselbach and Mr. D. Schäfer, Robert Bosch GmbH, Stuttgart; Mr. H. O. Meyer, Siemens AG, Bad Neustadt an der Saale; Dr. H. P. Euler, Institute of Sociology, University of Karlsruhe; Mr. R. Grevé, Deutsche Forschungs- und Versuchsanstalt für Luft- und Raumfahrt, Humanisierung des Arbeitsleben, Bonn-Bad Godesberg; Dr. W. Rohmert, Institut für Arbeitswissenschaft der Technischen Hochschule Darmstadt; Dr. H. J. Warnecke and Mr. H. Sauer, Institut für Productionstechnik und Automatisierung der Fraunhofer Gesellschaft zur Förderung der Angewandten Forschung e.V., University of Stuttgart; and Dr. R. Weil, Institut für Angewandte Arbeitswissenschaft e.V., Cologne.

design, work operations and the working environment. Under section 90 of the Act, the employer is required to inform the works council in due time of any plans concerning—

(a) the construction, alteration or extension of manufacturing, office and other business premises belonging to the establishment;

(b) technical plant;

(c) the work process and operations; or

(d) jobs,

—and consult the works council on the proposed measures, with particular regard to their effects on the nature of the work and the demands made on the workers. Also important is the express requirement by Parliament in sections 90 and 91 that, as regards job design, work operations and the working environment, due account must be taken of accepted principles regarding a humane approach to work. An Act of 1973 requires undertakings above a certain size to appoint industrial physicians, safety engineers and safety technicians or supervisors, whose duties are to include assisting the employer in pursuing a humane approach to work. Under section 3 of the Workplaces Ordinance of 1975, the employer must install and operate work stations in accordance with specified generally recognised standards of industrial safety, industrial medicine and hygiene.[8]

The essential thread running through all these statutory provisions is that the initiative for putting measures into effect for a humane approach to work lies with the owner of the business or the employer. The works council is granted participation rights: enforcement opportunities are accorded in exceptional cases. This means that the organisation of work in industry is a matter for co-management with the works council and trade unions, and that there is no place for new management methods or co-operative management styles unilaterally imposed by management itself. The intention is to lead to integrated co-operation between corporate management, the works councils, trade unions and research bodies, on an experimental basis supported by the Federal Government.

Specialised research aimed at "humanising the world of work" was encouraged by the Government at an early date. In its fourth research report, of 1972,[9] the Federal Government called for research on work and technical change in order to analyse the consequences of technical change for work and to provide a basis for the elimination of existing and the prevention of future negative influences. Research should be carried out into the whole range of problems associated with technological, economic and social change with a view to the continued development of social policy and an improvement in working and living conditions. The Government had already established an "Economic and Social Change Committee" in 1971. The Committee is an autonomous body comprising representatives of employers, workers and research bodies. Its terms of reference are to investigate the effects of technological, economic and social change and consequent requirements with regard to the continuing development of social policy, and to identify wherever possible opportunities for the future shaping of

..., ... purpose of such opinions is to provide expert advice for policy purposes. Responsibility for the programme does not, therefore, lie with the Federal Ministry of Research and Technology but with a secretariat set up for the purpose, which answers to the Federal Chancellor's Office. Although the opinions are not of a binding character in terms either of policy or of practice, by the end of 1973 they had led to an insistent movement for reform.

On 8 May 1974 the Federal Ministries of Labour and Social Affairs and of Research and Technology came forward with a "joint action programme on research to humanise work". The general aim of that programme is to examine the opportunities for increased adjustment of working conditions to the needs of working people. The research and development work is intended to lead to practical proposals. The particular aims of the action programme are as follows:

(a) the development of safety data, guidelines and minimum safety standards for plant, installations and workshops;

(b) the development of technologies commensurate with human capacities;

(c) the development of model codes for work organisation and job design; and

(d) the application and dissemination of technological findings and operational experience.

A basic requirement under the programmes is to design experiments through interdisciplinary research based on the application of the economic and physical sciences.

The Government invested substantial funds in the programme. During the first year, 1974, DM 9 million were made available; this amount was raised to DM 30 million for 1975 and DM 45 million for 1976, and some DM 47 million were earmarked for 1977. Current research projects concern measures to bring about improvements in—

(a) the functioning of labour and industrial organisations;

(b) ergonomics;

(c) technology;

(d) the diffusion and application of knowledge of labour matters; and

(e) related factors.

The emphasis is clearly laid on organisational and technological measures directly related to the production of goods. However, greater attention will be paid in future to projects to improve working conditions in the services sector, including offices and administration.[10]

Any enterprise may apply for support. Applications are checked by a special committee consisting of representatives of employers, workers (trade unions) and expert consultants. At the time of writing, about a third of the applications were meeting with refusals. The ministry concerned (chiefly the Federal Ministry of Research and Technology) then enters into a contract with the applicant whereby the latter undertakes to bear half of the project costs and to facilitate expert monitoring of projects. The function of the consultants in these projects is chiefly to contribute expert advice to industrial decision-making concerning new forms of work organisation. The consultants also follow the experiments in order to ascertain to what extent the results could be applied elsewhere.

Attitudes of management and of organised labour

Management has fully acknowledged work organisation as its traditional field of action. Consequently, employers and their representatives met the new challenge of the humanisation of work by referring to the fact that a search for optimum forms of work organisation had always been one of their chief aims.[11] Humaneness and profitability, they said, were complementary objectives, not conflicting ones. What was now referred to as humanisation of work had been an objective achieved by employers for decades through continuing reorganisation and improvement of conditions of employment. Furthermore, they said, the demand for humanisation gave the false impression that work was currently inhuman. In this connection, employers refer to a survey on the quality of life at work, which had been carried out by the Institute for Applied Social Science on behalf of the Federal Ministry of Labour from autumn 1972 to spring 1973; according to the results of the survey, most workers regarded their conditions of employment as being at least adequate.

An increase in operational flexibility in response to fluctuations in sales and in the employment market, together with improved quality control, are regarded by employers as particular advantages of new forms of work organisation, which can be achieved by measures such as—

(a) an enlargement of job content (through variety and job enrichment);

(b) flexible working hours;

(c) increased skills (through training, job rotation);

(d) delegation of responsibility; and

(e) selection of personnel on the basis of qualifications (aptitude testing).

As a rule, savings to be expected (through reduced labour costs and less capital tied up in work in progress) would be offset by increased investment in plant (which would, however, be subsidised up to 50 per cent under the Government's programme).

Up to the first half of 1973, the talks on such matters as co-management in the undertaking were marked by great concern with institutional aspects, which blocked the way to an understanding of the social and welfare consequences of new forms of work organisation. The trade unions were alleged to be using humanisation as a means of bringing about an even greater democratisation of the economy. The employers' federations warned of possible negative consequences if institutionalisation of new organisational forms and co-management went too far. One fear in this respect concerns reduced scope for corporate planning and decision-making and a watering-down of the principle of reward by merit. On the other hand, owners of enterprises seemed prepared to accept any measures that would not prejudice commercial success, particularly where they

... ... of .... and reducing it to the shaping of work content and structures.

A shift from the previous attitude of trade unions appeared in the speeches on Labour Day (1 May) 1973, when demands were made for further improvement in the living conditions of all workers, for restrictions on economic power through co-management and for humanisation of work. Critical voices, however, warned against strengthening the basically individualistic orientation of workers through a merely marginal improvement in the job situation. So-called "new forms of work organisation" would, they said, merely stabilise existing social relationships in favour of management and disrupt the solidarity and collective outlook of workers. It was argued that this development should be of special concern to trade unions, and that employers could draw far greater benefit from the new work structures than the workers.

A breakthrough to a more positive attitude towards measures to improve the work situation was made at a conference on "the humanisation of work as a task for social policy and the trade unions", which was held in Munich in May 1974 by the German Confederation of Trade Unions.[12] It was regarded as necessary to spell out the trade union attitude to the concept of humanising work, to give it vitality and to adapt it to realities. A clear trade union counter-concept was needed, since the term had by that time become relatively dog-eared, and to some extent it had been abused to propagate proposals that equated the humanisation of work with the application of new techniques and sophisticated methods of job evaluation. The aim of the meeting was first to give public emphasis to the appropriateness and urgency of trade union demands for more humane working conditions, and secondly to highlight the opinions and intentions current in the trade union movement in that respect. The result of the conference was the adoption of the following trade union objectives in connection with the humanisation of work:

(a) protection against and elimination of unacceptable intensification of work through suitable counter-measures tackling the causes, whether they be in the fields of employment, work content or methods of determining wage and salary rates;

(b) protection of the health and well-being of workers through the reduction of excessive stress and other harmful effects of the working environment;

(c) reduction in workload instead of financial compensation;

(d) upgrading and skill improvement; the introduction of wage and salary scales and job evaluation systems promoting these objectives;

(e) endeavouring to stabilise conditions of employment and remuneration, particularly earnings and job security for older workers; and

(f) securing and expanding trade union negotiating power in the spheres of collective bargaining and co-management.

The restructuring of work through collective bargaining seems likely to become a new field for trade union action to further development of humane working conditions. Agreements of broad territorial or occupational coverage, sometimes known as "blanket agreements", establish minimum general conditions of work in such respects as hours, salary and wage scales, holidays and leave, periods of notice, work operations and the working environment. Supplementary agreements of more limited coverage govern such matters as the level of individual rates of pay. Blanket collective agreements are drawn up for the long term, so that for the most part, such agreements concluded in the Federal Republic soon after the Second World War still apply today. An important exception is a collective agreement concluded on 1 November 1973 in the metalworking industries in the north of Wurttemberg and Baden, which was reached only after nine days of labour unrest. The following are the chief improvements secured by the agreement:

(1) All flow-line workers, all piece-workers and all time-plus-bonus workers are entitled to at least 5 minutes' break per hour. It goes without saying that workers on time rates are also entitled to a break.

(2) In the case of flow-line and time-work, existing times may not be further subdivided. Research findings regarding working methods must be applied in the enterprise, preferably to offset the unfavourable effects of monotonous tasks. This obligation binds employers especially in cases in which the job time amounts to less than one-and-a-half minutes. Employers and the works council must take every opportunity to see that this goal is attained.

(3) The pace of work at the flow-line is to be based on the time required for the longest operation.

(4) Workers aged 55 or over who have been with the establishment or undertaking for at least one year shall not have their earnings reduced. Anxiety in the face of old age, of reduced effective output and of loss of pension due to reduced earnings is a matter of the past.

(5) Jobs, working methods and the working environment will in future be designed with people in mind.

(6) During the first quarter of each calendar year, the parties to the collective agreement undertake to hold discussions and consultations on matters concerning a humane approach to work.

Current labour-management discussion on new forms of work organisation reflects a more down-to-earth approach and a real interest in improving the position of the worker.

Research projects

In the Federal Republic problems of work organisation are being tackled through a great many scientific disciplines: the subject in itself is regarded as an ideal field for interdisciplinary research. The difference in the recognised aims of the disciplines involved in this research process, however, hinders a common, uniform approach towards the analysis and definition of work situations. The increasing importance of man-machine systems in the field of industrial psychology and labour studies, the ever-increasing importance of alienation as a central concept of industrial sociology and of the social sciences, and the workers' own systematise the trend towards new ideas (e.g. humanisation) and concepts as to the restructuring of work organisation. The many forms of humanisation of work have been categorised as follows:[14]

(1) A means of promoting a humane approach to work (as under sections 90 and 91 of the Act concerning the organisation of the undertaking), e.g. through improved industrial safety, standards of industrial hygiene.

(2) A means of enlarging the scope for action, including decision-making, e.g. job rotation, job enlargement, job enrichment, co-management on the job.

(3) An aim to be achieved through political co-determination, e.g. through controls on management and increased government direction.

(4) An aim to be achieved through revolutionary destruction of class society.

(5) An aim to be achieved through socialisation processes preparing people for a revolution and a subsequent humane society in which there will be no domination of man by man.

The situation in the Federal Republic of Germany would appear to be that forms (1) and (2) are being actively pursued at the present time through legislation and the Government's programme of research into humanisation of work, while form (3) is being seriously discussed. Forms (4) and (5) are advocated only by a small group of Marxist academics.

The most recent contribution to an analysis of the various attitudes and attempts to justify measures taken for the improvement of work quality now under discussion in the Federal Republic is the following classification:[15]

(1) *Democratic and legal approach.* Based on an analysis of constitutional principles (e.g. articles 1 and 2 of the Constitution of the Federal Republic).[16] From these, requirements are deduced, e.g. concerning human values in the undertaking or co-management on a basis of representative democracy.

(2) *Anthropological or sociological approach.* First, the actual work situation is contrasted with anthropological concepts and a different, more responsible conception of work is identified; secondly, the relations between the work situation (job quality) and the social situation (quality of life) are analysed. New forms of work organisation are then proposed in the light of the discrepancies.

(3) *Motivational approach.* Job quality and satisfaction would be improved under this approach through the introduction of incentives offering the worker either intrinsic rewards (self-fulfilment) or extrinsic rewards (better conditions of work).

(4) *Economic approach.* The basic assumption for this approach is that, in practice, work organisation is the necessary outcome of economic conditions. Modified job-structuring principles are the consequence of economic pressures. They have been developed away from extending working times to a steadily increasing intensification of work, through the following stages:

(a) Taylorism;

(b) application of individual psychology (e.g. selection procedures, compensatory rest);

(c) application of group psychology (e.g. human relations measures);

(d) application of motivational psychology (e.g. broadening of the scope for activity, decision-making and control).

Economic determinism is in fact the description that comes closest to explaining the efforts made to improve work organisation in the Federal Republic. It is therefore useful to take a look at the current economic situation.

Economic conditions

There has been a substantial shift in emphasis in the investment activities of industry in the Federal Republic of Germany in recent years. Capacity has hardly been increased; stress is now being laid on rationalisation measures and adaptation to technical innovation. Environmental protection and the strengthening of the social infrastructure are becoming more and more important, as is investment to improve work quality. This can largely be attributed to the Government's action programme to humanise work and the new provisions of the Act concerning the organisation of the undertaking.

Other relatively favourable economic factors in the Federal Republic are overshadowed by the unsatisfactory employment situation. The risk of increased long-term unemployment continues. The fact that such reductions in unemployment as have occurred are to be attributed not so much to new engagements as to the disappearance of jobseekers from the active labour market gives cause for concern. The return of foreign workers to their countries of origin and recourse to flexible age limits has reduced the number of jobless persons. By the end of 1976 the unemployment rate among foreigners was lower than the average, partly because "foreigner-intensive" sectors of the economy, such as the automobile and building industries, had displayed above-average growth rates during the economic upswing preceding the current depression. On the other hand, the position with regard to unemployed women is particularly unsatisfactory. It may be noted in this connection that there are few part-time jobs, and that jobs with low skill requirements—which were largely held by women—are among those most affected by economy measures. All these problems have meant that the Federal Government has become more concerned with matters of labour policy. In this connection, such measures as reducing the statutory pensionable age and shortening working hours are as much debated as retraining and financial assistance to increase regional mobility. Since unemployment among the semi-skilled is above average, the demand for new training methods and further education appear more sensible than the measures to reduce manpower supply referred to above.

To understand the unemployment position in the Federal Republic of Germany it is also important to realise that, under the Employment Promotion Act,[17] workers who lose their jobs receive unemployment pay for one year at the rate of about 68 per cent of their last net remuneration. If they have still not found new jobs by then, they are entitled to unemployment relief at the rate of about 58 per cent of their most recent net remuneration. This being so, it is almost impossible rises, the level of their expectations and requirements with regard to jobs and remuneration rises similarly. Moreover, since no new foreign workers are taken on, the labour shortage is exercising a strong pressure on the development of new forms of work organisation in order to create more attractive jobs. This pressure, and the efforts of Government and Parliament described above, explain the unusual interest shown in the programme for humanising work.

CASE STUDIES

Projects to humanise work and attempts to modify the work situation have mushroomed in a variety of industrial sectors in the Federal Republic of Germany. Consequently, there is an abundance of case histories that can be selected through assorted criteria. As both practical and theoretical analysis show, the success or failure of a modified work organisation is determined by a large number of factors.[18] If "technique" is used as a criterion of selection, assembly processes may be used as good examples of restructuring of work, in the Federal Republic as in other countries. "Organisation" as a criterion is an obvious choice for case histories in which trends in the transfer from individual to group working are highlighted. Still another criterion is the financial support provided by the Federal Ministry of Research and Technology and the involvement of external consultancy research. Taking these factors into account, three case studies have been made:

(1) Blaupunkt (assembly of car radios, with state support and external consultancy research).

(2) Siemens (assembly of domestic appliances, without state support or external consultancy research).

(3) Volkswagenwerk (assembly of engines, with support of the State and with external consultancy research).

Blaupunkt: car radios[19]

Blaupunktwerke GmbH at Hildesheim is a firm that manufactures radio and television equipment, car radios and accessories, and traffic signalling and control systems. In 1975 it had a sales turnover of DM 782 million and employed 10,400 persons (12,400 in 1974). Three-quarters of the nominal capital of DM 80 million is held by Robert Bosch GmbH, mainly a supplier of electrical parts to the automobile industry, and 25 per cent by Bosch-Siemens Hausgeräte GmbH. The latter's capital is divided equally between Robert Bosch GmbH and Siemens AG, which is the major electrical engineering firm in the Federal Republic.

The change in work organisation in this case history is related to the assembly of car radios at the Hildesheim factory. Assembly is undertaken in a loose-linked flow-line structure and, simultaneously, experimentally in an autonomous sub-group. One belt is about 60 metres long and links 62 work stations, at which an average of 52 persons are engaged. The job cycle time is 1.02 minutes, with buffer periods of 3 to 4 minutes. Belt output is 470 items per day. Assembly of the car radios involves the following operations:

(1) *Pre-assembly.* Components of the base fitting, such as housing front, tuner drive and printed circuit board, are combined into one unit, the so-called tuning section, and are tested as such.

(2) *Assembly* of the complete set. The tuning section is fitted into the housing together with the moving parts and certain circuits and minor parts. This operation includes such activities as connecting, fitting and fastening components, wiring and soldering electrical circuits, and carrying out interim checks.

(3) *Adjustment and checking* of the complete set.

(4) *Fault elimination.* Faults in the set, in components or parts may be either due to assembly or already present in the parts supplied. These faults are eliminated in a repair operation independent of the assembly process.

Functions at the individual assembly lines require specific and different skills and entail different degrees of complexity, according to whether the work concerns assembly, adjustment, testing or repairs. Assembly requires relatively little skill. For pre-assembly, some ten days are sufficient to achieve normal output. The main requirements for assembly work are manual dexterity and a high degree of muscular co-ordination. As a rule, training of new workers is carried out by supervisors. In addition to persons employed directly at the production belt, the workshop personnel includes the foremen, section leaders and chargehands. A foreman directs the work of some 200 persons. Apart from the persons directly engaged on these productive tasks, there are indirect contributions such as the supply of materials on the one hand and maintenance and repair work on the other. Supervisory functions, repair work and testing are all carried out by nationals of the Federal Republic.

Nine-tenths of the workers are aliens (mostly Turkish women), whose ignorance of German hampers them from communicating their difficulties with the job to their German-speaking supervisors and fellow-workers. Social relations at work are similarly affected by the language barrier. The assembly lines are worked under a two-shift system. This means that workers receive shift allowances but must adjust to shift working, which may affect, for example, housekeeping arrangements, particularly if both husband and wife are employed, or the residential situation in foreign workers' hostels. In either case, an important factor is that the spouse or fellow-workers will as a rule be employed on different shifts or at different workplaces.

Production costs and labour productivity as such gave no cause for changes in the work organisation. Lost time and reject rates remained at normal levels. Problems tended to arise rather through the lack of flexibility of the production system. The existing time-based production structure was no longer able to cope with the varying requirements and conditions of the market as regards quantity, type and product variations, the more so since Japanese competition had increased. Although the assembly process was mechanised to a small extent, any adjustments caused substantial disturbances to the work flow.

.... could in no way be regarded as unsatisfactory. The undertaking was, and is, well known for its highly advantageous fringe benefits and progressive welfare policies. The jobs offered were not subject to harmful environmental influences (such as noise, dangerous substances or safety risks). Nor was the pay below average. Moreover, as the main employer in the region, the firm was not in direct competition with other employers. Yet although the regional unemployment rate was above average, at 6 to 7 per cent within the area of the factory, the jobs offered could not meet the expectations of nationals, and since they were in a position to decline employment not in line with their expectations, most of the vacancies were filled by aliens. In industrial centres of the Federal Republic today one notices that the age structure of factory workers has shifted in such a way that the nationals directly engaged in production are older than the aliens. A prime consideration in modifying work structures has accordingly been to improve career prospects, through opportunities for increasing skills and for promotion, both for aliens and for the school leavers of the Federal Republic.

In short, new forms of work organisation were required in order to ensure flexibility in the production system and to provide attractive jobs. In mid-1973 an internal project group consisting of production planners, designers, workshop management, personnel department staff and members of the central unit concerned with job design began to make plans for different assembly systems. The works council participated in the project to the extent that it was informed and consulted in accordance with its rights under sections 90 and 91 of the Act concerning the organisation of the undertaking.[20] In 1974 preliminary work by the team was integrated into the programme of the Ministry of Research and Technology. State support within the framework of the humanisation of work programme provided for a grant to the Robert Bosch Company in the 1974-77 period of—

(a) 50 per cent of the additional expenditure incurred for relevant projects in Bosch establishments; and

(b) 100 per cent of the cost of research assistance provided by external consultants.

The state support was spread over various work projects at Bosch, including car radio production at the Hildesheim factory. Work related to but extending beyond particular work projects was also financed by the State and covers tasks such as co-ordination of the programming schedules, data collection, development of work systems, development of organisational systems, preparation of training outlines based on work requirements, and development of procedures for the introduction of improved work structures. Company representatives and works council members were joined on the project by consultants from the Production Technology and Automation Institute[21] of Stuttgart, and the Working Party for Empirical Research on Training[22] of Heidelberg. The terms of reference of those bodies include advice on the development and introduction of improved work structures and external consultancy research to ensure communication of results. In the present case, the contribution of the consultants included advice on industrial training, financial management, industrial sociology and educational sociology, given to—

(a) 14 working parties whose terms of reference extend beyond any particular factory; and

(b) the special planning teams at the various Bosch Group establishments.

The purpose of the external consultancy research is to monitor the projects in accordance with the criteria of the various disciplines involved and with regard to their transferability to other undertakings. The social scientists carried out a survey of the situation before the new forms of work organisation were introduced, as well as several others after the changes had been made. These surveys covered some 1,500 persons, divided into subjects and controls.

The structure of the assembly process, i.e. organisation of the pre-assembly, assembly, adjustment, testing and repair activities, was first subjected to a series of tests. In particular, the system was to meet the following requirements:

(a) a high degree of flexibility with regard to quantity and type variations;

(b) adaptability of the system for training new members of the group;

(c) increased scope for individual action;

(d) enlargement of job content;

(e) creation of opportunities for skill development;

(f) transfer to the staff of responsibility with regard to quantity and quality; and

(g) expansion of communication possibilities and an acceleration of information transfer.

The organisational changes were not only to introduce technical improvements in the work system but also to provide scope for individual action and decision: the workers concerned were therefore to decide freely on their own field of work, and such a decision was to be reversible. This meant that new work structures could not be permanently established but should wherever possible to subject to any further changes required. Various possible work structures were developed on the basis of the above-mentioned objectives. Among the possibilities, the following arrangement appeared to be the most suitable. All of the various assembly functions were consolidated, and the workers involved were divided into groups, each collectively responsible for carrying out the entire assembly process on part of the plant's output. This arrangement was intended, in particular, to facilitate more rapid elimination of defects. A U-shaped bench arrangement was adopted, with an average complement of ten persons. The arrangement of the individual work stations is shown in figure 1.

The job cycle time was extended to about 6 minutes, buffer times being increased to 30 or 40 minutes per work station. The personnel skills requirement was to be achieved through a 30 to 40 per cent overlap of job content between adjoining work stations. It was thought that in this way a continuing and personally determined acquisition of a knowledge of the content of neighbouring jobs would

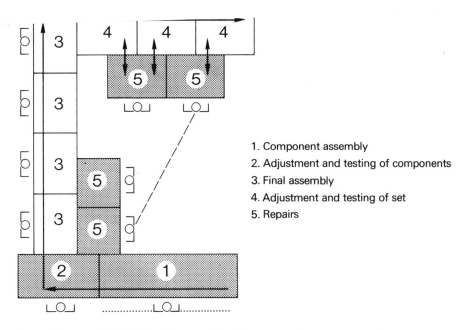

1. Component assembly
2. Adjustment and testing of components
3. Final assembly
4. Adjustment and testing of set
5. Repairs

Source: G. Isenmann, K. Podeschwik and E. Rost: *Höherqualifizierung im Arbeitsprozess,* Rationalisierungskuratorium der Deutschen Wirtschaft, National congress on humanisation of work held under RKW auspices in April 1976, Heft Stand 7, p. 8.

be ensured. The overlap in job content at adjoining work stations serves several purposes. First, it facilitates the training of new group members, since they start with simple jobs and can make progress by gradually extending the range of the work they do. Once the whole range of work has been covered, a change of station can be made with little additional learning. Secondly, such a work structure can adjust to absenteeism without disproportionate loss of time. Thirdly, an overlap of work creates a co-operative network that permits mutual support and consultation without exposing individual workers to the consequences of departing from a strict allocation of time. To improve communication it was felt that equipment mounted on work benches should be kept as low as possible, and should not exceed 30 cm above the work bench so that the workers in the group could easily maintain visual contact.

The possibility of gradual enlargement of tasks in the adjustment and testing stations is subject to other technical prerequisites. In order to create a progressive learning situation here too, the work stations in question were equipped for the full adjustment or testing procedure. In addition to these measures to extend the scope of tasks, decisions regarding indirect action, such as the supply of materials, simple maintenance tasks or co-ordination of work and quantities, were left to the group or to its members.

Group working began early in 1975. The workers concerned had a very instrumental attitude to their work. Dominance of the financial motive can be directly traced to the social situation of the foreign workers. Changes in work organisation, particularly when linked to higher skills, were therefore necessarily associated with corresponding financial expectations. Job allocations and transfers were made on a voluntary basis so as to avoid giving cause for resignations or for the development of negative attitudes because of the introduction of modified working conditions. Such negative attitudes were observed mainly where the changes threatened to affect personal relations or leisure time detrimentally. This was manifested principally on transfer from double-shift working to a single shift, in which this new form of work organisation was now tested. Supervisors, such as foremen, were rather suspicious of a change in work organisation. This may be explained both by additional pressures of a personal nature and by difficulty in adjusting to new work procedures.

During the start-up stage, opportunities for job enlargement were not actively considered. The workers were all chiefly concerned with learning the processes at their own work stations and with achieving the standard group output of 90 units a day. Only active leadership among the workshop staff created a willingness to learn additional work elements. Acquaintance with adjoining work stations was generally achieved in such a way that, initially, experience was gained of similar work on adjoining stations, i.e. assemblers changed places at the assembly stations. Only after they had learned the simpler jobs did they tackle adjustment and testing jobs. When the training stage was completed it appeared necessary to carry out continuous job rotation in order to avoid loss of experience. Consequently, the stage was soon reached where one worker had learnt to work at all stations; four workers could handle jobs at three or four stations, and five others became qualified to work at two stations. Because of an increase in skills, the management was clearly forced to open up appropriate opportunities for promotion within the workshop organisation for certain members of the group.

In terms of economic efficiency, expectations regarding flexibility have been fully met. This applies to quantity of output, product type adaptation and variations in the workforce. The absence of a member of the group no longer means a bottleneck for downstream tasks on the process line. As regards costs only a qualified conclusion can be drawn. Expenditure on equipment rises slightly (about 6-10 per cent),[23] as do wage and plant costs. On the other hand, some manufacturing overheads were reduced through group working. These include, in particular, the cost of workshop supervision and repair and subsequent labour costs. The reductions were achieved by improvements in the quality of assembled sets and a corresponding reduction in repair personnel.

Siemens: domestic appliances[24]

Siemens AG is the major electrical engineering firm in the Federal Republic of Germany, with extensive interests abroad. In 1975-76 it employed some 300,000 persons. Sales were about DM 19,000 million. The enterprise is organised into separate divisions, accounting for the following percentages of sales turnover: power engineering 32, information technology 24, data processing 15, electrical

	vacuum cleaners	vacuum cleaners	(including drive)
Number of types	1	5	50	4
Monthly No. of items per type	4 000	2 000-20 000	500-20 000	4 000
Number of individual parts	25	30	60	65
Weight of complete unit (kg)	0.3	1.0-2.5	3.2-9.0	1.0

Source: H. O. Meyer: *Erfahrungen bei der Einführung neuer Arbeitsformen in der Montage von Haushaltsgeräten*, p. 13.

installations 12, medical technology 9 and construction 5. The firm has tried out new forms of work organisation at a number of its factories throughout the Federal Republic without calling for financial support from the Ministry of Research and Technology. Chief among these measures is the conversion to small-group assembly of appliances and appliance parts.

The following case history describes a project in the electric motor works at Bad Neustadt an der Saale. In this factory there are 1,800 industrial workers, of whom 400 are assigned to the production of domestic appliances. The conversion concerned assembly work on rotary beaters and on small and full-sized vacuum cleaners (see table 1). In detail, the assembly covers—

(a) motors for floor units;

(b) drives (blowers) for hand and full-sized vacuum cleaners;

(c) final assembly of hand and full-sized vacuum cleaners; and

(d) final assembly of rotary beaters.

The assembly processes followed a timed flow-line. Each flow-line occupied 8 to 15 women workers (nationals of the Federal Republic) who were given short job induction courses. For normal throughput, the work cycle averaged 1 minute. The change in work organisation was planned as part of the relocation of production in a newly constructed workshop. Preliminary work was started at the beginning of 1973. Project development and implementation was left entirely to internal departments. The works council was informed of the intended conversion at the start of the planning phase. Project implementation was preceded by a survey of the workers concerned by the firm's own psychologists (personal, two-hour interviews with 80 workers). The findings did not, however, appear sufficiently reliable to the management for direct application to reorganisation measures.

Financial as well as psychological or motivational factors militated in favour of doing away with the flow-line system. Absenteeism and labour turnover were not such as to justify changes in work organisation. Financial factors, on the other hand, did require reorganisation of the assembly sections. The types of

Table 2. Group working arrangements for the production of rotary beaters and vaccum cleaners at the Siemens works at Bad Neustadt an der Saale

Item	Motors for floor units	Drives (blowers) for hand and full-sized vacuum cleaners	Final assembly of hand and full-sized vacuum cleaners	Final assembly of beaters (including drive)
Number of work groups	2	5	16	3
Work stations per group	1	3	3	4
Job time (min.) per work station	6	2.5	2.8-6.5	2.4
Supervision	Foreman	1 group supervisor per 3 assembly units		
Electrical testing	Included in assembly	At next point	At next point	Included in assembly

Source: H. O. Meyer: *Erfahrungen bei der Einführung neuer Arbeitsformen in der Montage von Haushaltsgeräten*, p. 13.

appliance to be assembled were relatively short-lived consumer goods subject to frequent changes, owing to marketing considerations, as regards aesthetic design, performance and handling characteristics. Further, a broad range of types was offered, varying in composition and production quantity. These requirements as to flexibility in production engineering could not be adequately met by the flow-line system: seasonal fluctuations and the introduction of new models led to adjustment difficulties, in the latter case because the training time required dislocated the assembly process. A further reason for changes in work organisation lay in the waste of capacity involved in time unproductively spent in transferring items between the belt and work stations (about 5 per cent of total cycle time). General losses in cycle time that were due to desynchronisation of work flow and that could not be eliminated by appropriate planning of the work sequence resulted in further waste of about the same amount. Particular difficulties always arose when assembly capacity had to be adjusted to market fluctuations (by shortening or lengthening the belt).

Besides increasing flexibility, it was hoped to bring about a reduction in workload. Work content was to be extended in such a way that—

(a) different kinds of skill could be deployed on any one job;

(b) a sitting posture would generally be possible, with changes of position provided for in the work flow; and

(c) workers could occasionally have time for a break.

It was also hoped that mutual contact, support and consultation would be achieved relatively easily by working in small groups. It was decided that each individual work group would remain in existence for some time in order to facilitate the establishment and maintenance of the necessary social contact. In addition, it was assumed that changes in the work flow that were left to the workers could be better organised in small groups, and the work groups were therefore

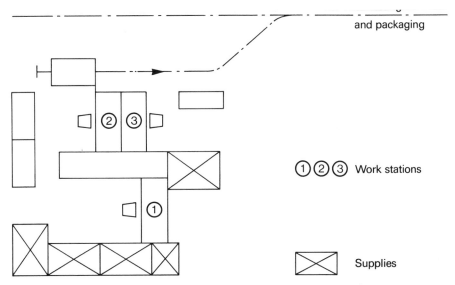

and packaging

①②③ Work stations

⊠ Supplies

Source: H. O. Meyer: "Erfahrungen mit Gruppenmontage-Plätzen am Beispiel eines Elektrogerätewerkes", in Institut für ange-
wändte Arbeitswissenschaft e. V.: *Arbeitsstrukturierung in der deutschen Metallindustrie* (2), p. 59.

made responsible for the co-ordination of tasks not linked to job stations. There
were financial inducements to encourage the groups to seize this opportunity
since remuneration was on a group basis. Quality control was also assigned to the
work group in order to promote group cohesion. However, an incidental requirement of job enlargement was the electrical testing of the vacuum cleaners. This
work was always undertaken at a single spot, so that for efficiency reasons it
could not be included within the range of tasks of all the groups.

Working within the new work structure (see table 2) began in May 1974. The
motors for the floor units were each entirely assembled and checked at two work
stations. The other products (except rotary beaters) were assembled by three-
person groups. These were linked by transit paths, with separate work stations for
product testing and packaging (see figure 2). Assembly of the beaters was undertaken by four-person groups with integrated product testing. A particular feature
of the new work organisation is that each product type can be assembled at any
work station. This is achieved by interchangeable bench tops and parts holders.

Group size was determined chiefly by technical and financial considerations.
Product design reflected the desirability of splitting the over-all production
process into three or four assembly stages, so that each member of a group would
always pass on a completed part. With groups of this size it is also possible to ensure that each group works longer on a particular model. Finally, a group of this
size fits in well, in conjunction with the design features, with the transport paths
and buffer times between group work stations.

In human terms, the results of the experiment were satisfactory after initial difficulties. When the changes in work organisation were introduced, a positive reaction to the work situation was shown by the highly skilled workers. The others grew accustomed to the modified working conditions only after a lengthy period of adjustment; this applied particularly to women who had already spent several years on the assembly line. A change in work or achievement motivation was reflected in the exercise of group responsibility, as could be seen from the co-ordination and agreement among group members. Opportunities for inter-personal contact were improved by the fact that the groups decided on their own composition. In contradistinction to assembly-line working, dissatisfaction arose where parts to be assembled proved faulty. The works management attributes this reaction to the fact that it is easier to learn how to deal with one and the same faulty part in a short cycle. Such a fault is felt to be less disturbing than faults affecting different parts and leading to a greater amount of work. It also appears clear that whereas on a short cycle faulty parts are regarded as providing welcome variation and challenge, they are a source of inconvenience and annoyance when the job content is enlarged. For these reasons, stronger action was taken to eliminate faults in parts manufacture, on the initiative of group members.

Despite the greater concentration needed and the correspondingly reduced opportunity of achieving the required results in a purely routine manner, the majority (about 80 per cent) of the women concerned felt at the end of the working day that they had been less "busy". This feeling can be attributed first to the reduced physical effort, since enlargement of the job content reduces the need to transport assembly parts at frequent intervals. The regular change from a sitting to a standing position and vice versa is also a contributing factor.

As management had expected, the requirements made of immediate supervisors increased with the conversion to group working. For this reason, such staff attended preparatory training courses beforehand. The women concerned were informed by their supervisors about the new assembly system and appropriately trained at the end of the planning stage. The role of group supervisors was much changed. By contrast with their previous functions of decision-making and monitoring or providing technical advice, they were assigned to handling personal cases. This new role could not, of course, be fully reconciled with their own image of themselves. It is therefore intended, in the long term, to fill these posts with specially skilled workers, thus affording promotion opportunities for group members.

The new form of work organisation has been evaluated by the management on the basis of two years of experience with this new arrangement. On the whole the corporate objectives with regard to group working were met. The increased flexibility was regarded as particularly valuable. The ability of assembly groups to adjust to market changes, i.e. meeting shifts in demand for different products, was found to have been achieved to the desired extent, so that it had been possible to reduce stocks of finished products. Even the most extensive model changes within the product programme were completed without major disturbance to the assembly process. In order to avoid capacity loss through conversion from one product type to another, work benches for one group were always left unoccupied, and new product types. Their assembly could be tested in small volume, and the suitability of tools and equipment could be checked. At that stage, working methods and work stations could be tried out without affecting the assembly of other products. As a further consequence of group assembly, a reduction was noticed in the time cycle loss and transit times. Over-all, the increase in output per product type amounted to between 15 and 20 per cent. One reason for this was thought to be the mutual support the workers gave each other in the course of the work (e.g. interchange of assembly functions). Finally, assembly errors were reduced, and consequently fewer persons had to be assigned to repair work.

While these results could generally be regarded as positive from the financial point of view, some costs were higher. The cost of tooling and equipment, for example, was estimated to be about 30 per cent higher, since product types with higher item volume necessitated provision of duplicate work benches. Similarly, the training period for new workers increased. Additional costs arose because of the need to have more materials on hand. The increased supply of materials to work stations (buffer stocks) further leads to greater space requirement (about 20 per cent) and to more expensive arrangements for the distribution of materials; in the present case computer support was required.

Volkswagen: automobile engines[25]

The Volkswagen company is one of the largest manufacturers of passenger cars in the Federal Republic, and also has extensive interests abroad. Sixty per cent of its nominal capital of DM 900 million is held in the form of so-called "people's shares"; of the remainder 20 per cent is held by the Federal Republic, 16 per cent by the Province of Lower Saxony and 4 per cent by the Volkswagen-werk Foundation. In 1975 the sales turnover of the Volkswagen group was DM 19,000 million (of which DM 6,500 million were generated through the domestic market). While group earnings rose by 11 per cent in 1975, the over-all production of vehicles at home and abroad fell by 6 per cent. The firm's share of the domestic car market was 27.3 per cent. The home establishment employed 118,000 persons. This was a reduction of 12 per cent as compared with 1974. Investments, also compared with 1974, fell by 51 per cent. The plant at Salzgitter, from which this case history originates, employs 5,400 persons. This level has been steadily maintained since sensational staff reductions in 1974-75, under which workers willing to retire were given large sums of severance pay.

In 1974 the company management began to discuss new forms of work organisation for humanising the world of work, after previously carrying out studies and taking measures to increase industrial safety and to improve the working environment. As part of a programme of "comparison of work structures in unit production", particular attention was devoted to group assembly of standard four-cylinder engines at the Salzgitter works. Engine assembly is chiefly undertaken on a continuously moving conveyor belt or, after recent changes, on transfer assembly lines. Cycle times, according to daily throughput on the conveyor belt, varied from 1.5 to 3 minutes, and in the case of transfer assembly from 0.8 to 1.2 minutes. Work was divided into two shifts. In terms of qualifications the workers ranged from unskilled to skilled. Ninety-eight per cent of workers at the Salzgitter works are trade union members, while in the company as a whole the proportion is slightly lower. The Salzgitter works are covered by a special collective agreement for the company as a whole. Foreign workers account for 27 per cent of the company's workforce. When the factory was newly built there had been a recruitment problem, which has since been eliminated even though alternative employment is available in the Salzgitter industrial area.

According to the management there were no compelling reasons, such as poor quality or high proportion of faults, for the experimental development and comparison of new forms of work organisation. The main aim was to extend the ergonomic research that had been conducted for some time. It was not denied, however, that competitive pressures (experiments in Sweden) and the growing popular demand for an improvement in the quality of work, especially in the automobile industry,[26] substantially assisted the launching of the project. The general objective of the project for the development and comparison of new work structures was to produce, on an experimental basis, 100 engines per working day in autonomous group working, with due regard to the structural conditions of a mass-production undertaking. The new structure was intended—

(a) to facilitate further training on the job;

(b) to secure maximum facility of communication;

(c) to allow some autonomy with regard to both work organisation and the actual carrying out of the work;

(d) to lead to an increased measure of job satisfaction; and

(e) to be applied on a flexible basis.

A task force was set up jointly by—

(a) the Volkswagen company, especially for the financial aspects;

(b) the Darmstadt Institute of Labour Studies,[27] especially for the ergonomic aspects; and

(c) the Department of Occupational and Industrial Psychology of the Federal Technical University of Zurich.[28]

Members of this task force were to produce as much reliable data as possible, within the scope of section 90 of the Workers' Representation Act, and to put forward solutions for the human, financial and technological problems that would arise. The ergonomic guidelines for the task force were:

(1) Manufacturing aims:

    (a) flexibility of production;

    (b) improvement in quality; and

    (c) reduction of labour turnover and absenteeism.

...~~improve workers~~ satisfaction; and

(d) to facilitate interaction and communication.

(3) Consequential reorganisation:

 (a) to give meaningful content to jobs;

 (b) to give the workers some freedom to organise their own work;

 (c) to provide rotation of tasks; and

 (d) to provide tasks requiring different skills.

The psychological guidelines were to bring about or to provide for—

(a) group autonomy;

(b) communication within the groups;

(c) scope for decision-making;

(d) optimum group size;

(e) participation in design.

To ensure proper project implementation, it was thought desirable to achieve a maximum of information flow, to co-ordinate expertise and to take as many decisions as possible on the spot. The project was organised in such a way as to provide participation, and the works council was involved from the start. A co-ordination officer for the project as a whole was appointed from the personnel and welfare division of the company. The partners in the project applied individually for financial support from the Ministry of Research and Technology in 1975. When funds had been granted, amounting to DM 12.5 million over-all, it proved possible to get the project under way in the same year.

Since experience of alternatives to the assembly line had in the past been extremely varied and to some extent contradictory, the firm felt it necessary to probe the multiple consequences of change and the opportunities for it. Accordingly, a comparison of various work structures was undertaken. The car engine assembly project falls into three phases during which the task force observed the work done under different working patterns:

(a) on a continuously moving conveyor belt (data collection: six weeks, 1975);

(b) on an intermittent transfer line (data collection: six months, up to March 1976); and

(c) in group assembly (was to be continued until 1978).

The assembly groups were formed towards the end of 1975, before the technical and organisational features of engine assembly by autonomous groups had been worked out in detail. It said in support of this step that—

(a) participation by workers employed in the new groups leads to constructive co-operation only if full information is supplied at a very early date (at least one year before production starts) and personal decisions can be taken on that basis; and

(b) the benefits of partly autonomous group working become apparent only if optimum conditions have been created from the motivational and training points of view.

Participation clearly had to be voluntary. Out of 450 workers approached in the engines section, 260 (i.e. about 60 per cent) said they were ready to take part in the experiment. However, they could not all be assigned to the project since only 50 were needed. These were selected after consulting the engines and personnel departments and the works council. In accordance with the proposals of the consultants concerned, four groups of seven persons each (i.e. two shifts of two groups each) were formed, three so-called "substitutes" being assigned to each group to ensure continuity of the experiment. The groups were formed without any intervention by the management, but with the aid and advice of the industrial psychologists, who also monitored the further development of the groups. A few potential group members did not participate for various reasons, e.g. as a result of staff surplus or because they did not feel at home within the group formed. The groups were monitored at the head office by a member of the Zurich staff. Internally, a system of group representation was created (e.g. group spokesman, representatives). The spokesman was integrated into the project organisation. No new personnel were recruited for the project. A comparatively small number of persons were hired to work on traditional production lines instead of the workers transferred to the project.

Parallel with and immediately after the formation of the groups had begun, the technical side of the experiment was developed jointly with the participants. The following objectives were laid down for each group:

(a) the complete assembly of an engine including preliminary work;

(b) running in and/or inspection;

(c) assumption of the decision-making and control functions required in this connection.

In accordance with these objectives two alternative assembly procedures were worked out (figure 3), one of them being based on proposals by one of the group spokesmen. The procedure subsequently adopted was similar to the first one shown in figure 3, which allows parallel production by several assembly groups.

This flexible form of organisation can, in fact, be transformed into a work-fragmenting system by making the individual assembly groups work in sequence instead of in parallel. In 1976 engines were fully fitted out by each of the four assembly groups. So far, the Salzgitter assembly procedure had been applied to the assembly of engines only. Running-in and testing were still carried out away from the assembly groups in other sections of the plant, the cost of which was not integrated with that of assembly. The reason given for this arrangement was the hitherto inadequate qualifications of the group members.

Special training courses were developed to prepare workers for their new tasks. The social scientists introduced a variety of new methods to raise the level of group members' qualifications to that required for the assembly of a complete engine. A few problems arose in this connection, so that the teaching methods ultimately used by the supervisory staff were the traditional ones. The research

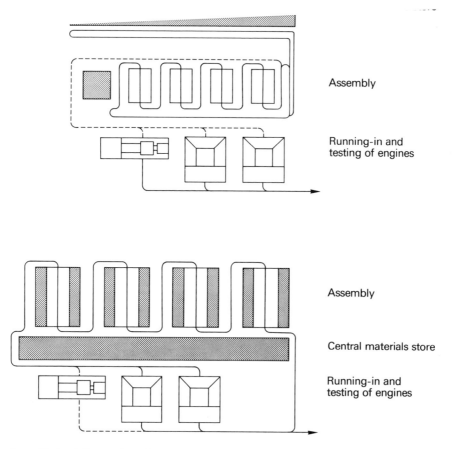

Assembly

Running-in and
testing of engines

Assembly

Central materials store

Running-in and
testing of engines

Source: M. Granel: *Gruppenarbeit in der PKW - Motoren - Montage,* Vortrage Nr. 10, Fachtagung Arbeitsgestaltung in der Produktion '76 des Instituts für Produktionstechnik und Automatisierung (Stuttgart, IPA, 1976).

workers were still working on the training processes and what can be learned from them. Various means of assessing new training courses were being used.

The groups were provided with their weekly programme in advance. Within those limits, group members themselves were allowed to determine their daily output and sequence of internal work pauses. Group members have the right to be heard on all matters concerning group work.

All four autonomous groups began working in June 1976. By the end of the year the project was in its third phase. At that stage additional cost had been incurred through investment in plant. Further labour costs had also been incurred for the planning connected with the conversion. No decisive improvement in quality had yet been recorded. It seemed that the horizontal and vertical enlargement of tasks had increased work value, so that corresponding increases in pay rates would have to follow. However, the development of new systems of remuneration had yet to be undertaken and was to be a matter for negotiation between the parties to any new collective agreements. With rising motivation on the part of the group workers and the reserve personnel, the level of expectations had also risen. Since it had not been possible for expectations to be entirely met, some frustration had arisen. A particular problem for the group workers' direct supervisors had arisen from the change in traditional, hierarchical management structures. During the first year the foremen had been in a very difficult situation, but they had since found a new niche as consultants, which was accepted by the workers as well.

Altogether, it was clear from a number of discussions that the initial euphoria had given way to more sober attitudes. It must be borne in mind that this project directly involved only 28 out of the 5,400 people employed at the Salzgitter works. It was also clear that, especially in the automobile industry, it is difficult to depart from the high degree of mechanisation of flow-line assembly, particularly when rising demand puts pressure on capacity. With production processes structured in this way, there are no clear economic advantages in converting to group production as was the case with Siemens. It appeared from discussion that a radically new form of working structure is not possible in the automobile industry in view of the relatively homogeneous nature of product types.

GENERAL CONCLUSIONS

The publicity given to the discussion of new forms of work organisation in the Federal Republic seems excessive both in volume and in degree. This applies not only to the treatment of the subject by the mass media but also to works published by the firms concerned or by outside authors.[29]

New forms of work organisation in the undertaking have been labelled and classified according to concepts which are not comparable because of the different initial situations prevailing. The variety of new forms of work organisation adopted in enterprises is largely the result of the diversity of the reasons for the change. Changes in organisation of work are generally initiated by the management of the enterprise or factory, and they reflect this management orientation. The basic objective is an increase in the flexibility of the assembly process, i.e. in its adaptability to fluctuations in demand, and this objective has, indeed, apparently been achieved. In addition, increased flexibility is designed to reduce the vulnerability of the work process to disruption. Finally, increases in productivity are obtained by the reduction in work stoppages and the improvement in quality. In most cases—although in a general and unspecified way—the desire to increase job satisfaction is given as a reason for the changes.

In addition, comparison of reorganisation measures and their effectiveness is difficult because of different points of departure. Thus partial transformation in existing undertakings cannot be compared with measures taken when new undertakings are set up. One thing, however, seems certain, namely that "humanisation measures" are approved of by all concerned when they are carried out in connection with the establishment of entire new plants. Generally speaking,

the introduction of alternative forn.
successful in improving working con,
with the planning of new production u
formation of existing ones. This is the
management and acceptability to the woi

In the Federal Republic new forms ᴖ　　　　　　　　　　.gely introduced in isolation. A certain transfer of knᴖ　　　　　　.ieved through
congresses and the meetings organised by ᴖ　　　　　.c research institutes. Even in the case of projects promoted　　　　　.orities the level of
exchanges of experience has so far left much　　　　／ith the exception of
the working party on new work structures in ᴖ.　　　.itomobile industry, to
which automobile manufacturers in the Federal ᴎ　　　and the firm of Bosch
belong, institutionalised co-operation between undertᴖ ngs or between management and workers is still in its early stages. The fact that programmes for the
improvement of working conditions are largely carried out in isolation results in
heterogeneity and general vagueness in objectives, methods and results. The
primary consideration is the application of tried and trusted humanisation
measures involving slight financial risk, and not innovation or risky experimentation. This policy can largely be attributed to uncertainty about financial consequences, group psychology, suitable forms of remuneration and skill improvement.

Reorganisation measures directed to specific objectives are introduced
primarily in large undertakings in connection with assembly activities and mass
production. However, organisational changes often affect only marginal areas of
over-all assembly. In the automobile industry, for example, it is considered impossible to do away with the assembly line because of the length of production
runs. Reorganisation measures are thus limited to the small-scale production of
specially designed models such as ambular ᴖes.

Attempts are often made to justify the limited introduction of organisational
changes on the grounds of lack of interest among the workers concerned. Nevertheless, positive results are reported on the ˙projects implemented so far
(increased flexibility, improved quality, fewer work stoppages, improved job satisfaction). Generalisations of this kind are, however, not entirely valid since—

(a) the success and efficacy of conversion measures depend on the situation in
the undertaking before they were introduced and the level of expectations of
the management;

(b) usually only "successful" action is reported, and action that is supported by
the public authorities is almost invariably given a favourable assessment;

(c) measures to improve the quality of working life are actively taken only
where the need for them seems obvious (in particular in the case of
fragmented assembly work), i.e. where the risk of failure is considered to be
slight; and

(d) it is extremely rare for whole factories to be converted, and the transforma-
tions are often limited to special production lines from which they cannot be
extended to other personnel and other tasks.

try for Research and Technology and its influence on crucial issues in humanisation measures call for a few remarks. The promotional policy of the Federal Government was initially directed towards individual branches and fields of activity. It concentrated on problems of noise, vibration and dangerous substances. In particular, research was commissioned for projects to improve working conditions in coal mines. In 1975 promotional activities were extended to cover manufacturing. As regards large undertakings, the main focus was on the electrical and automobile industries. In future it is planned to extend the promotional policy also to administrative services. The main features of the promotional policy may in general be described as—

(a) measures to give the workers greater latitude to take the initiative and organise their own work, with the aim of improving their skills;

(b) the elimination of excessive stress in repetitive, short-cycle tasks;

(c) measures to reduce combined physical and social stresses and fatigue;

(d) an investigation of the conditions favourable or unfavourable to the Federal Government's programme of action; and

(e) preparation of practical aids to the application of new forms of work organisation.

In connection with these objectives the Ministry intends to involve workers and their representatives more closely than hitherto in the implementation of projects under its future promotional policy. So far, the workers' contribution has often been limited to formal approval of experiments by the works council. Attempts are now to be made to give freer rein to worker initiatives when undertakings are reorganised.

Notes

[1] A brief description of the general system of collective bargaining in the Federal Republic is to be found in ILO: *Collective bargaining in industrialised market economies*, Studies and reports, New series, No. 80 (Geneva, 1973), pp. 253-258.

[2] In particular under the Collective Agreements Act of 1949. A translation of the consolidated text of the Act, incorporating amendments up to 1969, has been published in the ILO *Legislative Series*, 1969—Ger. F.R. 4.

[3] In particular under an Act of 1952 on the prescribing of minimum conditions of employment (ibid., 1952—Ger. F.R. 1).

[4] Until 1976 the conventional English translation, "co-determination", was used in the ILO *Legislative Series* for the term "Mitbestimmung" used in labour legislation of the Federal Republic. Since June of that year the English term used has been "co-management".

[5] English translation in ILO: *Legislative Series*, 1976—Ger. F.R. 1. See also M. Peltzer: *Mitbestimmungsgesetz/Co-determination Act*, Deutsch-englische Textausgabe des Mitbestimmungs-

gesetzes mit einer englischen Einleitung (2nd ed., Cologne, Otto Schmidt Verlag, 1976), and D. Hoffmann: *The German Co-Determination Act, 1976 (Mitbestimmungsgesetz)* (Düsseldorf, Metzner Verlag, 1976).

[6] Particulars of the respective functions of the main bodies concerned will be found on pp. 81-83 of Johannes Schregle: "Co-determination in the Federal Republic of Germany: A comparative view", in *International Labour Review*, Jan.-Feb. 1978.

[7] An English translation has been published in the ILO *Legislative Series*, 1972—Ger. F.R. 1. See also M. Peltzer and R. Boer: *Betriebsverfassungsgesetz/Labour-Management Relation Act*, Kommentar für die Praxis in Deutsch und Englisch und synoptischer Darstellung (Frankfurt am Main, Fritz Knapp Verlag, 1977).

[8] Translations of the Act will be found in ILO: *Legislative Series*, 1973—Ger. F.R. 2; and of the Ordinance in idem, 1975—Ger. F.R. 2.

[9] Bundesregierung: *Forschungsbericht IV* (Bonn-Bad Godesberg, Verlag Dr. Heger, 1972), p. 55.

[10] On promotion measures approved by the Federal Ministry of Research and Technology, see Deutsche Forschungs- und Versuchsanstalt für Luft- und Raumfahrt (DFVLR): *Statusbericht über bewilligte Förderungsmassnahmen des Bundesministers für Forschung und Technologie zur Humanisierung des Arbeitslebens* (Bonn-Bad Godesberg, 1976).

[11] See, for example, Bundesvereinigung der Deutschen Arbeitgeberverbände: *Humanisierung der Arbeitswelt* (Cologne, 1975).

[12] See H. O. Vetter (ed.): *Humanisierung der Arbeit als gesellschaftspolitische und gewerkschaftliche Aufgabe*, Protokoll der DFG-Konferenz vom 16. und 17. Mai 1974 in München (Frankfurt am Main and Cologne, Europäische Verlagsanstalt, 1974).

[13] E. Ulich: "Arbeitswechsel und Aufgabenerweiterung", in *afa-Informationen* (Ausschuss für Arbeitsstudien), 23 (1972), p. 163.

[14] B. Tietze: "Humanisierung der Arbeitswelt: Theoretisches Programm und politische Praxis", in *Arbeit und Leistung*, 1974, p. 311.

[15] J. Gohl: "Zu Ansätzen der Humanisierungsdebatte", in *Zeitschrift für Arbeitswissenschaft*, 1 (1976), pp. 2 ff.

[16] "1.(1) The dignity of man is sacred. To respect and protect it is an obligation of all State authority. . . . 2.(1) Everyone has the right to develop his personality freely. . . ." (ILO: *Legislative Series*, 1949—Ger. F.R. 1).

[17] ibid., 1969—Ger. F.R. 1.

[18] W. H. Staehle: "Die Arbeitssituation als Ausgangspunkt von Arbeitsgestaltungsempfehlungen", in G. Reber (ed.): *Personal- und Sozialorientierung der Betriebswirtschaftslehre* (Stuttgart, Poeschel Verlag, 1977), Vol. 1.

[19] This case history is based on information obtained in an interview with Messrs. Kieselbach and Schafer at Robert Bosch GmbH and from G. Isenmann, K. Podeschwik and E. Rost: *Höherqualifizierung im Arbeitsprozess*, Rationalisierungskuratorium der Deutschen Wirtschaft, Kongress 1976, Heft Stand 7; and K. Podeschwik: *Arbeitsgestaltung in der Montage unter dem Aspekt der Höherqualifizierung*, Vortrag Nr. 28, Fachtagung Arbeitsgestaltung in der Produktion '76 des Instituts für Produktionstechnik und Automatisierung (Stuttgart, IPA, 1976).

[20] See above, pp. 83-84.

[21] Institut für Produktionstechnik und Automatisierung.

[22] Arbeitsgruppe für empirische Bildungsforschung.

[23] See H. Zippe: *Wirtschaftsvergleich alternativer Arbeitssysteme*, Vortrage Nr. 17, Fachtagung Arbeitsgestaltung in der Produktion '76 des Instituts für Produktionstechnik und Automatisierung (Stuttgart, IPA, 1976), pp. 10 ff.

[24] This case study is based on information obtained in an interview with Mr. H. O. Meyer of Siemens AG and from two of his published works, viz. "Erfahrungen mit Gruppenmontage-Plätzen am Beispiel eines Elektrogerätewerkes", in Institut für angewandte Arbeitswissenschaft e.V.: *Arbeitsstrukturierung in der deutschen Metallindustrie (2)* (Cologne, 1975), pp. 55-62; and *Erfahrungen bei der Einführung neuer Arbeitsformen in der Montage von Haushaltsgeräten*, Vortage Nr. 19, Fachtagung Arbeitsgestaltung in der Produktion '76 des Instituts für Produktionstechnik und Automatisierung (Stuttgart, IPA, 1976).

[25] This case study is based on information from discussions with various persons at the Salzgitter works of Volkswagen AG and from M. Granel: *Gruppenarbeit in der PKW-Motoren-Montage*, Vortrage Nr. 10, Fachtagung Arbeitsgestaltung in der Produktion '76 des Instituts für

Produktionstechnik und Automatisierung (Stuttgart, IPA, 1976); and idem: *Vergleich von Arbeitsstrukturen,* Rationalisierungskuratorium der Deutschen Wirtschaft, Kongress 1976, Heft Stand 12.

[26] Increasing action for the humanisation of work in the automobile industry led up in 1972 to the establishment of a working party on "new work structures in the German automobile industry" which in November 1976, through Daimler-Benz, Stuttgart, issued a brochure summarising its activities. See Arbeitskreis "Neue Arbeitsstrukturen der deutschen Automobilindustrie": *Gestaltung der menschlichen Arbeit — Beispiele aus der deutschen Automobilindustrie* (1976).

[27] Institut für Arbeitswissenschaft der Technische Hochschule Darmstadt.

[28] Lehrstuhl für Arbeits- und Betriebspsychologie der Eidgenossischen Technischen Hochschule Zürich.

[29] Readers with an interest in the subject may none the less find it profitable to consult the following:

Bartölke, K., and Gohl, J. *A critical perspective on humanization activities and ongoing experiments in Germany,* Arbeitspapiere des Fachbereiches Wirtschaftswissenschaft der Gesamthochschule Wuppertal, Nr. 16 (Wuppertal, 1976).

Froemer, F. (ed.). *Arbeitshumanisierung — Eine Darstellung der Bestrebungen, die Arbeitswelt menschlicher zu gestalten* (Opladen, Westdeutscher Verlag, 1975).

Gaitanides, M. *Industrielle Arbeitsorganisation und technische Entwicklung* (Berlin, Walter De Gruyter, 1975).

Gaugler, E., Kolb, M., and Ling, B. *Humanisierung der Arbeitswelt und Produktivität* (Mannheim, Forschungsstelle für Betriebswirtschaft und Sozialpraxis, 1976).

Haug, G. *Kooperation von Betrieb und Wissenschaft,* Rationalisierungskuratorium der Deutschen Wirtschaft, Kongress 1976, Heft Stand 10.

Mann, W. E., Schäfer, D., and Metzger, H. *Auf dem Weg zu neuen Arbeitsstrukturen,* Rationalisierungskuratorium der Deutschen Wirtschaft, Kongress 1976, Heft Stand 9.

Mergner, U., Osterland, M., and Pelte, K. *Arbeitsbedingungen im Wandel* (Göttingen, Otto Schwartz Verlag, 1975).

UNITED KINGDOM

_____

UNITED KINGDOM

By A. T. M. Wilson*

NATIONAL CONDITIONS[1]

Industrial relations and the law

A country without a written Constitution, and with a devotion to case law, is by these characteristics alone bound to be different from many other countries not only in respect of law but in many related ways. The 1965-68 Royal Commission on Trade Unions and Employers' Associations[2] stressed the importance of custom and practice and voluntary collective bargaining in British labour relations and made it very clear that legislation played only a limited part in this field. Further evidence of the strength of this tradition can be found in the fact that the Council of the Advisory, Conciliation and Arbitration Service of the Department of Employment has undertaken to build up a set of "codes of industrial relations practice", jointly agreed by employers and trade unions. These will not have statutory power but are defined as a list of recommendations on "matters which will be taken into account" by any industrial tribunal, for example, in dealing with a labour-management dispute. These codes represent an effort to retain the principle of accepting custom and practice in the field of industrial relations while taking a step towards their rationalisation by agreement. The points made by the Royal Commission were later emphasised by Professor Kahn-Freund—he had been a member of the Commission—in a lecture entitled *Labour and the law: An ambivalent relationship.*[3] In this he considered a number of United Kingdom characteristics, including the widespread mistrust and unwillingness over going to law, and the equally strong preference for private negotiation or private settlement of disputes. He also noted that trade unions had been legally sanctioned institutions in the United Kingdom for over a century, while full parliamentary enfranchisement of members of the working class had a much more recent origin: the Trades Union Congress had been founded in 1868, much earlier than the Labour Party, and the relationship had been affected by this sequence.

---

*London Graduate School of Business Studies. The author's acknowledgement of his indebtedness to persons directly concerned with development of new forms of work organisation will be found in the notes. The draft of the four case studies included in this paper was approved for publication by both managements and trade unions concerned.

Employment and industry

The United Kingdom figure of about 1.4 million unemployed in 1976 in a economically active population of over 25 million[4] is perhaps open to a variety of controversial comments and interpretations. There still remain powerful memories of the extent of which the achievement of full employment was agreed policy in every year since 1950 at least. In part for this reason, recent legislation has sought to improve job security, to maintain employment at the highest possible level, and to create jobs for younger people wherever this could be done. It is significant that despite the high level of unemployment there is an obvious unwillingness on the part of younger people leaving school or college to enter industry, particularly manufacturing industry. This reluctance may have been rather more marked some years ago, but it is important that it still prevails in spite of the current unemployment.

Worker representation

There are over 400 unions in the United Kingdom, despite recent amalgamations—and of these 120 or so, covering over 12 million workers, are affiliated to the Trades Union Congress. The number of union members has risen recently, largely through the unionisation of white-collar, middle-management and professional workers. This multiplicity of individual unions, taken together with the importance of custom and practice, does not facilitate negotiation between a particular industry or company and the workers it employs. At company or unit level this difficulty is in part offset by the existence of trade union representatives, usually elected from among the workforce by the members of unions represented within it, and known as "shop stewards". With the spread of wage bargaining and much increased union activity at factory level, these representatives are coming to play an increasingly important role. They usually form a committee which elects a chairman, or "convener", from the main union concerned. It has often been observed that the formally agreed role of shop steward is usually much narrower than their accepted range of activities; also, they are not always on the best of terms with local trade union officials.

Questions of worker representation at board level in companies have been a matter of considerable debate. The Government has put one aspect of the issue to a special committee of a roughly bipartite kind confined by its terms of reference to considering the representation of workers at top level in companies. This reported in January 1977[5] on how such representation might be accomplished. A minority report and a note of dissent were not unexpectedly appended, but it is noteworthy that in broad discussions of the issue there is very considerable agreement among unions, managers, employers and government officials that no type of participation at the higher levels of a company is likely to be effective if it is not based on practical experience, over time, of what has been called "grass roots participation"—that is, decision-making processes which involve the workers at the level at which they actually work.

Attitudes of management and labour

A member of the Council of the Confederation of British Industry and of its Employment Policy Committee has outlined the general outlook of the Confederation on matters affecting the organisation of work in the following terms:[6]

> There are some who argue that the only practical way of furthering participation is by the extension of collective bargaining into matters which hitherto have not been the subject of negotiation. This is an inevitable trend and part of the evolutionary process of industrial relations; but I do not believe this development on its own provides the complete answer.
>
> It is important to recognise that consultation and negotiation, although closely interrelated, have separate roles to play. On many occasions an over-all objective can be successfully determined by joint consultation, often without conflict if the discussions start early enough. But the way in which the objective should be implemented and the share of the benefits have to be the subject of negotiation and compromise.
>
> One should also recognise that there is usually scope for an extension of joint regulation, which is a very positive way of giving employees a larger say in matters which have a direct bearing on their working environment—for example, a joint approach to the development of payment systems, shift systems, plant layouts, job restructuring, training and retraining, safety and health.
>
> . . . .
>
> Closer links need to be developed between machine and equipment designers and the people who have to operate them; the feedback often seems to be quite inadequate. And finally when designing new factories, a reappraisal is needed of the influence of size on the state of industrial relations in a plant. Many modern factories are much too large and the apparent economies of large-scale operation are offset by low productivity resulting from a lack of morale, poor motivation and failure of communications.

In this connection it may be worth mentioning an attitude familiar in middle management. It is only a slight exaggeration to say that there are many middle-level production managers, often engineers by background, who have become so convinced of the inevitability and regular recurrence of severe difficulties in their work that they have become specialists in trouble-shooting rather than in preventive action. To people of this background and outlook innovations in work organisation are obviously likely to seem hopelessly idealistic, and any success they may achieve is apt to be regarded as accidental and untypical.

The Trades Union Congress has been compelled to devote major attention to the level of unemployment; but senior members of its staff, and of many individual unions, have shown very considerable interest in the possibilities of innovation in work organisation—for a number of reasons, not excluding the possible contribution this can make to remedying the current situation of low wages and low productivity in the United Kingdom. The trade union position is exemplified later, in more specific terms, in the second case study.[7]

From the little information available, it would seem that members of management are generally the first to contemplate changes in work organisation, on recognising the emergence of such problems as recruiting and manning, low productivity and growing international competition—problems which some reorganisation of work, without changes in technology, could help to solve. This is not to say that trade union officers or shop stewards have not played a considerable part in the early stages of many of these developments, as the case studies show; but is is understandable that the general attitude of trade unions in the United Kingdom to such possibilities should be one of caution at a time when there is much unemployment and attempts are being made to follow counter-inflationary wage policies.

Activities of specialised bodies

Both the Confederation of British Industry and the Trades Union Congress have nominated senior representatives to the Department of Employment Tripartite Steering Committee on Job Satisfaction. Taking its origin from a report by N. A. B. Wilson on the quality of working life,[8] this Committee has since sponsored a booklet entitled *Making work more satisfying*.[9] They have also set up a work research unit that has a ten-project programme of wide range, and is engaged in a considerable volume of associated advisory, training, and publishing activities.

The Social Science Research Council recently set up a working party to consider research on the quality of working life, and the Science Research Council, even more recently, has become interested in fostering improvements in the quality of production management—an area in which, as noted earlier, trouble-shooting in situations of difficulty is often regarded as inevitable, and has often been more valued than planning of innovation to avoid familiar troubles.

The National Economic Development Council—also a tripartite body—has sponsored a considerable number of economic development committees, each of which is concerned with a particular industry. One of these, for mechanical engineering, has for some ten years been greatly concerned with production planning and, more recently, with the possibilities of the "cell system" of group technology in engineering, a sector of manufacturing that is of particular importance in the United Kingdom. In 1975 this committee published a report[10] which summarised the experience in this field of some 50 companies, and described the committee's discussions with trade union officials and consultants, reproducing their comments on factors likely to have influenced the slow adoption of its recommendations on the use of cell methods by the 5,000 engineering companies in the United Kingdom with more than 25 employees. Only some 150 companies had been actively concerned with these recommendations; and the committee listed the difficulties which had led to this situation as follows:

(a) the suspicion created by early and extravagant claims for these cell methods of work organisation;

(b) the highly technical ensuing debate which, it feels, had little meaning for senior management;

(c) fear that these innovations—an unnecessary fear, the committee noted—would involve major organisational upheavals;

(d) the low level of competitive pressure in the industry;

(e) fear of the power of traditional attitudes and practices, and of industrial disputes arising from experimental changes on the shop floor; and

(f) "the conflict of interest which arises from the transfer of responsibility to the shop floor and the simplification of planning and control procedures".[11]

People who have considered these innovations, the committee noted, believed that the factors that have just been listed were at the root of much of the resistance to the spread of significant re-structuring of work on the shop floor, or reduction in administrative overhead costs. These attitudes and feelings present very genuine difficulties to companies; and the committee noted that the slow adoption of their recommendations could not be attributed to official union attitudes. They concluded that the system of group technology "was likely to be accepted, and the flexible use of skilled men on machines agreed, provided that sufficient attention was given to the involvement of the workers in group design, and to negotiation over manpower flexibility".[12]

Experiments to date

For reasons which have been outlined, companies and other employing organisations in the United Kingdom do not always find it easy to be forthcoming about changes and innovations at present, or to give full accounts of their activities and results in this field. This compels the making of estimates which, in turn, requires at least a rough definition of the area of interest. It must be realised that the experience of many organisations in designing and operating a new form of socio-technical system has been acquired in the office, and around the computer, and not on the factory floor. In the direct manufacturing field almost the only available public data are those given in a report by Professor Burbidge on a particular form of innovation—the cell system of group technology—in one form of production, batch production, largely in engineering.[13] He lists over 100 United Kingdom companies that are experimenting with this system, among them the company which provides the second case study in this paper. The figures from this company exemplify a further source of difficulty which companies have had to face in recent years in consistent reporting of developments over time—the difficulty created by the profound disturbances and changes in the conventions of accountancy brought about by inflation.

Professor Burbidge's figures do not include activities in large units or entire corporations in process industries, such as are reported in the case study concerning Imperial Chemical Industries, in which wide programmes of job re-structuring had gone on in a manual operative establishment of 85,000. Beyond this, there are known to be extensive programmes of an experimental kind in the public sector of industry, and within both central and local government; and, once again, a large labour force is potentially concerned. Finally, there has been a recent postal survey of company work in these fields, undertaken by the Institute of Personnel Management.[14] The most that can be said of these different indications is that they could be held to support some rather vague statement, to this effect, for example: some hundreds of organisations in the United Kingdom are concerned to explore, in a relatively serious way, the possibilities of new forms of socio-technical system or of work organisation.

It is no easier to make more than a general guess with respect to the location and pattern of these explorations and developments. Clearly, for reasons which are not identical certain categories of organisation have been active in this field: organisations handling large volumes of routine data; large continuous process production units; and smaller engineering units. Only a minority of these organisations have published accounts of their experiments or their results. It seems possible, however, that whatever the significance of a particular form of technology in these matters, characteristics related only indirectly to any particular type of industrial or commercial work may well be of major significance in the determination of this pattern. For example, commercial success and other features of a particular company may have led to innovation in work organisation, rather than general characteristics of its particular industry; for even within a single industry companies differ greatly in their interest and achievements in the field under discussion.

Among the examples of innovation which have not so far been publicly reported, there are known to be developments that have been highly successful as well as experiments that have manifestly failed. From what can be picked up indirectly about situations of this second type, it seems likely that many could be described as rather desperate efforts to deal with great difficulties in conditions that were unlikely to be at all favourable. The proportion of the total labour force in the United Kingdom affected by innovative experiments remains small, and the significance of the successful innovations is still, very largely, that they help to remove the rather extraordinary incredulity which exists about the reality of such possibilities, and thus, for example, allow inquiries and experiments to clarify the situations in which new forms of work organisation are possible, or in which they can, in time, become so. It is of special importance that interest in these matters, and in their wider political, economic and social implications, shows every sign of growing despite the widespread problems of trade and industry that have been so prominent in recent years.

CASE STUDIES

The following case studies take the form of extracts from available reports, in each case with some additional information from the organisation concerned and from public sources. They deal with developments and activities in United Kingdom work organisation which have the particular characteristic of being comprehensive in the sense that they concern company-wide innovations.

A productivity bargaining agreement in a petroleum refinery[15]

The first case study reported in this paper covers research undertaken in a British Petroleum oil refinery by W. W. Daniel, of Political and Economic Planning, an independent social research organisation with much tripartite support. As part of a much wider research project, information was obtained on contrasts between initial, hypothetical views and subsequent reactions based on experience, concerning a productivity bargaining agreement. The agreement provided for unit-wide efforts to bring about changes in job content and in the structure of work, with considerable wage increases. In 1968 the workers concerned, operators engaged in process work, had salaries ranging from £1,350 to £1,525 a year, according to seniority. (These figures would need multiplication in 1977 by a factor of about 2.) These earnings were based on a 44-hour week with no overtime and paid sickness leave.

Conditions in control rooms were clean, pleasant and noise free. The working atmosphere was relaxed, not to say leisurely, under normal working conditions, and the job rarely if ever involved hard physical labour. Overalls and protective clothing were provided free and renewed frequently for work outside the control room on the plant itself. Meals were provided at a nominal charge and the firm had what must be the equal of any industrial sports and social club, with indoor swimming pool, squash and badminton courts and so on. It was not surprising that in these circumstances the men were generally well satisfied with their job, even if, equally unsurprisingly, they were also convinced that the firm could and should pay them more in view of company profits and the comparative earnings to maintenance and day men.[16]

"The only consistent and persistent complaint" that emerged in the early stages of these productivity and payment negotiations related to—

shift working and working on weekends and holidays; and this came up almost universally as a main disadvantage in the job. Apart from shift work the men were well pleased with their lot. But this is a very different thing from the experience of gratification or deprivation in the work itself. . . . Here too, however, the findings gave substantial support to the optimistic vision of semi-automated process work. With a very few special exceptions, the men found the work itself interesting and rewarding. The chief sources of satisfaction were the opportunity provided by the job for using their minds and brains in learning and problem resolution.[17]

These men had modest levels of education and skill. Owing to their type of background, there had been little opportunity for them to use or develop their abilities; and the transition into jobs in the petrochemical industry had often been a great awakening. They found the opportunity to help, train and advise young entrants to the industry an even greater source of self-respect. At the same time the most unsatisfactory feature of the work was that once the workers had learnt the job they might find it tedious and boring, when everything was running smoothly, to be restricted to a control panel governing one part of the process. Moreover running alongside the satisfaction with so many features of the work and workplace, and particularly the consciousness of general conformity of interests at work, went a militant and widespread feeling of inherent conflict with management on economic issues. This led to a well developed policy of securing collective advancement through active trade unionism and resistance to any innovations, such as promotion on merit, that might weaken collective solidarity.

The agreement that was proposed was of the classical type. As far as the men in the plants covered in the interviewing were concerned, it sought chiefly a reduction in manning; more flexibility among operators so that they would carry out a wider range of tasks at different levels over a broader span of the process, and including some simple maintenance tasks; a simplification of the grading system by substituting five basic grades for the 19 different rates of pay previously operating; a slight weakening of the seniority rules; and a stable 40-hour week with no overtime or additional payments. In return they received increases in pay ranging from £4 to £6 a week, which represented proportions ranging from 15 to 30 per cent of their previous remuneration, and conditions of employment more akin to those of staff employees which included a guaranteed annual salary paid weekly, full pay when sick and an end to clocking in.

Relationships in the plant between management and men and between supervisors and men were excellent, reflecting the mutual respect and reciprocity characteristic of work in continuous-process technology. Despite this, the changes sought in the agreement were fiercely resisted. It appeared through retrospective interviewing that the resistance was largely due to the fact that the agreement was seen as a threat to security of employment and job opportunities, even though it carried a no-redundancy guarantee. Indeed, the reduction of job opportunities in the local labour market that resulted remained the chief source of any residual hostility towards the agreement even nine months after it had been introduced. Thus the agreement was initially greeted with hostility and resistance, and it was only pushed through eventually on the basis of tough bargaining over the men's share of the savings in terms of increases in earnings and fringe benefits, in relation to the new skills they would have to learn and the new responsibility they would have to carry.

The interviewing was carried out nine months after the agreement had come into force. Questions about the agreement were incorporated into a pilot interview schedule with a 10 per cent representative sample from a total workforce of 600. The study was not specifically designed to explore the effects and implications of productivity bargaining, nor workers' attitudes and feelings about them. It was built around a very different series of topics, but since an agreement had been made so recently before interviewing was carried out, it was thought useful to make a general inquiry on how it was working out. The questions in this request were first "How do you find this new agreement?", followed by a series of probes of the type "What makes you say that?" The men's answers provide a broad picture of how the agreement was viewed after nine months' experience, and of the reasons for favouring and disfavouring it.

In fact, although mixed feelings were widespread, there was a substantial majority (65 per cent) who broadly favoured the agreement and found it was generally working out to their advantage. At the same time a substantial minority (25 per cent) remained unfavourably disposed to it, and the residual 10 per cent saw both advantages and disadvantages associated with it that were so evenly balanced that they were unable to decide whether they were in favour of it or not.

The most frequently mentioned items related to the job enrichment that the agreement had . . . brought about. The most commonly mentioned sources of satisfaction were the ways in which the changes in working practice defined by the agreement had made work in the plant more interesting and satisfying by giving operators more chance to use and develop their abilities through learning and carrying out a wide range and higher level of job—both simple maintenance tasks and operating jobs covering a broader span of the process.[18]

It is particularly interesting that the changes in conditions of employment and fringe benefits, designed to represent a substantial move towards staff status, with a number of new privileges for the men, hardly featured at all among their reasons for now approving the agreement.

But certainly the most striking and interesting aspect of these findings is that factors related to job interest and satisfaction were those most frequently mentioned—by 68 per cent of all respondents. The proportion is more than double those spontaneously mentioning "more money", despite the fact that every man interviewed had received a pay increase of at least 15 per cent and most had received increases nearer 30 per cent. Indeed the proportion mentioning items related to job interest or satisfaction exceeds those mentioning all other items, including money.

Here we have a strange paradox. The agreement had been negotiated and implemented in the face of strong opposition and only after hard wage-work bargaining backed by a national incomes policy. Yet nine months after the agreement, the majority of the men favoured the changes because of job enrichment, heightened interest and satisfaction in their work rather than because of increases in wages.

The point, of course, is that in the negotiating context they were not more—perhaps even not at all—interested in job satisfaction. They wanted to make the best deal in the terms that the negotiating context defines: increased earnings in some currency in relation to increased responsibilities and workload, with clear reference to the social and cultural implications.

But once agreement had been reached and once the changes had been implemented, the formal benefits that it had furnished were taken for granted and what then became important were the changes that had been generated in the context and meaning of their day-to-day activities and relationships at work. In practice this meant that there was virtually a complete reversal in priorities when the reference point was the work rather than the negotiating context.[19]

The general point quoted in the last paragraph has wide implications for the timing and design of changes in work organisation and payment systems. Another point illustrated by this case is that verbal comments and questionnaire replies on jobs and working conditions may vary in important ways, depending on the expectations and perceptions of the respondents. Replies also vary greatly with the context in which, or of which, the respondents are speaking. Beyond this, difficulty can arise when their views are sought on hypothetical questions, on matters of which they have not had actual experience. The reality and importance of such difficulties in assessing statements about work are illustrated in a brief example given[20] in a discussion of "job satisfaction" studies. A worker had been invited to say whether he found his work satisfying and his job a "good" job: "I've got a pretty good job", he said. "What makes it such a good job?" he was asked. "Don't get me wrong", he said, "I didn't say it's a good job. It's an OK job—about as good a job as a guy like me might expect. The foreman leaves me alone and it pays well. But I would never call it a good job. It doesn't amount to much, but it's not bad." Points of this kind are intended to be covered in design of surveys: but it is not always clear that this has been done effectively.

Cellular production in a medium-sized engineering company[21]

In the United Kingdom some 80 per cent of engineering products are the outcome of batch production, i.e. the manufacture of varying numbers of a wide variety of articles—often component parts of a final product which may be assembled elsewhere. A medium-sized engineering company, Serck-Audco, was engaged in this type of work, making batches, each often of some hundreds, of a wide range of different kinds of metal valve parts; it exported some 50 per cent of its output. Export trade is particularly sensitive to competition over keeping delivery dates, and at the end of the 1950s the company found itself in difficulty on this score. An examination by the managing director, Mr. G. M. Ranson, of the flow of different products through the company's manufacturing system made very clear the extent to which time was being lost by the familiar, traditional and rather inefficient use of machining capacity. The materials being transformed into a large number of products spent an average of 80 per cent of their total factory life in queues, waiting for the completion of other batches of components of a different kind, and for the necessary adjustment and re-setting of the machine tools for each batch. This examination led him to develop the idea of "cellular" manufacture, or "cellular group production", a comprehensive socio-technical innovation which involved every function of the company. (To avoid confusion, it must be noted that earlier than this development various studies and experiments, of a purely technological character, and covered by the generic term of "group technology" had been initiated in many countries; these were based on the use of improved systems of classification and coding of machine processes into "families", with a view to rationalisation and reduction of the range of components needed for particular products.) The basic points about the cellular system of production are described in the two following quotations; it will be seen that the first of them uses the words "group technology" in a socio-technical sense. "Group technology", says a 1975 report of the Economic Development Committee for Mechanical Engineering[22] is "the organisation of production facilities in self-contained and self-regulating groups or cells, each of which undertakes the complete manufacture of a family of components with similar manufacturing characteristics. The cell staff are often each capable of using several machines or processes, so that there are usually fewer men than machines". The socio-technical nature of the concept is described as follows[23]: "The fundamental principle behind cellular manufacture, which it is much more important to grasp than the mechanistic nuts and bolts of the process itself, is that it consists of pockets of self-contained responsibility in which man's skill, intelligence and enthusiasm are harnessed in somewhat specialised working groups, which can extract the best possible result from the level of manufacturing technology in the context of the particular circumstances which apply at the time."

Within the Serck company, the idea of this new system of production was conveyed to a total of some 1,000 workers with very little difficulty. At that time, half of the workers were members of the Amalgamated Union of Engineering Workers. The problem of training people for the new system seems also to have presented little difficulty, and the supervisors, whose role was changed in various ways, were entirely agreeable, for they were given the objective of achieving a specified output over successive two-week periods, unless the necessary raw material and equipment were not available. A job evaluation scheme was introduced, with the agreement of the trade union, and overtime working was reduced except in the event of sudden market changes. The results are given in table 1.

The monetary values are at current prices and therefore reflect inflation, but there is no denying the improvement in output per worker in terms of tons of valves. This clearly shows that the initial spurt of 50 per cent improvement over four years up to 1965-66 did not level off, as might have been expected, but was maintained as operations and methods within the cells continued to improve. Additional information previously published by the National Economic Develop-

Table 1. Serck Audco valves performance record, 1961-71

Year	Net despatches (£m)	Value added (£m)	Average no. of workers employed	Total wages and salaries (£m)	Despatches per worker (£)	Output per worker (tons)	Value added per worker (£)	Average income per worker (£)
1961-62	2 220	1 615	1 001	0 714	2 218	4.0	1 613	714
1962-63	2 184	1 580	952	0 700	2 294	4.5	1 660	742
1963-64	2 585	1 872	903	0 752	2 863	5.5	2 073	833
1964-65	2 922	2 007	941	0 844	3 105	5.8	2 133	897
1965-66	3 363	2 303	992	0 951	3 390	6.0	2 320	953
1966-67	3 768	2 616	987	0 979	3 818	6.5	2 681	992
1967-68	3 576	2 519	906	0 951	3 947	6.9	2 780	1050
1968-69	4 984	3 117	1 130	1 338	4 411	7.4	2 759[1]	1 184
1969-70	6 008	3 786	1 181	1 578	5 087	7.5	3 206	1 336
1970-71	6 727	4 374	1 179	1 787	5 706	7.9	3 710	1 516

[1] During this period the progress in value added per worker was retarded by the problems associated with the transfer of £1.3 million of ball valve production to another plant.

Source: G. M. Ranson: *Group technology* (London, McGraw-Hill, 1972); National Economic Development Office: *Production planning and control* (London, 1966).

ment Office, relating to the period from 1961 to 1966, and updated by Mr. Ranson for 1967, can be summarised as follows:

— sales, up 70 per cent;

— stocks, down 44 per cent;

— stocks-sales ratio, down from 52 to 22 per cent;

— manufacturing time, down from 12 to 2½ weeks;

— overdue orders, down from average of 6 weeks to an average of 2½ days;

— worker output, up 70 per cent; and

— capital investment, cost recovered four times by stock reduction alone.

This company received a Queen's Award for Exporting in 1970. (Such an award is preceded by an independent evaluation of a company's performance.)

There are many reasons for believing that negotiations between management and trade unions over jobs, wages and conditions in batch production companies have particular interest and importance. For this reason, the Mechanical Engineering Development Committee, who produced a report on cell production in group technology, decided to include as an appendix a statement by an anonymous trade union. The statement is relatively complete and has importance beyond this particular system of manufacturing. Extracts from it [24] are reproduced below:

> From the start it must be understood that the trade union movement has never stood in the way of technological progress. On the contrary, where there has been an obvious gain to working conditions then the trade unions have been in the forefront of those seeking its introduction. All the evidence confirms that there has been massive co-operation from trade unionists in the bringing into being of techniques which have brought huge productivity gains.
>
> When trade unions have been accused of approaching new methods with caution it must be understood that it has not been because they resent the favourable economic consequences for industry or the nation, but because they have reason to believe that such benefits may not be shared with the degree of fairness they consider right and proper. Indeed, quite often the historical moment of technological change may play a vital part in how the change is met.
>
> . . . .
>
> . . . We are . . . fully aware of the potential of the [group technology] technique. We are also conscious of the fact that with the past and current low level of investment in the engineering industry, along with the comparatively advanced age structure of our machine tools, group technology offers a low cost approach to increased productivity, in a way which has been shown to be feasible in selected areas.
>
> For our part any reservations we express concerning the introduction of group technology do not stem from whether it is, or is not, a worthwhile production method but from how it will affect our people, especially in the light of present day feeling in the industry. First, then, we seek involvement in this and other radical changes at all levels long before plans for its introduction are detailed. This means involvement at two levels at least. First is at national level, in order to set such guidelines as may prove necessary to both sides so that the second level, of plant introduction, may go ahead on the basis of agreed negotiatory principles. In this way agreements that will stick will be more likely to accrue.
>
> At plant level many obvious questions will be raised. Among them there will be some common to most situations such as:
>
> *1. Incentive schemes.* Where these are reduced or their eventual abolition sought then negotiations on at least two principles will be involved. One is the replacement with an

earnings level which will reflect the change; and [the] second is . . . the right of the individual worker to have a degree of control over his job, which was part of the old payment-by-result system.

2. Setters. With new methods of grouping of machines, perhaps coupled to numerical control, then the setter becomes an immediate[ly] redundant worker who has to be placed elsewhere. And it will take more than vague talk of absorption through expanding production or loss through natural wastage to get past this corner.

3. De-skilling. This is similar to the setter category. It will no doubt result in some job simplification at some stage, with the threat to the skilled man's status and the position of his union in the negotiating body.

4. Throughput. This will naturally be quicker than before (or what is the exercise for?). Then questions will be asked about plans made for marketing the increased output, and if this has been taken care of (and it does not always happen), has the extra shop loading exercise (if there is one) been implemented? Plans for the implementation of group technology should be thorough, taking into consideration possible effects over all areas.

5. Training. Just as with productivity bargaining, it was found that the most successful schemes contained plans for extensive and progressive training of personnel, so the workers undertaking a change to group technology would feel easier if they knew that retraining was well planned and readily available both to ease them into the situation and to provide continuity as teething troubles were encountered and the new system became established.

And again as with productivity bargaining there will need to be a continuous monitoring committee set up as watch-dog, to see that the running of the scheme constantly reflects the nuances of changing application. This is the type of committee ideally fixed to negotiate comprehensive benefits spreading across all the workers engaged in the exercise rather than the few readily identifiable as the basic core of the gains.

Work re-structuring in Imperial Chemical Industries[25]

Imperial Chemical Industries is a large multinational chemical company, based in the United Kingdom. In 1975 it had assets of £2,748 million, a turnover of £3,099 million, and 129,000 workers in the United Kingdom itself. The company has made highly successful use of a very broad range of technological processes, and has widely dispersed plants. The programme to be discussed is regarded as the first extended attempt in the United Kingdom to apply newer ideas of productivity bargaining to the whole workforce of a large multi-unit company. The management initiated the process but the trade unions were consulted almost at once. The scheme was jointly sanctioned throughout.

The origins of the experiment lay in the company's recognition, in 1964, of the inadequacy of its responses to increasing commercial competition and economic threats. This led to a range of decisions by the board of directors; for example, to examine the efficiency of plant manning. The experiment eventually covered about 90 per cent of the manual workforce, and took place as a two-stage process, with lessons learned from the first stage used to improve the design and operation of the second stage.

The company's outstanding growth record over more than 40 years goes with a long tradition of rapid response to changing technologies in the chemical industry. At the initiation of the experiment to be described, the former traditions of paternalistic management were still strong. In the depression of the 1930s the company had been an unusually good employer, and the loyalty this produced in the workforce persisted in the older plants. An employee profit-sharing or bonus scheme has been in existence since 1954. In general, managers took it for granted that they alone had the right and the power to make all the necessary decisions about how the company should be run, but in practice the influence of the trade union shop stewards, and of the shop-floor workers whom they represented, had increased considerably, while the power of the immediate first-level shop-floor supervisors had dwindled. By the time the experiment took place, the ability of management to implement decisions largely depended on the consent of the manual workers and their representatives.

By national standards, the company had experienced very few strikes. This was not regarded as indicating the existence of widespread satisfaction in the workforce but was related to three factors: first, the power and ability of shop stewards to settle disputes as they occurred on the shop floor; secondly, the vulnerability of the chemical industry to pay claims because of the high costs of stoppages in its continuous-process plants; and thirdly, the relatively low contribution of wages to the over-all costs of a generally capital-intensive production industry. Personnel management was taking up an increased proportion of the managers' time, but managerial concern and skills in this field were not outstanding. Nevertheless, there had been doubts over the years about the equity and suitability of the rigid division of the company's workers into those paid weekly, according to hours worked, and those on staff salaries, which assumed regular hours and payments.

A high percentage of the manual workers belonged to trade unions, and their shop stewards were officially recognised as worker representatives in dealings with management, though only at shop-floor level. The manual workforce was clearly divided into general and craft workers, the former being mainly process operatives and the latter the men who maintained the plants. This division was also reflected in the organisation of management.

Bargaining with the trade unions was mainly carried out at the centre of the company, where top-level representatives of the 11 main manual unions with members in the company's employment negotiated and concluded company-wide agreements with management. In this way, uniform pay and working conditions had been established. However, the system was extremely complex: it included different pay systems for craft and general workers; different combinations of basic pay rates; extra rates according to the position of jobs in the 22 categories of the grading structure; incentive bonuses related to individual or group productivity; overtime payments; and many special allowances.

There were considerable variations between the different divisions and units of the company—for example in the technologies employed, the degree of labour intensity, the amount of mass production, the working environment and local traditions, attitudes to work and social organisation. In commercial terms, good over-all results had been achieved, particularly through the development of new products and high capital investment in plants to produce them. However, new jobs in new technologies were leading to problems with the old arrangements for demarcating work between different crafts, and between craft work and general work. Moreover, as jobs became more technically demanding, managers were finding that the company pay structure was too rigid to allow appropriate rewards for the changing work that was increasingly required. To overcome these difficulties, the system had to be manipulated in ways which were not provided for in official agreements; and the incentive bonus scheme, under which payments were partly related to productivity, had become ineffective.

The directors were shocked by the findings of studies made in the company in the early 1960s, particularly the results of a detailed comparison with a United States company. In 1964 a management study group of six members from the personnel and production sides was asked to focus its attention on labour productivity and on the possibility of introducing a system of more stable rates of pay for some of the hourly paid workers. When the panel began its work, it widened its terms of reference to include work organisation, and launched research projects, including one under which each of five plants was asked to devise ideal manning arrangements—that is, systems of manning that would ensure maximum cost effectiveness. The results of this study showed that improved manning could bring large financial savings to the company over the years. The panel's report to the board was approved early in 1965. Its main recommendations were that—

(a) manning should be made more efficient by allowing general process workers to carry out the simpler plant maintenance jobs which had until then been reserved for craft workers;

(b) supervision should be simplified and reduced; and

(c) the boundaries between different crafts should be made more flexible so that each category of craftsmen could be permitted to do some of the simpler jobs formerly reserved for the other categories.

It was recommended that these changes should be achieved by raising job status and security as well as rates of remuneration. The first stage in the process of implementation should be the negotiation of a central agreement with the 11 trade unions to allow this new approach to be tried out in a small number of plants.

In April 1965 the first discussions between the management and the unions took place in the firm's trade union advisory council. This council consisted of senior board members and the chief national administrators of the relevant trade unions. It provided a forum for general discussion of broad policy issues rather than for the negotiation of agreements, which was governed by established procedures. The council approved the holding of discussions with trade union national officers, that is, with the union representatives with whom actual bargaining usually took place. Talks with these officers started in May. They were initially rather uneasy over the unusual proposal of an open-ended agreement—that is, the initiation of a continuous process of review of work organisation, jobs, and systems of payment—rather than the customary negotiation on immediate specific issues.

Imperial Chemical Industries' "manpower utilisation and payment structure" agreement was made public and signed by the company and the union representatives in October. Under the agreement the company and the unions agreed to aim at higher efficiency in the utilisation of manpower by reducing demarcations between craft and general work and between the different kinds of craft work. Demarcations were to be reduced by local plant-level and shop-floor level discussions and decisions, both on what reductions to make and on how to bring them about. Once agreed, these local arrangements would need central ratification by the company and the unions. These methods of improving efficiency were tried out in a few plants. In 1966 suggestions were invited and received from divisions of the company regarding other units in which the proposed structure could be tried out; plants not included in the early trials were becoming interested as a result of what they had heard from plants where experiments had already taken place. Early in 1967 new units were selected and approved by the board. These further experiments began in 1968; more units were then allowed to volunteer, and many of the experiments were successful in spite of some continued resistance. In all, the experiments covered 5 per cent of the company's total manual workforce at that time. The more general lessons learned from these experiments were these:

(1) The old management ways of operating were no longer appropriate, and modern social science could at least point the way to new and better ways of working. (This discovery in itself increased the management's confidence in the project.)

(2) Useful lessons could be drawn from difficulties encountered in implementing organisational change when such difficulties were examined in the light of social science concepts.

(3) For participative methods to be successfully introduced, the actual process by which they were introduced had to be participative in itself.

(4) Besides providing the opportunity to learn these lessons, the experiments had allowed old and persistent conflicts to come to the surface, be expressed, and at least be better understood.

It was realised that it would not be possible to return to the forms of work organisation that had prevailed before the experiments, if only because the new and higher pay levels established in the experiments could not be reduced and they provided precedents for other units. In July 1968 the main board of the company set up a committee of directors to review the application of the first agreement. They agreed that future changes should be designed and carried out in a fully participative way, so that shop-floor workers and division-level managers, as well as trade unions, could contribute to new plans. The committee made two more decisions: first, that more of the savings achieved by the company through work reorganisation should be passed on to employees in the form of increased pay; and secondly that management training should be increased.

In September of that year the trade unions responded by an official request for negotiations on a new agreement. Over the next few months many meetings were held, at all levels, between trade union and management representatives. There emerged a general consensus to continue this process, in search of a new and wider agreement. There were some new trade union demands—for increases in pay, no redundancies, eventual 100 per cent trade union membership among the manual workers, and control by the individual craft unions over which parts of their work should be relinquished to others. During February and March 1969 a drafting committee set up jointly by the trade unions and the management produced a new provisional agreement for consideration. In April more meetings and discussions were held in all plants to consider the draft. The major recommendations received widespread approval; a few adjustments were made to the draft. The new agreement—now known as the "weekly staff agreement"—was approved by the joint drafting committee in May, jointly signed by the 11 relevant unions in June, ratified by each individual union in July, and shortly afterwards approved wholeheartedly by the main company board and the boards of the various divisions.

The new and much wider agreement repeated support for the aims originally stated for the earlier programme of pilot studies—improved efficiency through a change in demarcation practices; and—a more fundamental point—the extended and continued use of participative decision-making in discussion and negotiations of work reorganisation and payments systems. The agreement had other points: new pay increases; acceptance by the company of the principle that every new worker should join the relevant trade union; agreement that there would be no redundancies, but retraining and re-allocation; and that trade union control would be increased over the extent to which demarcation constraints would be reduced. The new agreement was a much longer document than the earlier one; it was legislative in tone; it included relatively long—and unusual—passages of explanation; and it included a statement that, for the implementation of the agreement, management retraining would be as necessary as worker training. There was also an important point on job and work structures: these would need to be continuously re-examined in the future, if the company was to keep pace with continuing social change.

A target was set for the implementation of the agreement: 40,000 workers, about 85 per cent of the company's United Kingdom manual workforce, should if possible have gone through the job re-structuring process in the 18 months up to the end of 1970. In the event, this target was exceeded. Because of the volume and location of work required by the participative approach, control of implementation of the agreement was inevitably taken over by the division and plant-level personnel staff. The process was carried out quickly and professionally, in part as a result of lessons learned from the earlier programme, and in part because implementation of the new agreement could to some extent follow patterns of implementation that had grown up for previous company-wide agreements. After 1970 it was not easy to maintain the momentum of change, but a national conference between company managers and trade union officers was held in 1972 to consider the continuation of job re-structuring; and more changes followed.

The process by which the agreement was implemented in one chemical works, a process production plant with 3,500 manual workers, is outlined below:

(1) Initially, district trade union officials were called in, and gave their approval to the handing over of responsibility for introduction of the new system to the shop stewards at the works.

(2) A programme for implementation of the agreement was agreed upon between management representatives and the shop stewards. The programme identi-

fied the many different stages which would need to be gone through, but did not constitute a timetable.

(3) Training courses on topics relevant to the new system were held for management and for shop stewards.

(4) Job analysis was carried out throughout the plant by study groups consisting of the relevant operatives, craftsmen, shop stewards, foremen and managers, and with the aid of work study specialists. Discussions took place with other job analysis study groups, new job descriptions were drafted, and wider and more far-reaching proposals were made for the introduction of new machines and equipment which could improve efficiency and, in the longer term, reduce manning requirements.

(5) The newly designed jobs were carefully assessed, to decide their position in the company's new and simplified grading system. The initial assessments were returned to each job study group for approval or review.

(6) These new arrangements were then formally approved by management. They were implemented as each group was ready; and many of the proposals for new machines and equipment were carried out.

What has just been said refers to jobs at operative level. There was also a "programme of controlled experimental studies" in specialised and supervisory groups. In one experiment a group of design engineers were given a much increased independence in running the projects on which they were working. They were encouraged to become experts in special fields; they were made responsible for choosing the outside consultants who would be used; they were allowed freedom in the setting and spending of cash budgets on equipment and on the employment of their staff, and they were given a serious share of responsibility for recruitment and management of their staff. The results included savings in supervisor time, for the design engineers consulted their supervisors for help and advice less frequently; time was also saved that would previously have been spent on obtaining approval to spend money. After the experiment, all those affected wanted to keep the new arrangements. There was no evidence of any decline in the quality of the decisions taken, and no over-all increase in unit expenditure.

A group of engineering maintenance foremen was given increased responsibility for preventive work. In addition, they were consulted on planning, on changes in working arrangements, and more than before on matters of design. They were given specific innovative projects to work on—projects which required them to consult other categories of employees. They were allowed to deputise for engineers, and given control of their cash budgets, together with complete disciplinary control over the people working under them, short of dismissal, and formal responsibility for training their subordinates. Results included a reduced incidence of cases of indiscipline among the subordinates; large cash savings to the company from the innovatory work; no increase in expenditure; and, according to their supervisors, considerable improvement in their performance as foremen.

It is not easy to arrive at a precise judgement of the total effect of the wide-ranging and protracted efforts that have been described above. In the company there were some specific changes—to be listed in a moment—which can with certainty be regarded as due largely or entirely to the two agreements. Other, less easily definable, changes in the same period were probably due to the second agreement, although they might well have occurred in the longer run in any event. From the point of view of the company—and perhaps of any company—the impossibility of exact measurement of results is not necessarily a fatal difficulty. It is the business of management to live with various degrees of uncertainty, and it is seldom possible to be absolutely sure that some specific line of action in a complex situation has produced the hoped-for specific results. Both success and failure are often partly compounded of mysterious elements that operate in unrecognised ways. It is this point of view which has made one very experienced executive entitle an important paper on planning "The science of muddling through".[26] In any event the following specific changes that have occurred by 1972 are attributable to the second agreement:

(1) There was an end to the complex pay structure, with separate arrangements for craft and general workers. A simpler system was introduced; but its many advantages were offset by a still further reduction in the extent to which unit managers could provide a flexible payment system to meet local needs.

(2) Not unexpectedly, as a result of years of work study and work simplification, first-line supervisors became a main target for manning reductions.

(3) The old "works councils", concerned only with "welfare" and unable to tackle any matters directly affecting the wage system, were superseded by plant-level joint consultation committees on which the operatives were represented by the shop stewards of their unions.

(4) The manual workforce became virtually 100 per cent unionised.

(5) The company gained increased expertise in analysing and changing industrial organisation. Almost all managers attended training courses, and to some extent changed their views of their own function. The techniques for change which were previously available in the company were tested and found wanting, and others were substituted.

(6) Substantial job enrichment and job enlargement took place, and demands from workers for yet more change of this kind persisted in many places.

(7) Among managers, the custom was established of consulting shop stewards, and of seeking their help in coping with important managerial and plant problems.

(8) In negotiations over precise but minor differences in shop-floor workers' pay, the power and influence of shop stewards was somewhat reduced.

(9) The number of industrial disputes over pay bonuses was reduced.

(10) The work of the engineering maintenance (craft) workers and the process (general) workers was more fully integrated.

(11) Even though the demarcations were now fewer and more sensible, the introduction of officially recognised lines of demarcation between work—which

was the effect of the agreements to new job structures—led to a reduction in local flexibility of manpower development.

(12) In the company, the official responsibility for decision-making on work content of jobs was shifted from management to joint management-worker groups, by whom the responsibility for implementing their decisions was now jointly and formally accepted.

(13) As a result of the second agreement there was some spontaneous movement towards the introduction of autonomous group working where this form of work organisation was possible.

(14) In most plants and units absenteeism and labour turnover went down; overtime working went down; and pay levels rose and became more stable from week to week. Many workers changed to a fortnightly payment, through banks rather than in cash.

It will be recalled that a central aim of the long two-stage process of participative work reorganisation described in this case study was the initiation of a continual process of consultation within the company on all matters affecting its efficiency. This aim is still being maintained by the corporation.

Group working in the Durham and Northumberland coal fields[27]

The coal mines of the United Kingdom were nationalised after the Second World War. More recently, the industry's prospects have been affected by the discovery of oil fields under the North Sea and by the development of nuclear power. The National Coal Board's workforce was run down from 703,900 in 1947 to 247,800 in 1975, and investment at each operating coal face was much increased. The study from which various points are given below was made in the 1950s, when the technology of coalmining in the United Kingdom could be described as "partial mechanisation" as against the "comprehensive" mechanisation of more recent years.

Where coal face operations have become comprehensively mechanised, work groups are beginning to establish themselves which have wider autonomy, greater powers of self-regulation, and a fuller commitment to more holistic tasks than those associated with partially mechanised methods. Such characteristics . . . are also the characteristics of pre-mechanised face groups. A tradition deeply embedded in the industry is being rediscovered and adapted to new circumstances.

An understanding of this tradition and the relevance of its application, appropriately transformed, is becoming even more important as mechanisation of the industry proceeds—whereas in 1960 under 40 per cent of output was power-loaded, by the end of 1961 it was over 50 per cent, and rising steadily.

It may be asked how the tradition came to be lost. The answer can only be that the loss of the more organic type of working group was difficult to avoid given the extent to which an ideology of extreme work breakdown accompanied the introduction of mass production methods in industry generally. But now that the validity of this ideology has been called into question, much may be learnt concerning the optimum organisation of working groups from an industry such as mining. Having always possessed latent traditions in an alternative direction, it has a creativeness which is bringing into existence models relevant in other contexts.

Of particular interest to the student of social process is the ability of quite large primary work groups of 40-50 members to act as self-regulating, self-developing social organisms able to maintain themselves in a steady state of high productivity throughout the entire period of their "missions".[28] These missions, which involved the daily management of a three-shift work cycle by the group itself, lasted for nearly two years—the life of the coal faces concerned. At the end of this time the groups were still growing in their capacity to adapt to changes in their task environments and to satisfy the needs of their members. Autonomous groups of this size are not usually thought capable of succeeding with a task of this complexity or a mission of this duration. The degree of success actually attained varied widely among several such groups studied. Through a comparison, however, of the conditions attendant on these different degrees of success, some at least of the factors crucial for the effective functioning of large autonomous work groups have been identified.[29]

The main findings of this study were derived from multiple comparisons, particularly between two types of organisation during the period of "partial mechanisation" in the United Kingdom coalmines—the "conventional long-wall system" and the "composite long-wall system". The study illustrates, in considerable detail, the potential and limitations of the two types; the contrasting ranges of flexibility in dealing with various forms of stress on the system; the inter-group dynamics of each type of work organisation; and the potential and actual productivity of the two types. The studies permitted observation of mining operations with the same level and type of technology, in the same coal seam, at the same time; only the work organisation differed. The contrasting structure of these two types of organisation is shown in table 2. This table summarises the main factors affecting day-to-day experience of face work. Men working under the conventional long-wall system did their one main task on one or other of two shifts, always with the same group of fellow workers. Under the composite system men rotated between several main tasks and all three shifts, and moved from one activity group to another. (The activity groups are differentiated work groups within the team as a whole.)

Table 2. Variety of work experience under the conventional and the composite long-wall systems of coal mining in the United Kingdom
(Averages for whole team)

Aspect of work experience	Method of working	
	Conventional	Composite
Main tasks worked at	1.0	3.6
Different shifts worked on	2.0	2.9
Activity groups worked with	1.0	5.5

Source: Trist, E. L.; Higgin, G. W.; Murray, H.; and Pollock, A. B.: *Organizational choice: Capabilities of groups at the coal face under changing technologies* (London, Tavistock Publications, 1963).

A second important aspect of these two systems was the extent to which under the conventional system, unlike the composite system, the different groups working on different shifts in the same 24-hour cycle had difficulty in adjusting their output so as not to break the flow of production. This difficulty is reflected

Table 3. State of cycle progress at end of filling shift under the conventional and the composite long-wall systems of coal mining in the United Kingdom
(Percentage of cycles)

State of cycle progress	Method of working	
	Conventional	Composite
In advance	0	22
Normal	31	73
Lagging	69	5
All cycles	100	100

Source: Trist et al., op. cit., p. 124.

Table 4. Absence rates under the conventional and the composite long-wall systems of coal mining in the United Kingdom
(Percentage of possible shifts at work)

Reason for absence	Method of working	
	Conventional	Composite
No reason given	4.3	0.4
Accident	6.8	3.2
Sickness and other	8.9	4.6
Total	20.0	8.2

Source: Trist et al., op. cit., p. 123.

in table 3, which shows the relative frequency of falling behind under the two systems.

The individual stress engendered by these two systems can be seen by a comparative set of figures of rates for three types of absence (table 4).

Before mechanisation came into mining, the traditional system was "single-place working", in which work proceeds in a continuous manner with each successive shift taking up the cycle at the point left by the previous shift; the cycle operations are not governed by a time schedule. A worker in this system—a "single-place" worker—must therefore possess the necessary range of skills to carry out all his tasks, for sooner or later he will be required to do them all. He is a "complete miner". It is experience from this tradition which has largely contributed to the development of the composite system, in which a group have "responsible autonomy" for their operations and work on a single shared-out pay note (i.e. a financial contract with the mine management to produce an agreed amount of coal from a particular coal face, with other agreed conditions).

A second contribution from this tradition—of great importance to composite working—is that of the self-selected team, a primary work group of men sharing the same pay note, who work on the same coal face, either on the same or on different shifts. The activity groups who together make up a shift team may vary in number from two to six. These teams select themselves by choosing "mates" of the same standard and work performance as themselves, taking account of an individual's capacity for physical effort, his skill as a workman, the standards of performance he sets for himself, his known pattern of attendance, his age, and so on. Because men of like capacity tend to work together, the earnings of the teams, under the agreement, vary widely, even from the same workplace. Men were found earning scarcely more than the statutory minimum wage; others were earning between two and three times as much. These extremes were partly the result of differences in conditions and partly of differences in ability and stamina. The process of self-selection gives the group a sanction which can be either implicitly or explicitly applied in order to maintain its standard. A man failing to meet the group's standards will be warned informally by the other members; if improvement does not occur he will be told to look for another team for the next quarter. If the man is unsuccessful in finding other men to work with him, he may be placed by management in a group with others in a similar position to himself, where each man is on his own rather than on a shared pay note; or he may find himself on a different kind of ancillary work, which is less remunerative than face work. The small group, capable of responsible autonomy and able to vary its work pace in correspondence with changing conditions, is a type of social structure ideally adapted to the underground situation. The existence of the self-selected teams has given the Durham face worker great experience in handling relations in the small group.[30]

The special contemporary interest of these almost traditional methods of handling individual differences in working capacity is the possibilities they suggest for resolving this frequent problem of innovation in work organisation. The miners working a coal seam constitute a formal social group, membership of which confers rights and imposes obligations. A man taking up mining in fact joins a seam rather than a pit. He graduates through a series of roles to the higher-paid coal face work in his own seam, and when he is older and seeks less arduous work, it is into the ancillary tasks of his own seam that he moves. Within the seam unit there are rules governing the equitable sharing of workplaces, so that every group has an equal chance of working in good and bad conditions. This sharing system, known as "cavilling", is a unique feature of the Durham and Northumberland coal fields. With a few specialised exceptions, all workplaces are pooled every three months and the individual miners who will work in these places are drawn by lot in a formal ceremony at which both the management and the trade union branch are present. This procedure was highly adaptive to single-place working, since there were large numbers of places, with wide differences in conditions which directly affected earnings. What cavilling does ensure is a random allocation which provides a safeguard against favouritism and victimisation over the workplace to which a man is allocated. It is really based on a folk custom concerned with obtaining justice at the hand of chance.[31]

It was traditional in these pits for workers and management to deal with each other through the "lodge"—the trade union's local unit—to a far greater extent than in most industries. The slowness of the production tempo deriving from the absence of mechanisation made co-ordination relatively simple in single-place working. The coexistence of a well developed trade union structure with an undeveloped management structure was a central feature of the social system of collieries as these had been fashioned by the earlier and simpler forms of mining. The wage system that emerged in those circumstances is based on the idea of the "price agreement", i.e. a negotiated payment for a specified task, e.g. the amount of coal produced, or a defined volume of this type of coal face work. This contractual emphasis led to a tradition of management through the wages system rather than through direct control of the working group, which remained autonomous. "It is management by negotiation between two independently constituted 'powers' who are yet mutually dependent, and whose relative strengths have varied considerably over the course of time."[32]

"Composite long-wall working depends on successfully binding together into a corporate whole the rather large over-all group comprised by the successive task groups of the three-shift cycle" (i.e. a total of 39-41 men, in activity groups of from two to six members each). Among both miners and managers widespread scepticism exists that this can be effectively done. It is argued that in the conventional long-wall system the need for smaller activity groups who follow each other in the three differently structured shifts of such a cycle varies widely, as does group performance, so that if they were treated and paid as one group either the pace would be that of the slowest or the merger would split up through internal disagreement. There is force to these contentions. But they overlook a fundamental point: the members of each of these conventional long-wall activity groups perform tasks that are identical, not complementary. Composite long-wall organisation, by contrast, involves the relating together of individuals performing different tasks. The over-all cycle group which comes into being is composed of the activity groups which, under the conventional long-wall system, had only separate existence. Under the composite system, these groups are willing to share a common payment in as far as all their members believe that the level of their personal earnings is kept up by a regular completion of the over-all shift and cycle task, perceived as an outcome of interdependence rather than of separate individual achievement. "The essential concept is that of the multi-skilled face worker, interchangeable with others according to need, all such men being regarded as making an equivalent contribution and therefore as meriting the same reward."[33]

GENERAL

Even if it is no longer accepted that technological requirements and the design of technological equipment are conditions from which there is never any significant organisational escape, what has also become clear is that many past technological designs were based on unstated, and indeed unrecognised, assumptions about individual human capacities and about the properties of working groups and production systems. There can be little, doubt, for example, that many of the traditional sequences of machine-processing in batch manufacture represent, at the group level, a fragmentation of work which has features in common with the fragmentation of the work of an individual operative; and at both group and individual level there can be gross under-use and misuse of skill, flexibility and potential of both machines and men. Considerations of this kind lend particular interest to situations in which a completely new manufacturing unit is to be designed and brought into operation. In these circumstances, there is much less of the past to be dealt with; and it is certainly true that one of the permanent results of, for example, the Volvo experiment in car assembly at Kalmar, is that no one will now build a plant of this kind without at least thinking over the possibility of making the socio-technical modifications which stem from the developments on that site. The re-design of machine tools is now also of wide interest; and it is important to record the concern of distinguished technologists with the human and social implications in the design of new forms of working group as well as with the scope and limitations of automation and of mechanical robots for routine production.

With respect to smaller changes—for example, job enlargement or job enrichment for operatives—it can be said that where they have been undertaken almost on their own and not as part of a broader innovation of a kind to be discussed in a moment, there has been a strong tendency for the change to be abandoned after a few years, with a return to the previous norm. On the other hand, after a time some of these small initial innovations and developments have come to be regarded by the company concerned not as ends in themselves but as a first step towards the discovery of some of the ultimate implications of such changes. In one large electronic manufacturing company, for example, a senior executive said: "When we started off we really had no idea how far we might have to go; we are now convinced that in the end—not unwillingly but perhaps unexpectedly—we will have to go the whole way in re-design of the socio-technical system, including the nature and organisation of the managerial and technical staff."

This last quotation defines the nature of a "comprehensive" innovation, of a kind which is likely, if it is successful, to continue and to develop further; and this point is made clear in the case studies reported earlier. Innovations of this kind need to include a minimum of elements: the design of whole tasks at the operative level; the introduction of multi-skilled working teams with a high degree of self-management; maximum flexibility in work assignments; changes in the roles of supervisors and managers; changes in the information system; and changes in systems of remuneration and fringe benefits in the whole operational unit concerned. (The last of these items is a source of frequent difficulty if it has not been considered at an early design stage of a project in this field.) In addition, of course, nearly all of these basic elements of a successful innovative design involve modifications of education and training, and have a considerable effect on the manpower planning and the career development systems of the organisation concerned. It will be recalled that in the various cases studied these conditions had to a large extent been met. However, these cases also make clear a more basic point: an innovatory project in work organisation is not like a rail journey, for which to go from point A to point B one merely selects a suitable train on an existing line; with a little exaggeration it can be said that such a project is rather more like the construction of a railway line from A to B; for it is the design and management of the change, not a choice among existing ready-made solutions, which constitutes the problem and provides the challenge and the satisfaction to all concerned.

Sometimes one or other of the elements just listed has not been included in the design of a work innovation, with consequent difficulties. For example, there is no reason to disbelieve that a number of mechanical engineering concerns in the United Kingdom set out to introduce cell groups and group technology methods without fully appreciating the need to select and train group members and types of supervisor who would be appropriate for their new roles. The first case study, for instance, describes workers who were almost actively hostile to the changes proposed but after nine months found themselves largely in support; and the same is likely to be true of a considerable proportion of supervisors of innovations in work organisation. Where a situation of this kind exists it is obvious that changes in the role of supervisors will only be brought about with considerable care—and over time, as the trade unions report on cell systems in mechanical engineering emphasises at the end of the second case study.[34]

A number of issues of importance arise in connection with the evaluation of the results of innovations in work organisation. First, comparisons of the state of affairs before and after work reorganisation experiments are often difficult, or even misleading, in circumstances in which it is not possible adequately to describe, quantify or control the other variables operating, over the relevant period, outside and around the immediate experimental group and its activities. Detailed study of the interplay of factors in a change while it is going on (i.e. the features of the various stages of a move from one particular form of work organisation to another) may yield more significant information than comparisons of the state of affairs before and after a change, which often involve so many explicit or implicit assumptions about the relevance and stability of variables as to raise grave doubts about their conclusions. This does not mean that such comparisons are not of interest; but it does mean that without knowledge of all that has been going on in the meantime the findings they provide may often be misleading.

This leads to the question of the Hawthorne effect.[35] It has become almost customary to regard such effects as unlikely to continue for long after withdrawal of the external stimulus—for example, the concern and interest shown by a consultant in a work group; and it has become usual to accept, as a rough empirical rule, that if a total work situation has remained relatively stable, and if an innovation has been introduced and some improvement has persisted for longer than about 18 months after removal of such a stimulus, the improvement can with some likelihood be attributed to the innovation.

In the case studies reported earlier there is evidence that socio-psychological characteristics of a particular company or operating unit, related to its technology by only indirect links, influence the likelihood of innovation in work organisation; and there is even more evidence that success in many kinds of innovatory projects is more likely in organisations where learning to foster innovation is an aim of the organisation itself. There are obviously organisations that are not given to learning and innovation; and in some of these, a sudden revelation of the need for change may occur. In these circumstances the prospects of success are best in small companies;[36] in large organisations, flashes of delayed insight are usually accompanied by the dismissal of top managers, and the whole organisation takes quite a time to recover. Small companies have certain advantages in matters of innovation; and there is a growing awareness of the existence of these diseconomies of scale. With a considerable degree of over-simplification, the factors favouring successful innovation can be listed as follows:

(1) *Recognition by a network of key employees, at all levels and in all functions of the company, of the importance of environmental changes as a factor regularly leading to important internal decisions.* These changes in the company's environment may, for example, be changes in demand, in the amount of competition, in the technology available to the industry, or in the availability of labour or capital. In relation to changes in work organisation, there are sometimes problems over internal discussion of such matters; for some works councils, by agreement with the relevant trade unions, may be debarred from discussing matters which might have a major effect on a wages agreement. This situation would make it difficult in the United Kingdom to introduce compulsory worker representation at board level; participatory decision-making over job content and work organisation at "grass roots" level is also a problem.

(2) *A long history of contact and discussion with the relevant trade union officers and internal stewards over present and future situations affecting the company concerned and its industry.* It is important that these discussions, which have a mutually consultative character, be separate in time from those concerned with negotiating conditions of employment. The first case study illustrates this point; for it is not possible to plan an actual game of poker while at the same time discussing the theory of games. This second favourable factor represents, in effect, the record of the company with regard to the development and operation of agreed procedures to seek the comments and co-operation of unions on aspects of company planning in which they have a special interest, and also to develop agreed procedures for applying such decisions as may be agreed between management and unions. The range of these agreements is increasing. In companies that are successful in growth and innovation in general, long-term manpower planning in particular is not a mere adjunct of corporate planning but a fully integrated part of it. Moreover, such companies have not relied on the personal support of a single senior workers' representative with regard to changes in work organisation. The process of approving innovations has been entrusted to a group of interested parties including trade union representatives or shop stewards, usually forming a "steering committee".

(3) *The existence of a company scheme of career and promotion planning.* There is an inherent and continuing conflict between, on the one hand, the changing needs of an organisation of employees of all kinds and at all levels and, on the other, the changing skills, experience and aspirations of its employees. The limitation of such conflicts is a main function of schemes of manpower and career planning. When they are successful they become widely agreed means to widely agreed ends.

This last point is especially relevant to the career opportunities of first-line supervisors and lower-middle management. In years gone by, one of the effects of the fragmentation of work at the operative level was to produce a need for first-line supervisors, in considerable number, to control the re-integration of work which had been fragmented. It can now be seen that supervisors and lower-middle management in manufacturing industry can be regarded as even more unfortunate victims of (an earlier) Taylorism than the operatives they were brought in to control. As already mentioned, it was relatively infrequent, in the past, to promote supervisors even to lower levels of management. "For the foreman", it was often said in the past, "the career ladder has only one rung." In many of the new forms of work organisation the supervisor's pattern of responsibility has of necessity changed a great deal. The supervisor's new role is less controlling, more advisory, more technical, and more concerned with the relation between working groups. The foreman becomes more like a minister of foreign affairs than a prime minister. Such a pattern of responsibility and experience is more directly related to those of middle management and is likely to have a much greater attraction for many of the entrants to industry. It should make it easier to recruit people with career aspirations which are well above the supervisory level; and if so, this could have a very wide significance for industrial career paths in general.

The emergence of these notions of factors favouring success raises a considerable number of related and extremely important questions. For example, how far are such factors of importance only for industrial units over a certain size? Would it be of any help for change in general, and innovation in work organisation in particular, if arrangements to foster development of the three factors were encouraged by legislation? Why is commercial success, in the larger companies, so frequently associated with developments and activities which, though not expensive, seem to be unconsidered by other and less successful organisations? (It is hard to avoid the conclusion that effectiveness of management, particularly at the top, is an essential element in this familiar state of affairs.)

If the three factors listed above as fostering successful innovation in work organisation were studied in conjunction with wider points made in the statement of trade unions' views on group technology (referred to in the second case study) that a growing volume of trade, an expanding industry, and a developing firm make innovation in work organisation very much easier, it might be possible to evolve a rough set of general hypotheses about the social ecology of innovation in work organisation. Such an ecology, of course, would provide a basis for a social pathology of innovations that failed.

It may be useful in this connection to examine the idea that a company can be viewed as a political system. This idea must first be distinguished from what is usually described by the word "politicking"—that is, a kind of "black market" in power and influence, associated with cliques and cabals, which exists in varying forms and degrees in most organisations. This is not what is meant by "political system" in the present context. What is meant is the relationship between the power and influence of different functional and hierarchical groups within an organisation, and in its external relations. In successful organisations there is a direct and accepted connection between the priority and continuity attributed to the need to deal with different environmental situations and the political power of different internal groups—functional or specialist—concerned with each of these external situations; and there is an analogous situation with respect to the priority of internal problems of any organisation. At any one time there is usually an agreed balance of power and influence between the constituent integrative, functional and specialist personnel of an organisation. One of the important questions about innovation in work organisation is its effect on this balance; but another equally important one relates to its effect on the "black market" in power and influence of the private, informal "politicking" whose range, importance and proportion, as compared with the formal, public, political system of a company, is one index of organisational health. Without too much difficulty, some of the basic notions of political science can be used with advantage in thinking about such matters. For example, the "constituency" of a group, or of an individual member of an organisation, can be regarded as consisting of the people and groups, primarily within the organisation, from whom something less than hostility needs to be obtained if that group or individual is to be enabled to operate effectively. In a slightly different setting, this same point was made very clearly by Dubin[37] in a comment on decision-making that was based on a behavioural study of this process:

Two simple and supplementary points . . . derive from studies of the behaviours of decision makers in operation rather than the study of simulating models of these decision-making operations. The observations are *(a)* that the time scale of decision is very much (and I want to underscore the "very much") longer than the formalistic analysis of decision making would lead one to expect, and, *(b)* that organisational decision making is fundamentally a political process.

By the "political factor" in decision making we mean that disparate and even conflicting interests of individuals or groups are accommodated in the decision itself. These differences first have to be searched out through discussion and analysis, the disparities among them made clear, and the points of compromise and accommodation determined. Finally, the actual decision incorporating the balance points among the interest has to be reached. These steps, taken together, involve political processes.

It should be made clear that time is necessary to play politics. This suggests that the analytical problem of time scale is really coupled with the analytical problem of the politics of decision. The linkage can be expressed as follows: the greater the need to accommodate differences in a decision, the more time may be consumed in reaching the decision.

These remarks lead on to another useful idea which represents the general point just made, in rather different language, namely the formal and informal sides of organisation. Detailed study of the day-to-day working of any organisation will usually disclose the existence of a variety of informal activities, procedures and influences which, as has just been said, are not fully represented in any public description of its affairs. These activities continue for long periods and represent a special aspect of the structure of an organisation. This point has been fully documented in most countries.[38] At operative level in manufacturing industry, for example, there are often worker-initiated and worker-controlled modifications of their formal job activities—modifications designed to cope with some inadequacy of equipment or of work planning, or to produce some individual benefit. Under-reporting of completed work can be used to help maintain stability in weekly earnings, or to make optimal use of an incentive scheme. Activities that are identical in nature but different in content—for example, techniques for getting round a budgetary control system—are familiar in the work of managers and specialists in industry; it is even rumoured that they exist in government service. In general terms, some students of organisation feel, no formal organisation could work effectively—and in some cases could not work at all—without informal procedures of various kinds. It is obvious that a full knowledge of any existing work organisation, including these informal aspects, is important in planning innovation; for difficulty over accepting change, or unexpected willingness to accept it, may well be related to features not visible in the formal structure and procedures of an organisation.

The two aspects of organisation that have just been briefly noted—first "political" activity and "politicking" and secondly the existence of important "informal" influences and procedures within an organisation—may well have some relation to a suggestion made by Roeber in his study of the extended programme of job re-structuring in Imperial Chemical Industries[39] which is briefly summarised in the third case study. He puts forward the hypothesis—perhaps he might prefer a stronger description—that the increase in participatory decision-making at operative and supervisory levels in the units of this company, and by implication elsewhere, may most easily be understood as a shift of certain forms of power and procedure from the informal to the formal level. There can be no doubt whatever that this is a useful idea for understanding existing forms of work organisation and planning new forms. However, it is even more important to consider what is meant by "power" in different contexts and at different levels of social organisation. This is an extremely wide and popular issue. In relation to a single industrial organisation, people concerned with conflicts over changes in the balance of power, and in the sharing of power, sometimes see it as being almost a fixed quantity, so that struggles to alter the sharing of power constitute a zero-sum game, and any absolute or relative gain in power for any one group means an equivalent loss in power for others. From an empirical point of view, it is more than obvious that there are considerable fluctuations in the total power and capacity of a company to handle both environmental and internal situations in ways which accept conflicting interests but can avoid disaster and permit survival or growth; and the total amount of this power depends greatly on the perceptiveness, the skills, the willingness of its members to co-operate in these matters, and on their development of means to contain conflict within certain limits. In as far as these over-simplications are accepted, increased sharing of power within an organisation can be regarded as strengthening one group or individual without of necessity producing an equal and opposite weakening of others. The sharing of power may be little more than a diminution of conflict to permit an increased expenditure of energy in more appropriate directions. With the development of professionalism, many managers and executives in industry appear to be increasingly willing to spend a higher proportion of their time and energy in tackling awkward problems at the environmental boundary of their company, or between groups within it, without feeling undue alarm over giving to other employees increased responsibility and power to help them deal with tasks and problems within their own sphere of immediate concern.

Notes

[1] It may be useful to record at this point the almost simultaneous appearance of two volumes which between them give an unusually comprehensive account of important aspects of social, economic and industrial change in the United Kingdom. The first is No. 7 in the series of annual reviews of *Social trends* by the Central Statistical Office (London, H M Stationery Office, 1976); the second is E. G. Wood: *British industries: A comparison of performance* (London, McGraw-Hill, 1976).

[2] Royal Commission on Trade Unions and Employers' Associations, 1965-68 (Chairman: Lord Donovan): *Report,* Cmnd. 3623 (London, H M Stationery Office, 1969).

[3] Otto Kahn-Freund: *Labour and the law: An ambivalent relationship,* Third Woodward Memorial Lecture (London, Imperial College of Science and Technology, 1975).

[4] From ILO: *Yearbook of Labour Statistics,* 1977.

[5] *Report of the Committee of Inquiry on Industrial Democracy (Chairman: Lord Bullock),* Cmnd. 6706 (London, H M Stationery Office, 1977).

[6] Paul Bradbury: "The changing balance: Industry and the worker", in *CBI Review* (London, Confederation of British Industry), Spring 1976, pp. 8-9.

[7] See pp. 124-125.

[8] Department of Employment: *On the quality of working life,* by N. A. B. Wilson, Manpower Paper No. 7 (London, H M Stationery Office, 1973).

[9] Department of Employment Work Research Unit: *Making work more satisfying,* Report of the Tripartite Steering Committee (London, 1975).

[10] Mechanical Engineering Economic Development Committee: *Why group technology?* (London, National Economic Development Office, 1975).

[11] ibid., pp. 9-10.

[12] ibid., p. 10.

[13] John L. Burbidge: *Final report on a study of the effects of group production methods on the humanisation of work, . . .* prepared at the completion of a study executed under contract to the International Labour Office by the International Centre for Advanced Technical and Vocational Training (Turin, International Centre for Advanced Technical and Vocational Training, 1975).

[14] Institute of Personnel Management: *Job redesign in practice,* Report of a working party, by Keith Carby (London, 1976).

[15] For the long extracts used in this case study, the author wishes to thank Mr. W. W. Daniel of Political and Economic Planning. For more extensive descriptions of the case the reader is referred to W. W. Daniel: *Beyond the wage-work bargain,* Broadsheet 519 (London, Political and Economic Planning, 1970); W. W. Daniel and N. McIntosh: *The right to manage?* (London, Political and Economic Planning and Macdonald, 1972); and G. Strauss in J. M. Rosow (ed.): *The worker and the job: Coping with change* (London, Prentice-Hall International, 1974).

[16] *Beyond the wage-work bargain,* op. cit., p. 43.

[17] ibid., pp. 43-44.

[18] *The right to manage?,* op. cit., p. 34.

[19] ibid., pp. 35-36.

[20] By Strauss, op. cit.

[21] This case study is drawn essentially from the following sources: J. L. Burbidge: *The introduction of group technology* (London, Heinemann, 1975); idem: *Group production methods and humanisation of work: The evidence in industrialised countries,* International Institute for Labour Studies, Research Series, Developments in the fields of humanisation of work and quality of working life, No. 10 (Geneva, 1976); Economic Development Committee for Mechanical Engineering: *Why group technology?* (London, National Economic Development Office, 1975); G. M. Ranson: *Group technology* (London, McGraw-Hill, 1972); and D. T. N. Williamson: "The anachronistic factory", in *Proceedings of the Royal Society of London,* A 331 (1972), pp. 139-160.

[22] op. cit., p. 3.

[23] Williamson, op. cit.

[24] Economic Development Committee for Mechanical Engineering: *Why group technology?,* op. cit., pp. 31 and 33-34.

[25] The author expresses special thanks to Mr. Trevor Owen and Mr. Arthur Johnston, senior officials of the company, for their observations in respect of this case study. Recommended additional readings for this case are: W. J. Paul and K. B. Robertson: *Job enrichment and employee motivation* (London, Gower Press, 1970); and J. Roeber: *Social change at work: The ICI weekly staff agreement* (London, Duckworth, 1975).

[26] C. E. Lindblom: "The science of muddling through", in Ansoff (ed.): *Business strategy* (Harmondsworth, Middlesex, Penguin Books, 1967), pp. 41-60.

[27] The information and concepts that follow are taken from studies undertaken by members of the Tavistock Institute between 1950 and 1958, and reported in E. L. Trist, G. W. Higgin, H. Murray and A. B. Pollock: *Organizational choice: Capabilities of groups at the coal face under changing technologies; the loss, rediscovery and transformation of a work tradition* (London, Tavistock Publications, 1963), to which the author is particularly indebted.

[28] Agreement between management and such a group to undertake defined tasks (with a group financial contract) dealing with a particular coal face.

[29] Trist et al., op. cit., pp. xii-xiii.

[30] ibid., pp. 33-34.

[31] ibid., pp. 34-35.

[32] ibid., pp. 35-36.

[33] ibid., pp. 76-77.

[34] Change at supervisory level in industry is more fully discussed in K. E. Thurley and H. Wirdenius: *Supervision: A re-appraisal* (London, Heinemann, 1973).

[35] So called from an important and unexpected finding of the 1929-31 Harvard Business School studies at the Western Electric plant of that name in a Chicago suburb: it was found at one stage that a mere display of interest in the activities of a group of workers, without any change in their conditions of work, improved their willingness to co-operate and their efficiency.

[36] It is significant that Scanlon plans—agreements over division of improved gains from an agreed change of some kind—have in the past been most obviously useful in companies of this size. See Frederick G. Lesieur: *The Scanlon plan* (Cambridge, Mass., Massachusetts Institute of Technology Press, 1967).

[37] R. Dubin: "Business behaviour behaviourally viewed", in Strother (ed.): *Social science approaches to business behaviour* (Irwin Dorsey).

[38] T. Lupton reports and discusses them in a study of two United Kingdom units, entitled *On the shop floor* (London, Pergamon Press, 1963).

[39] Roeber, op. cit.

UNITED STATES

UNITED STATES
Paul S. Goodman* and
Edward E. Lawler III†

Experiments with new forms of work organisation have proliferated in the United States since 1970. The experiments have taken many forms in many different kinds of organisations, and their effect on the nature of work, the character of the work environment and the nature of labour-management relations is potentially very significant.

As used in this monograph, the expression "new form of work organisation" denotes the outcome of changes affecting a number of aspects of the organisation, and includes the establishment of machinery to introduce the changes and ensure their permanence. All of the new forms of work organisation considered here, whether introduced in new plants or in existing ones, are distinguished by these two characteristics. The changes in question are directed at the organisation as a total system rather than at any one of its aspects: they will affect, for example, authority, decision-making, rewards, communication, technology, selection and training. The general aim of the changes is usually to democratise the workplace, and to ensure greater control for the workers over their environment and more joint problem-solving by labour and management. The machinery for the introduction and maintenance of change is established to identify organisational problems, introduce and monitor changes, make adjustments, and institutionalise the process of change. It will be noted that on its own, a programme of job enrichment or supervisory training does not fit this definition.

NATIONAL CONDITIONS

The participation of labour and management in experiments with new forms of work organisation has been influenced by the fact that there have been no major ideological conflicts within the unions and no bitter conflict between labour and management, while labour-management relations have reached an advanced stage of development. Inflation, unemployment and foreign competition have also provided a stimulus for such participation. The use of labour-

* Graduate School of Industrial Administration, Carnegie-Mellon University.
† University of Michigan and Battelle Memorial Institute.

management committees outside the traditional collective bargaining arrangements parallels the design in many new forms of work organisation. All these factors constituted necessary though not sufficient conditions for the experiments.

Economic conditions

Since 1970 there have been several recessions in the United States: unemployment rates have been abnormally high, and inflation has been acute. Real gross national product per head, which had been rising slowly during the 1960s, dropped slightly during the first recession in 1969-70; in 1971-72 it began to rise again, levelling off in 1973, and it dropped again at the beginning of the second recession in 1974. The industrial production index, another measure of real output, shows the same trend. A comparison of actual and potential real gross national product shows the magnitude of the economic downturns. From the end of 1965 to 1970 the actual and potential values were very similar. The discrepancies were most marked at the end of 1970 and in 1975. The latter trough was the largest since the period immediately after the Second World War.[1] Whereas about 75 million persons were engaged in non-agricultural activities in 1970, by 1975 the number was slightly over 80 million. The unemployment rate mirrors the two recessions. In late 1969 the total unemployment rate was less than 4 per cent. By the end of 1970 it was close to 6 per cent, where it remained until 1971. There was then a slight reduction of total unemployment until the beginning of 1974, when the rate increased, to reach about 9 per cent by 1975. Inflation, as measured by the rise in the consumer price index (all items seasonally adjusted) was of the order of 11 to 12 per cent at its peak in 1974, while the index of total private non-farm output per man-hour (1967 = 100) rose from slightly over 100 in 1970 to 110 in 1975. In short, economic conditions since 1970 have generally not been good.

Labour-management relations

Developments in labour-management relations since 1970 have also affected the current spread of experiments with new forms of work organisation. These relations in turn were clearly affected by the economic conditions that have just been discussed: it was in response to growing inflation that in 1972 the Nixon administration introduced a three-phase programme to limit wage and price increases. In the first phase there was a freeze on wages, in the second increases in wages had to be justified to a pay board, and in the third there was voluntary control over wage increases. A requirement of the programme was that wage increases should be justified by increases in productivity. This programme was followed by growing use of labour-management committees at both the industry and the local level. Committees in the construction, food and steel industries dealt with a variety of issues such as wages, technological change and employment security. Such committees are an important aspect of most experiments with new forms of work organisation.

A joint concern of labour and management for productivity also became evident during this period. In the past, productivity had been a problem for management. However, as foreign competitors made greater advances in the United

States market job security was threatened, and a stimulus was provided for both labour and management to focus attention on finding ways to increase both productivity and job security. The Experimental Negotiating Agreement in the steel industry[2] is one example of this trend. Increasing productivity is one of th: goals of many of the work re-structuring experiments. Economic conditions also account for some other features of current collective agreements. For example, the use of cost-of-living adjustments in agreements is not new, but high inflation acted as an incentive to include escalator clauses in agreements. Unemployment during this period also increased the emphasis on job security. The experiments with new forms of work organisation also reflect the current issues in collective bargaining within individual industries. For example, employment security, emphasised in the Bolivar project,[3] is a central theme for the United Automobile Workers, whereas improving safety, a central concern of the United Mine Workers, is the major goal in the Rushton experiment.

The design of some of the experiments has also been affected by legislation enacted during this period which set limits to collective bargaining, particularly in the fields of safety and equality of opportunity in employment. For example, selection, promotion and termination have been affected by equal employment opportunity legislation, which also affects agreed seniority arrangements.

The introduction of new forms of work organisation has also been influenced by the state of the trade union movement. The proportion of trade unionists in the total labour force has remained low: from 1970 to 1974 union members constituted about 27 per cent of the workers employed in non-agricultural establishments. However, there has been much unionisation in the public sector, and increasing numbers of policemen, firemen, teachers, nurses and other state and municipal workers are covered by collective agreements. Some experiments with new forms of work organisation have been initiated in the public sector with union co-operation. There have been no major political or ideological changes in the leadership of most of the larger unions. This absence of major ideological conflict creates a setting in which experiments with new forms of work organisation can be more readily accepted. In one union in which a major change did occur, the United Mine Workers of America, the leadership change heralded a more democratic form of organisation which was congruent with the Rushton experiment made in a unionised coal mine.

Bodies promoting new forms of work organisation

Work re-structuring in the United States is sponsored by a variety of bodies, to some extent geographically dispersed, only one of them being a central government agency. The general objectives of all these bodies are similar—to increase productivity and enhance the quality of working life through new forms of work organisation. However, they differ in the relative importance they attach to these two aims and in the means chosen to attain them: some of the bodies concerned disseminate information, others stage experiments, while yet others stress educational activities or research. All of these bodies are non-profit-making. Some are run independently while others are associated with universities. The bodies first set up had nation-wide interests, whereas some of the newer ones confine themselves to particular states. The principal sources of funds are government, private foundations, the business community and unions.

The major bodies that advocate and design projects relating to new forms of work organisation in the United States are listed below. (Other bodies at the national and state levels—e.g. in Massachusetts—are involved in similar activities but on a smaller scale.)[4]

1. *National Center for Productivity and Quality of Working Life.* This is the only government agency connected with projects concerning new forms of work organisation. It was established by an executive order in 1970 and given statutory authority by Congress in 1971. Under its current mandate[5] the objective of the Center is "to focus, co-ordinate, and promote efforts to improve the rate of productivity". The Center's other activities include sponsoring conferences and studies concerned with productivity and the quality of working life, and disseminating information. Special committees have been set up, in particular, to cover the development of labour-management committees and productivity programmes in transport, the public sector and the health sector.

2. *National Quality of Work Center.*[6] This Center was founded in 1974 and is affiliated with the Institute of Social Research of the University of Michigan. Its primary objective has been to launch a set of demonstration projects, provide technical assistance to those projects and disseminate information about them. All projects are jointly sponsored by unions and management. Some of the projects involve the Tennessee Valley Authority (TVA), the TVA Engineers' Association, and the Office and Professional Employees Union;[7] Harman International and the United Automobile Workers (Bolivar project);[8] Rushton Mining Company and the United Mine Workers of America;[9] and Weyerhauser Corporation and the International Woodworkers of America. The Institute for Social Research conducts evaluations of the demonstration projects and is also involved in a set of related projects on such matters as person-environment fit, conditions facilitating organisational effectiveness, control structures and performance in work organisations.

3. *Center for Quality of Working Life.* This Center is affiliated with the Institute of Industrial Relations of the University of California at Los Angeles, and was formed in 1975 to formulate and publicise approaches that will enhance the quality of life at the workplace. The work of the Center involves technical assistance through research and consultation with management and unions, training of professionals, managers and union officers, in-depth case studies on designs to enhance quality of working life and dissemination of knowledge through conferences.

4. *Work in America Institute.* The objectives of this Institute are to improve the nature and organisation of work, and to increase productivity and enhance the quality of life. Other activities are concerned with bridging the gap between education and employment, facilitating labour-management co-operation, and assessing national manpower policies in terms of productivity and quality of life. The principal activities include clearing-house and communication work, technical assistance, and education and training through conferences, seminars,

and specially designed programmes. The Institute brings together representatives from management, labour and the government. It has received funds from both the private and the public sector.

CASE STUDIES

There were two criteria for the selection of the four cases described in this monograph. The first was availability of information: the cases chosen were ones on which extensive information was available. The second criterion was the existence of some implications for the labour movement in terms of the structure of the local union branch, relations between the local union branch and the national federation, new topics for collective bargaining, or future unionisation. (Experiments in non-union plants can affect the attempts to organise membership drives in such plants. For example, if a major corporation has union and non-union plants, and an experiment is conducted with some degree of success in a non-union setting, this might limit the union's ability to organise that and other non-union plants.) The authors of the present monograph have been directly or indirectly involved, as the principal research workers reporting on an experiment, in some of the cases selected. Although a selection of cases as a function of availability of information or of the authors' own direct involvement presents a possible selection bias, the authors nevertheless consider that the sample cases selected are representative of the major experiments currently being conducted in the United States with regard to new forms of work organisation.

Work reorganisation in an existing unionised coal mine (Rushton)

The Rushton Mining Company operates a unionised coal mine located at Osceola Mills, a small rural community of about 1,700 people in north-central Pennsylvania. In 1973 the presidents of the company and of the United Mine Workers of America agreed to try out a new form of work organisation in the mine. A labour-management committee with an external research team devised an over-all work re-structuring programme which brought about a substantial change in the communications, decision-making, authority and rewards systems at the mine. Autonomous group working was central to the programme of change. The results of the change effort include increases in safety, better work attitudes, greater amounts of job skill and no change in productivity.

The mine is a smallish one producing steam coal for the generation of electric power. Prospecting for the mine began in late 1962, and production commenced in 1965. Although the firm is part of a mining corporation owned by the power company which provided the initial backing for the mine, from its beginning it was run as a fairly autonomous unit; even after the power company took over formal ownership of the mine, it was run independently, and the main decisions continued to be taken by the founder and current president of the firm. A plant superintendent is in charge of the day-to-day operations. Under the superintendent there is a general foreman who supervises the underground work. The pit is divided into sections, each worked at any one time by a crew of six or more men supervised by a foreman; since the mine operates around the clock, each section

147

is manned by a number of crews, which rotate weekly. Mining has often been described as a transport system, since a mine is organised to transport coal from the face to the consumer. The coal is removed at the face with the help of a continuous miner, and transported to a conveyor belt which carries it to the surface. There it is transferred to a cleaning plant where the rock is separated and the coal washed and dried, and then transported by conveyors to a finished coal pile. Subsequently it is loaded on coal cars for transport to the power company. There is a separate maintenance service. Supervisors from both these latter sections report to the mine superintendent, as do members of staff management such as the safety director, training director and purchasing agent.

At the time of the experiment there were about 180 employees. Of these some 30 were classified as managerial. The remainder were production workers and members of the United Mine Workers of America. (By the end of 1976 the number of employees had risen to about 200, of whom 35 were managerial.) Culturally, the area is a relatively closed and isolated one devoted to mining and farming. The workforce is fairly well distributed over the adjacent towns. Although there are not a large number of mines located near Rushton, most of the men have mining backgrounds. Absenteeism and turnover rates have been relatively low. Rushton is the biggest and highest-paying employer in the area. Even before the experiment, the mine had a good safety record, and at the beginning of the experiment (between January and November 1973) there were only six lost-time accidents in the major mining sections, which have about 60 men.

The mine was started as a non-union mine. After a major strike over unionisation in 1967, a local branch of the United Mine Workers of America was established. During this early period labour-management relations were bitter and punctuated by many strikes, but in the early 1970s there were fewer strikes and more labour-management co-operation. Collective bargaining and the determination of general union policy take place at the national level. Though not a member of the employers' association that negotiates the national contract, the company none the less adopts that model contract as its own. The local union branch is involved in the day-to-day application of that collective agreement through its officers, and through committees such as the safety committee. District officials of the union monitor the activities of local union branches in the area and report to the national headquarters.

The experiment at Rushton began in a mining section. The physical conditions in the section are generally unfavourable. There is complete darkness. The ceiling height is around 1.65 m, wet areas are common, and there is a noticeable amount of dust. Each of the three crews in the section includes a continuous miner operator and his helper. The continuous miner is an expensive piece of machinery, about 7.6 metres across, which scrapes the coal from the seam. Two car operators then transport the coal to a feeder. Meanwhile two bolter operators are placing bolts in the roof to prevent roof falls. When special work is required (e.g. moving belts), general labourers are assigned to the regular crew. A maintenance man who reports to the maintenance supervisor is assigned to each crew, bringing the number of men to eight (counting the foreman) in each crew. The average age of the miners in the three crews working the section is 35, and on the average they have had 10.8 years of schooling; 89 per cent are married and all are white. The physical environment and the technology are such that—

(a) the physical working conditions are adverse;

(b) there is a high degree of uncertainty surrounding the mining operations (e.g. chances of roof falls, changes in the coal seam);

(c) owing in particular to the darkness, it is difficult for supervisors to direct the workforce;

(d) there is a high degree of interdependence within a crew, since if the continuous miner stops, production stops;

(e) there is a high degree of interdependence between crews in the same section, since failure to co-ordinate increases downtime and lowers production; and

(f) there is a high degree of interdependence between the mining crews and the outside sections, which must in particular see to it that the underground workers are never short of supplies.

The initial stimulus for the company's participation in the experiment came from a training programme conducted at Penn State University by Mr. Grant Brown early in 1973: the president of Rushton, Mr. Hinks, was attracted by some of the novel ideas put forward. Subsequently, Mr. Brown, Dr. Gerald Susman (Penn State University), and Dr. Eric Trist met Mr. Ted Mills, Director of the National Quality of Work Center, to consider the possibility of a quality of work project in a mine. The research team of Trist, Susman and Brown was formed. Through Mr. Mills, Mr. Hinks and his co-owner, Mr. Cimba, learned more about the concept of autonomous work groups, and the United Mine Workers became interested in participating in a quality of work experiment. In April 1973 Mr. Hinks and Arnold Miller, president of the United Mine Workers of America, signed a letter approving the purpose of a quality of work experiment and agreed that each of the parties should be entitled to withdraw if it saw fit. The Rushton president's values bear heavily on his decision to participate. Autonomy, responsibility and freedom of choice are essential aspects of the Rushton experiment. These are the values that are held and frequently given expression by Mr. Hinks. At a more practical level he is concerned with attracting young miners to Rushton in the future. The problem is that younger, better educated miners bring higher expectations to the job, yet the current state of work in mining does not match such expectations. He sees the experimental project as a way of attracting younger workers. The experiment attracted the union since it embodied an attempt to improve safety conditions and practices. Also, it reflected some of the values of the current union leadership; the union has been undergoing a process of democratisation which parallels this attempt to democratise decision-making at the workplace.

The experiment drew heavily on the theory of socio-technical systems. As already stated, the technology of the mine is marked by a high degree of uncertainty, much interdependence, and little opportunity to supervise directly or control the workforce. Given this technology, the research team needed to design a system that would facilitate co-ordination and flexibility of the workforce to meet uncertainty and to provide control at the appropriate levels of decision-making.

A joint committee composed of six members of management and ten from labour was set up to direct the necessary changes by diagnosing existing conditions, developing a change plan, adopting it, evaluating its outcomes and modifying it as necessary. The research team's role was to put up ideas to guide the labour-management committee. The committee began its work in August 1973, and a proposed plan for the experiment was subsequently adopted. The major characteristics of the plan were as follows:

(1) *Goals.* There were five major goals: safety, increased productivity, higher earnings, greater job skills, and job satisfaction.

(2) *Focal unit.* The plan dealt mainly with the section. The object of focusing on the section instead of the crew (in evaluating performance, for example) was to reduce competition and promote inter-crew co-operation. Traditionally there were six production workers in each crew. In the experimental section two support men, who laid track and transported supplies, were added to the crew. Previously, such support men had traditionally been drawn from the general labour force and assigned to a section only when support work was needed.

(3) *Supervision.* Responsibility for daily production and directing the work was delegated to the crew, which became an autonomous work group. The foreman was no longer responsible for production: his prime responsibility was safety; in addition, he was to become more involved in planning and in integrating the section with the rest of the mine.

(4) *Training and job switching.* A major part of the change was to train the men to become professionally skilled miners. The training included training in safety law and practices, ventilation and roof control. In addition, all men were expected to exchange jobs and learn the jobs of other members of their crew so that any crew member would be able to do any of the other members' jobs. Movement between jobs did not require observance of the formal procedures for filling vacancies provided for in the regular contract.

(5) *Pay and allocation of gains from productivity increases.* All workers in the experimental section received the same rate, the top rate for their crew. The rationale for the same pay and high rate was that all men in a crew assumed equal responsibility for production and maintenance of equipment. Also, they agreed to perform multiple tasks. Concerning productivity increases, no detailed gain-sharing plan was worked out in the initial agreement, but some general principles were established: if no gains resulted, the company would meet all the costs of the experiment, whereas if gains did occur the company's costs would first be reimbursed and the remaining net gains would be shared between labour and management.

(6) *Joint committees.* A smaller labour-management committee of five representatives of each party was set up 75 days after the experiment began for its day-to-day supervision, while the larger committee remained in being to deal with broad policy issues.

(7) *Grievances.* At first grievances were not to be dealt with through the traditional machinery. They should be dealt with in the experimental section

itself, and if that did not prove possible they were to be brought to the joint committee. Only if the joint committee failed to settle the issue should the traditional grievance machinery come into operation.

The initial plan for change is a significant document for various reasons. First, it represents a contract between labour and management outside the existing union-management contract. Secondly, both union and management gave up rights they previously enjoyed (for example, in respect of the procedure for filling vacancies). Thirdly, the changes discussed above represented a major alteration in the way in which work was conducted.

The experiment was launched in December 1973. The miners were given the option to volunteer for work in the one section that was selected as the experimental group. The concepts involved were expounded through a series of training sessions and "section conferences", which were day-long (eight-hour) meetings of all the personnel of the experimental section. The purposes were to review past performance, solve problems and plan future activities. In February 1974 the experimental section was declared officially autonomous. Other meetings in the form of section conferences, foreman training sessions and the mine labour-management conferences continued throughout the experiment. In October 1974 a new section was opened in the mine and it also was designated as an experimental section. Therefore a new programme of training and section conferences was instituted.

April 1975 marked the end of the experimental period for the first section. At that time the union asked for the whole mine to participate in the experiment. Subsequently a series of labour-management planning meetings were conducted to draw up a suitable agreement for the whole mine. A series of meetings were held with miners not already participating in the experiment to explain the proposed new document. On 20 August 1976, with all the miners voting, a quality of work programme for the whole mine was rejected in a close vote (75 to 79); the two autonomous sections voted for the programme. An analysis of the reasons for this result would be beyond the scope of this monograph. Briefly, it can be noted that some members of the workforce simply did not trust management. Others were irritated because the experimental programme had created wage inequities throughout the mine. Others simply did not understand the new programme. The president decided to continue the programme in the entire mine because of the closeness of the vote and his conviction that the experimental plan was beneficial to the workers and management. This decision was in conformity with the terms of the national union-management contract. The same procedures of training and section conferences were initiated to extend the programme to all sections and outside areas of the mine.

The Rushton project is probably the most evaluated of any of the past or current experiments with new forms of work organisation in the country. An independent evaluation team has monitored all the major results (e.g. on productivity, safety, attitudes), in some cases (e.g. for productivity) on the basis of elaborate analytical models. The immediate results of the original experiment from December 1973 to April 1975 are reviewed overleaf.[10]

(1) *Productivity*. The experiment did not significantly increase productivity. This finding was arrived at after intensive testing of a variety of economic models (production functions); the experimental section was compared with a variety of control groups.

(2) *Earnings*. Members of the experimental section earned more money.

(3) *Safety*. Six indicators of safety were considered. The experiment did not significantly affect accident rates. There were significant reductions in the number of violations of federal and state mining regulations. For example, violations of federal regulations dropped by about 10 per cent in the experimental section while increasing by about 85 per cent in the other sections. Safety practices and attitudes toward better safety practices improved as a function of the experiment.

(4) *Job skills*. One of the purposes of the experiment was to develop mining skills. Miners in the experimental section reported that the programme had substantially increased their job skills. There is general agreement on this point. Management received additional training.

(5) *Job attitudes*. Using a variety of multivariate models, the effects of the experiment on job attitudes was assessed. Greater feelings of responsibility, more interest in work, more positive feelings about one's work group seem to be attributable to the experiment. The whole experimental section developed a strong team spirit.

(6) *Communication and co-ordination*. The experiment had several indirect effects on the functioning of the mine. There was much more communication both vertically and horizontally, whereas previously communication had been primarily from top to bottom. Co-ordination between crews in the experimental section substantially increased.

(7) *Supervisory and managerial stress*. On the negative side the programme increased stress for the supervisors of the experimental crew and some middle managers.

(8) *Unionism*. The experiment did not affect the organisational structure of the local union branch or the rate of participation in union affairs. It did, however, increase conflict within the union because of the pay differentials between the experimental sections and the others.

(9) *Labour-management relations*. There were no changes in traditional indicators of labour-management relations such as the number or content of grievances, but there was some evidence of improvement in the approach of union and management officials to their problems. This improvement is attributed to the greater interaction between labour and management brought about by the experiment's labour-management committees.

Introduction of a Scanlon plan in an existing
non-unionised chemical plant (De Soto)

In 1971 a Scanlon plan was introduced into a plant of the Chemical Coatings Division of De Soto Chemical Corporation. In 1971 the sales of the parent company, De Soto, Inc., amounted to $214 million. The plant had not been affected by an economic crisis of the kind that is often given as a reason for introducing a Scanlon plan. It is one of nine geographically dispersed factories producing essentially the same products, and produces paints and other coatings, primarily for the mail order firm of Sears, Roebuck and Company, as well as for some industrial markets. It is located in a small town near Dallas, in Texas, a state whose reputation as one of cowboys and oil wells is justified more by the outlook of many of its inhabitants than by the actual structure of its economy, which is increasingly diversified. In 1971 the plant employed about 145 workers, mostly of the lower middle class; 17 per cent were managerial, 13 per cent were in the office and the remainder were in production. On the average, the production workers had received 11 years of schooling; 32 per cent had had a rural upbringing and 87 per cent were married. For most of the workers employment in this plant was their first experience of factory life. Unlike other plants within the Division, the plant is not unionised, although there had been some organising attempts before 1971.

The main office of the Chemical Coatings Division takes most of the major decisions, regarding new products, changes in quality control requirements, new processing procedures and changes in reporting procedures. The number and type of paints to be produced are largely determined by the Division's major customer. Most of the decisions at the plant level relate to the production of paints meeting the requirements of orders received, prescribed technology and quality control procedures. The small size of this plant precludes any elaborate organisational structure. The main decisions within the plant are taken by the plant manager, who is responsible for the operation of the whole plant. At the next lower level the plant manager's staff is responsible for the major units of the plant. The staff in question includes the production superintendent, the head of the quality control laboratory and the controller, as well as supervisors of sales and personnel. Foremen who represent the major production departments report to the production superintendent. Some of the larger departments have assistant foremen.

The plant in fact consists of a resin plant and an adjoining paint plant, and the technology is a mixture of batch and mass production. The resin plant can be described as being engaged in batch production: it is full of large kettles in which chemicals are "cooked" to produce one of the basic ingredients for the paint plant. The paint plant is divided into six departments. The production of paint begins in the mixing and grinding department where the chemicals are prepared. Water or oil is then added to bring the paint into its liquid form. A shader brings the batch up to specifications and then the paint goes to the filling and packing department, where it is put into containers. A laboratory department is engaged in quality control, and a receiving and warehouse department supplies raw materials for paint production and stores the finished product. A maintenance group takes care of the machinery, and an office group processes all the information necessary to keep the plant going.

The President of the Chemical Coatings Division first became interested in Scanlon plans during a class for business executives taken by Dr. Brian B. Moore at the University of Chicago. Additional reading strengthened the President's interest in how such a plan could be used in his Division. The concepts of a plan were then explored with the managers of the paint plants. The interest of the manager of the plant described here provided an opportunity of trying out a Scanlon plan in one plant. At that time the individual plants had lost some of their autonomy through general centralisation; participation by this particular plant in a new programme was one way in which its manager could re-assert his control over the plant. Another factor favouring the experiment was that the management of the Division has generally been open to organisational innovations and willing to make a variety of experiments (e.g. with shorter work weeks).

The gist of a Scanlon plan is its philosophy of co-operation between management and workers. The basic premise is that such co-operation can bring gains to management in terms of increased performance and to workers in terms of increased earnings and improvements in the quality of working life. A problem in most organisations is that labour and management are either hostile or indifferent to each other. Consequently the workers, who represent a major source of knowledge that could substantially affect the operation of the organisation, do not volunteer to put these resources at the organisation's disposal. The object of a Scanlon plan is to create an atmosphere in which labour and management freely share information. The essential elements in this atmosphere are mutual confidence and trust that sharing of information and knowledge will benefit all concerned. The information-sharing cannot be one-sided. As the workers share their knowledge with management, management must give access to information not previously shared with the workforce. Hence not only must communication channels change, but also certain rights or perquisites held by management; in particular, there must be joint decision-making.

Two specific features that are characteristic of every Scanlon plan are a suggestions system and a company-wide bonus system. The suggestions system is a new formal communication and decision-making system that permits information to be exchanged and managers and workers to participate jointly in certain operating decisions. It is superimposed on the existing systems. As under most Scanlon plans, a production committee was set up in each department or functional area of the plant. Members of the production committees were elected by the workers, and the department foremen or supervisors were also members ex officio. The major function of the production committees was to solicit, review and evaluate suggestions submitted by labour or management from the department concerned. The production committees were empowered to accept suggestions if they did not cost over a certain amount and did not affect other departments. The second component of the suggestion system is a screening committee consisting of an equal number of management and of worker representatives from the production committees. The activities of this committee include reviewing suggestions that either lie outside the jurisdiction of the production committees or on which the production committees have been unable to make agreed recommendations. The screening committee has a broader perspective, and reviews over-all company performance, changes in the organisation's environment and any major issues affecting general policy. Both the production committees and the screening committee meet at least once a month. It is important to note that these committees are active bodies which solicit, review and communicate decisions. A suggestions system under a Scanlon plan is much more elaborate than a traditional suggestions scheme.

The other distinguishing feature of a Scanlon plan is a company-wide bonus system. The premise underlying this system is that if labour and management cooperate, the performance of the company will improve and all should share in the benefits. Individual incentives, on the other hand, foster competition within the company, and are therefore contrary to the basic philosophy of Scanlon plans. The bonus system is established by determining a base ratio between labour costs and sales value of production (net sales plus inventory changes) from the company's past record. This ratio is a measure of labour productivity, and it is used to determine the company-wide bonus in a subsequent period. If the base ratio of labour costs to sales value is 40 per cent and if the actual ratio during a subsequent year of operation is 35 per cent, then 5 per cent of the sales value of production will be distributed to labour and management. In the plant considered here these calculations were made on a monthly basis. Twenty-five per cent of the bonus pool was put in reserve, and the remainder divided between labour and management in the proportion of three to one.

The plan was introduced in 1971. Mr. Frederick Lesieur, one of the leading Scanlon plan consultants in the United States, was brought in to help. He held a series of meetings with the workforce to explain the purpose and nature of the Scanlon plan. A vote followed in which the workers decided to adopt the plan for a trial year. The consultant then began work with management on developing the base ratio for the company bonus. Also, the production committees began to meet and some training was undertaken to teach members of these committees their roles. On the whole, the introduction of the plan was very rapid, taking only four to six weeks. (This is in sharp contrast to the establishment of the Rushton project, which cost labour, management and the consultants a great deal of time over a period of almost two years.)

The plan has since continued to be followed in this plant. Given the method for evaluating its effect, it is difficult to distinguish what proportion of the changes in productivity and work attitudes is directly attributable to the experiment. However, there have been positive changes which seem to have persisted over time, and the costs of the experiment have been quite low. From all accounts this experiment with new forms of work organisation has benefited both management and labour. As regards economic results, a Scanlon plan provides a unique means of measuring productivity changes, namely the bonus. The basic assumption is that given an accurate base ratio of labour to sales values of production, changes in the current ratio reflect changes in productivity. Therefore, payment of a bonus reflects positive productivity changes. The only major problems facing the plant since the introduction of the plan have been due to fluctuations in the demand for the goods produced: since the plant is largely dependent on one major customer, changes in demand by that customer affect sales and thus the bonus system. For example, early in the plan's operation there was a fall-off in demand which affected the existence and size of bonuses: in 1971 an average bonus of only 3 per cent of payroll was paid for six months. The bonus averaged between 7 and 8 per cent in 1972, 11 per cent in 1973 and 5 per cent in 1974. From 1971 to 1974 bonuses were paid in 70 per cent of the months. Other analyses of company records seem to confirm that productivity increased over the first three years of the programme.[11] (While the data seem to support the existence of productivity improvements for this plant, it is important to note that the analytic techniques used to isolate the productivity effect of the intervention at the Rushton mine, where no differences were found, were not employed in the analysis for this chemical plant.)

As already stated, suggestion-making is a cornerstone of Scanlon plans, and one of the best indicators of whether such a plan is working. The number of suggestions generated during the first three years of operation remained quite high: there were 231 in 1971, 201 in 1972 and 179 in 1973. Although the figures for the succeeding few years are not available, it seems that the rate of suggestions was about the same. Although the absolute number dropped slightly, the nature of the suggestions changed. Whereas many of the initial suggestions concerned how to improve the environment at work (e.g. a new fan) but did not relate to productivity, as time went by the number of such suggestions fell and the number of suggestions aimed at increasing productivity rose. Another indicator is the number of people making suggestions. In 1971, 82 per cent of all the hourly and salaried personnel made suggestions. This high rate of individual participation has continued. In short it seems the plan generated a good many suggestions, which had some effect on the bonus. They also provided opportunities for the workers to participate, to generate ideas about improving work, to learn about the functioning of the plant and to receive recognition for their contributions. The proportion of suggestions accepted by the production or screening committees exceeded 80 per cent.

Data on safety, turnover and absenteeism were not available. However, work attitudes were measured before the plan had been introduced and twice after it had been in operation (the last measurement taking place 11 months after the plan had been introduced). Analysis of work attitudes before its introduction indicated that there was a high degree of satisfaction over the plan (over 90 per cent expressed satisfaction). This contrasts with other situations in which it is not uncommon for a Scanlon plan to be introduced where there is much conflict between labour and management. Given this high level of satisfaction there was not much room for further improvement. However, after 11 months 100 per cent of the managers and 82 per cent of the workers reported that participation had increased. Both of these groups (93 per cent of the management, 72 per cent of the workers) felt that communication had improved. In terms of co-operation, 77 per cent of the managers and 71 per cent of the workers felt there was an improvement. Not only had participation, communication and co-operation increased, but also the respondents felt at the third measurement that these features would continue to improve. In general the atmosphere was one of continued trust and high satisfaction.

Another way to assess the effectiveness of a Scanlon plan is to see whether it is adopted in other plants. The manager of this particular plant voluntarily opted to try the plan in 1971, and the eight other plant managers in the Division had the same option. In the three following years a Scanlon plan was introduced in three other plants. Since these were voluntary decisions, it would seem the plant managers felt the plans would benefit them.

Autonomous work groups in a new processed food plant with a non-union workforce (Topeka)

In the United States the manufacture of dog food is a large and highly competitive industry. In the late 1960s the General Foods Corporation, which is one of the major food manufacturing and marketing firms in the United States, decided to set up a dog food manufacturing plant within its Gaines Pet Food Division. The plant is located in Topeka, a town of about 100,000 people and capital of the State of Kansas, in the Middle West of the United States. The town is the site of the state university, and the local educational level is high. The surrounding countryside has long been a very rich farming area. This kind of local setting provides what most people would regard as an attractive example of "the American way of life". In the past 20 years a considerable number of large factories have been built, and at present several of them employ over a thousand workers.

The General Foods Corporation maintains fairly close control over its subsidiaries. In order to take advantage of centralised purchasing, shipping and production planning, the corporation's central staff makes a number of decisions in these respects. Its operating plants are also normally expected to follow a set of procedural arrangements with regard to personnel and other matters. In addition, the Corporation tries to ensure that its managerial staff move from plant to plant so that they will maintain a sense of identification with the Corporation as a whole. Since this particular plant is only one of several similar plants owned by the Corporation and making the same single product, it must compete with its sister plants in order to be assigned favourable production quotas by the corporate office. Thus the objective for the plant is not sales volume or profit, but cost of goods produced: its managers have no control over such things as sales price or purchasing decisions; all they can do is try to ensure that it produces the final product at as low a cost as possible on the basis of the raw materials that are purchased for it.

Although the technology is fairly complex, it is not nearly as complex as that of a chemical plant or a petroleum plant. There are only minimum standards with respect to the quality of the product, and the technology is a fairly established one. The basic raw material is grain, which is cooked and transported through the plant by a substantially automated process. At the end of this process the dry dog food is bagged and taken to a shipping room, from where it is typically despatched by rail. Many of the jobs in the plant are of a monitoring and maintenance type, but a few jobs at the end involve relatively repetitive packaging and warehousing tasks. The plant has about 75 manufacturing and 35 office, professional and managerial employees. Most of them are white males in their first or second manufacturing job. There is a plant manager and an assistant to him. Reporting to them are the team leaders, each of whom is responsible for one of the three teams that operate the plant. There are about 25 workers per team.

The plant operates around the clock, and the teams rotate shifts every six weeks. There is no union in the plant. Although there have been a few occasions in which preliminary soundings have been taken by unions, no formal organising drive or election to certify a union as a bargaining agent has ever taken place. Other plants in this corporation are unionised.

There had been some previous experiments with work re-structuring in the corporation, but none as extensive as the project described here. The particular individual who persuaded the corporate management to launch the project had been a plant manager and had begun to look for a new and better approach to managing as a result. He became acquainted with work re-structuring and was able to convince others that it should be tried out. It was decided to operate a new plant with a new work structure from the beginning. The plant was not to be just a better place to work: it was to combine a better quality of working life with economic effectiveness. Although there may have been some thought on the part of the creators of the plant that it would provide a chance for them and others in the corporation to learn about new management approaches, economic effectiveness was the real justification for the plant. Apart from that, the guiding principles that seem to underlie most of the organisation of the plant are those of personal development and human resource utilisation: both the management and the non-management personnel talk about skill building and skill utilisation, and the person who advocated the idea of the plant continually emphasises the importance of making use of people's skills and utilising the full potential of individuals. Participation in decision-making is also regarded as important. The design of the plant reflects an egalitarian outlook: all the people working in the plant share the same eating areas, rest rooms, entrances, parking spaces and other physical facilities.

A strong and successful effort was made at the beginning to hire suitable managers. The top two managers showed much concern with the human factor and were committed to individual growth and development. From the very beginning the plant management tried to make the workers understand that the plant would be unlike the typical factory in the United States. Jobs were initially advertised as providing more meaningful work, and a large number of applicants applied for them. Employees were selected with an eye to whether they would be suited to a participative organisation. In addition, hiring decisions were made primarily by the individuals with whom the new workers would have to work: production workers eventually became involved in interviewing job candidates and making hiring decisions. The plant is basically organised around self-managing, autonomous work teams. Individuals in the teams are cross-trained so that they can do most of the production jobs in the plant. To learn all the jobs, the average person takes about three years. A few individuals have gone on to learn special skills such as electrical work or plumbing; these individuals do the maintenance tasks, since there is no special maintenance staff. To complement the autonomous work group structure and to encourage individuals to learn a variety of jobs, individuals are paid for the number of jobs they can do rather than for the particular job they may happen to be doing at the time. In addition, decisions about whether an individual has learned a particular skill are made by the work group, which is also responsible for handling absenteeism and other personnel problems.

Particularly at the start, the plant used a number of outside consultants. The managers and the teams went through extensive training programmes and drew quite heavily on what was known of the new practices they were trying to institute. They visited other plants, and members of the corporate staff also visited the plant and offered advice. It was always clear, however, that the administration of the project rested with the people in the plant, not with the external consultants.

The plant began production in 1971. Since it was one of the first in the United States in which a new form of work organisation had been tried out on a large scale, it was given wide newspaper and television coverage. Literally hundreds of articles have been written on the plant, and it has been deluged with visitors. This caused some problems for the managers. They were regarded by some others in the company as seeking too much publicity and as not identifying well within the Corporation as a whole. About four years after the plant began operation both the plant manager and his assistant left the Corporation. To some extent this reflected dissatisfaction on their part with the failure of the rest of the Corporation to adopt some of their practices and their inability to introduce further innovations in the Topeka plant. The plant seems to have successfully survived the departure of these two key individuals, and continues to function well. All the original novel features of the plant have been maintained, although the diffusion of the innovations to other plants remains limited. Some people within the Corporation think that resistance may have been built up in the rest of the Corporation because of the large amount of nation-wide attention paid to the innovations.

There is every indication that the plant is a success. Production costs are extremely low (about 30 per cent less than in a sister plant), absenteeism and turnover rates are also low (both about 3 per cent), and attitude survey results show very high job satisfaction. Few dispute the success of the plant, but there has been a considerable amount of speculation about the reasons for it. Some writers have tried to explain its success in terms of finding just the "right kind of workers", while others have tended to explain it in terms of the high level of freedom that the workers have to plan and organise their own work. There seems to have been a successful blending of a particular approach to management with a particular set of people to produce an extremely effective combination. It remains to be seen whether this particular approach is transferable to other parts of the organisation and to other organisations.

Quality of work programme for unionised white-collar
workers in the Tennessee Valley Authority

The Tennessee Valley Authority is one of the largest power generating utilities in the world. Its annual production through hydro-electric energy, fossil fuel and nuclear power amounts to 116 million megawatt-hours, with revenues of about $1,500 million. The Authority's power transmission network is interconnected with neighbouring power systems serving areas from the Gulf of Mexico to the Great Lakes. It employs over 24,000 people, all in the Tennessee Valley. The Authority is a corporate agency of the federal Government, and was created by an Act of Congress in 1933. It has a high degree of autonomy, and in many ways has the characteristics of a private corporation. All the powers of the corporation are vested in a three-member board of directors appointed by and reporting to the President of the United States. The general manager, who is the principal administrative officer, is appointed by and responsible to the board.

From the beginning, the Authority encouraged the formation of employee organisations. Between them, seven different bargaining unions represented almost all of the employees by 1943. "Co-operative conferences" were formed early in the history of the Authority as a part of the basic structure of labour-management relations. They are composed of managers and non-management employees in approximately equal numbers. There has usually been a conference in most of the Authority's workplaces, and there are 90 such conferences at present. The establishment of such co-operative conferences has been the outcome of formal negotiations, and they deal primarily with the kind of local problems that develop in any workplace and cannot be solved by collective bargaining. However, the co-operative conferences covering the Authority's workforce have often dealt with matters of only minor importance, because the collective agreement prohibits them from discussing remuneration or other conditions of work that might be matters for collective bargaining.

In 1973, discussions concerning a quality of work programme took place between the National Quality of Work Center and some members of the top management of the Authority. Strong suport for the project was found among the appropriate union officers in one of the Authority's 27 divisions, namely the Division of Transmission Planning and Engineering. That division is responsible for planning and designing transmission facilities for the Authority's entire network, which includes some 17,000 miles of high-voltage transmission lines and 640 sub-stations. More specifically, the division is concerned with transmission siting, environmental impact analysis and the design of sub-stations and other physical facilities, and prepares final designs, specifications and cost estimates for equipment and material. The division is located in Chattanooga, Tennessee, a historic old town with about 200,000 residents. The division is made up of some 380 white-collar workers—about 50 management and supervisory personnel, 145 engineers, 145 general support workers, and 40 clerical and administrative personnel. This number has remained fairly constant over the past decade. The workers of the division are represented by the Tennessee Valley Authority Engineering Association and the Office and Professional Employees International Union. The former is an independent union, while the latter is an affiliate of the national trade union confederation, the AFL-CIO. In view of the union support it seemed logical to launch the programme within the division. A representative of the National Quality of Work Center visited the site and obtained formal local approval from both union and management representatives, and the approval of the presidents of the appropriate unions and of the management of the Authority as a whole was also forthcoming.

The main aim of the programme was to make work more rewarding and satisfying. A secondary aim was to create a more effective work organisation in order to hold down costs and increase productivity in the face of high inflation. Thus, improvements in both the quality of working life and organisational effectiveness were seen as legitimate outcomes of the programme. There also seemed to be a related desire on the part of both union and management to strengthen the co-operative conferences. There is strong support within the Authority for labour-management co-operation, and acknowledgement that the conferences have not been as effective as they might have. The quality of work experiment was based on a strong commitment to the idea that workers should be involved in decisions that affect their day-to-day work life, and that a joint body comprising representatives of management and workers should control the changes that take place because the workers have both the skills and the information required to solve their own problems. There is also a strong commitment to the idea of human growth and development, and to the belief that there are within the organisation considerable human resources that could be put to better use if an appropriate organisational design is developed by the people who will be affected by it. It is also felt that unions and management can co-operate in bringing about organisational change.

It was decided to set up a quality of work committee to guide the over-all change process, and to hire an independent consultant team to assist the committee. The 14 members of the committee were elected by the union and appointed by management in May 1974. The committee quickly selected the consulting team to work with it, and the team gathered a considerable amount of data on the existing situation through questionnaires and interviews. The committee met weekly and, in addition, a week-long workshop was organised for it. During the first six months of the project over 7,500 person-hours were spent in meetings concerning quality of work, and in November 1975, for example, such meetings were attended by 103 members of the personnel. The workshop seems to have played a decisive part in stimulating interest in the programme. It established a procedure for problem solving and identified eight problem areas.

An independent assessment of the programme by the Institute for Social Research was not yet completed at the time of writing. However, probably the most significant change resulting from the programme concerns co-operative conferences. The Authority's union-management contracts were amended in that respect in 1975. The revised contracts provide that co-operative conferences may discuss and make recommendations to the respective labour and management representatives on negotiable matters. This change seems to be directly attributable to the quality of work programme. In addition, the Authority's upper management seemed very satisfied with the progress of the programme, and was endeavouring to extend it to other divisions. Such an extension will be the main criterion of success within the Authority as a whole. At the time of writing it was not clear what the nature of the extension would be. The management decided to extend the programme in the Division of Transmission Planning and Engineering till the end of 1977. The project also seemed to have continuing union support. The original consulting team left after about a year, but the Authority was considering the employment of other external consultants, and hired an organisation development specialist as a regular member of the staff in order to facilitate the progress of the quality of work programme.

Within the division a number of changes were introduced as a result of the programme. These changes include a flexible work schedule, a change in the performance appraisal process and methods, a change in the pay system so that merit can be better recognised, and the setting up of a new department to handle environmental impact problems and a committee to work on problems of productivity measurement. The quality of work committee continued to meet and to deal with problems. Probably the most significant issue that emerged from the programme concerned decision-making. Basically, the issue is whether the quality of work committee is a decision-making body as such. Resistance appeared among middle managers in the division to the whole idea of the committee. Efforts were being made to define more clearly the authority of the quality of work committee to implement change, and to organise the committee in such a way that it would have the support needed to make further organisational changes.

GENERAL CONCLUSIONS

Although the cases that have been reported on in this monograph provide good examples of major types of work re-structuring experiments in the United States, they do not cover the full range. The following conclusions are based on the authors' direct knowledge of 25 of the 70 to 90 experiments with new forms of work organisation which they estimate to have originated between 1970 and 1976 (25-30 in new plants, 15-20 in old unionised undertakings and 30-40 in old non-unionised undertakings). The authors fully realise that they may be unaware of some important events and trends connected with cases of which they have no definite knowledge. Moreover, they would point out that the study of new forms of work organisation in the United States is hindered by a lack of sufficient information to evaluate the effectiveness of projects in the organisations in which they are conducted and in the broader social context (e.g. in the community or the industry). The supply of information on projects over the past seven years is not too encouraging. There are few, if any, projects that have generated data with sufficient controls to permit an objective assessment. Many of the accounts are very impressionistic.[12] The case studies in which much of the information has been made available are, of course, useful in themselves, but since different observers of the same projects report different results, the reliability of those accounts is open to question. In some cases an effort has been made to measure attitudes systematically, but often such data collection has not been frequent enough or has not extended over a long enough period.

A major theoretical problem affecting the initiation and evaluation of projects concerning new forms of work organisation in countries such as the United States is the definition of effectiveness or success. This is partly a matter of identifying the appropriate constituencies. The workers and the company represent two constituencies which are probably concerned with different outcomes of a project; productivity is traditionally a goal of the company, while increased earnings and job security typically enter into the worker's definition of a successful programme. For many projects the union is a third constituency; it is likely that the company and the union will define success differently. Moreover, within the company and the union organisations, the local manager and the local union branch may assess effectiveness differently from top management or the national union leadership. Customers or regulators (e.g. government agencies) will evaluate the effectiveness of a project in yet another light. The costs and benefits of a project could even be examined from the point of view of society as a whole.

One approach to defining effectiveness has been suggested by Goodman.[10] Under this approach effectiveness can be assessed in terms of explicit and implicit goals. Explicit goals are derived from the major constituencies and explicitly stated by the constituencies in their agreement to participate in an experiment with new forms of work organisation. For example, in the Rushton project, labour and management agreed to five goals: safety, productivity, earnings, job satisfaction and job skills. These goals were incorporated in a written document. The existence of implicit goals has been pointed out by writers on organisational effectiveness. All organisations have explicit goals, but in addition they need to maintain internal and external adaptability if they are to survive. Therefore the effectiveness of a project can also be assessed in terms of how the project affects relations within an organisation and the external relations between one organisation and another. A project could enhance the internal adaptability of the organisation, as in the Rushton project in which workers learned to perform multiple tasks so that absenteeism or emergencies were quickly adapted to. As regards external relations, a project might introduce certain methods of working that might increase conflict between an organisation and a government regulatory agency concerned with safety; this would be a negative consequence. The point is that an organisation's adaptability (and, thus, survival) is not always closely connected with the achievement of its explicit short-term objectives, and that changes in adaptability are not exclusively related to changes in productivity or quality of work. In any event, however, even once objectives are identified, their relative importance still needs to be determined. The following generalisations are made in full consciousness of the fact that this conceptual problem is still unresolved.

Location and scale of experiments

It is difficult to generalise about where work re-structuring projects are taking place in the United States: they seem to be spread across a number of different industries, types of organisations and geographical areas. A few exceptions, however, are worth noting. The new plant projects, like the Topeka plant experiment described earlier, all tend to be in manufacturing plants that are subsidiaries of much larger organisations. In addition, many of them (perhaps 20 or more) are located in the southern or south-western parts of the United States, where industrialisation is relatively recent.

Relatively few experiments with new forms of work organisation are taking place in undertakings where the workforce is unionised. The exception to this generalisation is the series of eight projects (one of which is the Rushton project) sponsored by the National Quality of Work Center and the Institute for Social Research.

Another noteworthy characteristic of the experiments is their relatively small scale. Experiments directly involving more than 500 workers are extremely rare, and none seem to involve more than a few thousand. Thus, large undertakings in the United States with 5,000 or more workers are relatively untouched by the experiments. In some cases small parts of large entities have undergone change, but in no case has this change affected the undertakings as a whole. The potential for such an extension seems to exist in the Tennessee Valley Authority and in some other quality of work projects in which organisation-wide labour-management committees have been created.

There are slightly more projects in the private sector than in the government sector. At least one reason for this seems to be that the private sector employs most of the organisational change experts.

Reasons for participation

It is impossible to ascribe decisions to participate in experiments with new forms of work organisation to any single predominant factor. There are, however, several common patterns. One of these patterns emerges in cases in which new plants have been opened by firms in which the older plants were rent by union-management strife and the management saw no better way of motivating the workers, achieving high product quality and recruiting an adequate workforce. In such circumstances, if some member of the management strongly advocated a new approach, firms have in a number of cases made experiments of the kind undertaken in Topeka. Some organisations may have tried work re-structuring in an effort to avoid unionisation; the management may have acted on the assumption that a new form of work organisation would create a more satisfied workforce and that as a result unions would be unable to organise the workers. It is true that most of the new plants in which work re-structuring has been tried were not unionised. It is very difficult to determine to what extent this factor has influenced managerial decisions to experiment with new forms of work organisation. In some cases it probably played a major role, but there is evidence that in other cases it played no role at all: in several cases the management has in fact lent support to union organisation drives in a new plant, and in one case (Rockwell International) the union was involved from the beginning.

In the Rushton Mining Company, like a number of other companies, the origins of an experiment can be traced to a particular individual, who was the chief operating officer of the company and who personally decided on a change. In the Rushton case, and in many others, such a decision was based not so much on an economic crisis as on a system of personal values that did not square with traditional approaches to management. The innovator therefore decided on his own to try running his organisation in a different way. This same pattern has emerged in a number of other work re-structuring efforts in relatively small undertakings. Surprisingly few projects seem to have started in the United States because of economic problems. Indeed, with the exception of a few experiments with Scanlon plans, by and large the projects have started because a single manager or set of managers were tired of the old ways of doing things or had experienced a value crisis. This motivation has had some interesting consequences in terms of the kind of results that are expected from the projects. Although it has not eliminated a desire for improved operating results, it has led to some emphasis on non-economic outcomes. Thus, in projects like the Topeka one, managers frequently talk about greater opportunities for personal growth and development, better workforce utilisation and people leading better lives as important outcomes of the work re-structuring effort.

The commitment process

Commitment to new forms of work organisation seems to be achieved in two ways. The first might be described as "top-down": the top decision-maker (or makers) is won over to the idea of a work re-structuring programme and essentially orders it into existence. In the second case, although discussions may begin at the top, an effort is made to gain broad scale commitment in the organisation to the change project. Usually a vote is taken of all members of the organisation to see if they wish to go ahead with the project. This is typically done, for example, before the introduction of a Scanlon plan and on many of the quality-of-work programme sites, such as Rushton. The rationale behind a ballot in these cases is that change can take place only if the desirability of change commands widespread acceptance and commitment.

Role of consultants

Most work re-structuring projects in the United States have been carried out with the assistance of professional consultants. In most cases these consultants have not been employees of the company. External consultants have usually come either from private consulting firms or from a university. It is not unusual to find that a succession of consultants have been associated with a project. The typical consultant is so specialised that no single one is likely to feel comfortable dealing with the broad range of issues that are involved in a comprehensive organisational change. Thus, as work re-structuring projects expand to cover a wider range of subjects, new consulting help is sometimes brought in. At present there is little evidence on the comparative effectiveness of specialised internal advisers and external consultants. In fact, it is only recently that companies have employed significant numbers of internal advisers to help them with work re-structuring projects. It is also interesting that, with few exceptions (e.g. a project at Rockwell International), unions have not provided consulting help for work re-structuring efforts. Most unions in the United States do not have on their staff people with expertise in new forms of work organisation.

Communication

Almost every experiment with some new form of work organisation has been marked by an increased effort to provide individuals with information about their own and other people's performance. It has also included collecting and reporting data on work-team performance so that autonomous work groups may be in a better position to govern their own performance. In some cases organisations have provided a wider range of information. For example, they have provided information on pricing policy, purchasing, marketing, and have generally tried to help individuals to understand the over-all operation of the organisation better. These organisations have, in short, become more open. In some firms even information on individual salaries has been made public, a hitherto unheard-of practice in most large firms in the United States. It should be noted that many of these communication changes have come about not because they were originally planned by the organisation but because as workers have become more involved in such work re-structuring activities as the re-design of jobs and pay systems, they have requested this information to be able to function more effectively.

Decision-making

In almost every experiment with new forms of work organisation there has been a change in the nature of decision-making. Usually individuals are given more scope to decide how their work should be done. This kind of change is discussed below under the heading of re-design of jobs. Some companies have also made considerable efforts to involve their workers in the elaboration and application of personnel policy and in a host of other decisions concerning the future of the organisation. The quality of work programme of the National Quality of Work Center and the Institute for Social Research probably carries this approach further than any other. A quality of work committee is used to represent workers throughout an organisation for decision-making purposes. These joint labour-management committees make a whole range of decisions about their workplace. Although only eight projects exist in the United States which formally use this model, there are a growing number of cases in which organisations are using committees of their employees to design anything from pay systems to personnel policy.

Re-design of jobs

The re-design of jobs has been a feature of almost every experiment with new forms of work organisation. However, several different approaches have been taken. In most of the early work re-structuring efforts, a strong emphasis was placed on individual job enrichment; in these cases an effort was made to provide as much responsibility, autonomy, and feedback as possible for each individual job. More recently, a considerable number of projects have emphasised autonomous work group or teams. In the Topeka and Rushton projects, for example, the idea was to make them responsible for production, and in this way to give individuals, as members of their teams, more feedback and autonomy and a better understanding of what they were producing. The team approach has typically been taken in plants that are new or use process technology. At present both individual job enrichment and the promotion of more autonomous work groups are still at an experimental stage, and it is hard to say which of the two predominates. To some extent, it seems that an effort is being made to diagnose the weaknesses of the work situation and to decide which approach is likely to be more effective. On the whole, this solution has led to team projects in process production and individual job enrichment in most other cases.

Selection and training

The selection system used in the Topeka plant has been fairly commonly followed when new plants entered production. However, in most change projects the selection process has not been dramatically affected by work re-structuring, apparently because in existing plants little new personnel is required. Almost regardless of the nature of the work re-structuring effort, however, a higher priority seems to be attached to training. In most of the projects workers have been trained either to do other jobs in rotation or to cope with an expansion of their own previous assignment. In some cases, training in team work has also been included. This has usually involved training in interpersonal skills, team functioning, and how to make meetings effective. Career planning has been added in some organisations, as have courses in economics so that the workers can better understand the nature of the enterprise they work for.

Evaluation systems

In relatively few of the projects has the performance evaluation system been affected: by and large it is still a process in which superiors analyse the performance of their subordinates. In a few cases, however, evaluation has progressed beyond trait rating, in response to the requirements of management by objectives. In the Topeka case, for instance, individual evaluation decisions are now taken by the peer group. This seems to be a particularly common practice in new plants, but is otherwise rare.

Reward systems

There has been a substantial amount of change in reward systems. In some cases the system is changed to correspond more closely to an already evolving work re-structuring programme. Typical of such changes are payment for skills rather than for the actual job the worker may happen to be doing and, in some cases, the re-evaluation of a job in order to pay for additional duties that may have been added as a result of job enrichment. In a few cases, such as in the UAW-Harman Industries project at Bolivar, Tennessee, or the Rushton project, the over-all work re-structuring programme has led to consideration of a gain-sharing plan. It is important to note, however, that in such cases gain-sharing is usually a purely incidental result of the change introduced.

In other cases the main initial change introduced in an experiment related specifically to the reward system. Probably the most common project of this type is the company-wide bonus system of the Scanlon plans. It is generally agreed that there has been a tremendous though unquantified surge of interest in Scanlon plans. This interest seems to stem from their participative nature and the fact that they promise increases in productivity.

There are several other new approaches to reward systems that should be mentioned. A number of organisations have abandoned the traditional distinction between wage earners paid by the hour and salaried employees paid by the month, and a few organisations are experimenting with programmes that allow workers to pick their fringe benefits. It is also becoming a very common practice to display notices of job openings. This allows people to apply for the positions they want, and often makes salary information more public. Finally, a few organisations have made successful experiments with employee participation in the designing of pay systems, in respect of either base pay or bonus plans.

Plant layout

In a few cases, as in Topeka, an effort was made to adapt the layout of the plant to the practices that were to be introduced. This has usually meant more equal access to physical facilities. In a few cases (e.g. a Mead paper plant) the layout of machinery and work spaces conforms to the theory of socio-technical systems and thus leads naturally to the formation of teams and an improvement in communication. In a few cases the workers have also participated in decisions concerning the design of the work space they were to occupy in new or remodelled facilities. On the whole, however, the modification of physical layout and facilities is not a major feature of most of the projects.

Work scheduling

There have been quite a number of experiments with unusual hours of work in the United States—probably over a thousand. All sorts of systems have been tried, including a four-day work week; part-time working by two people to fill one full-time job; allowing workers to set their own starting and finishing times during the day; and allowing workers to set the length of their own work day. In most cases, however, these experiments have not been part of larger projects of work re-structuring.

Effects on the workers

It is too early to make a final assessment of what can be exepcted from new forms of work organisation, though certain tentative generalisations can be made. Increases in productivity seem to result from about half the projects, while in the other half no change occurs. Most of them seem to create more skilled and flexible workforces. Most projects also seem to result in increases in job satisfaction, and in feelings of personal growth, job involvement and organisational commitment. Absenteeism, turnover and lateness of arrival at work seem to be very much reduced with most of the projects; this tallies with the finding that job satisfaction increases.

In assessing the potential of new forms of work organisation, it is important not to lose sight of the problem of individual differences. The characteristics of work tend to match characteristics of the individual doing it (e.g. the worker's needs and abilities). The rationale for many of the experiments with new forms of work organisation is that current forms of work are incongruent with characteristics of the individual. The argument is that people want greater opportunities for achievement, growth, and control over their environment, and that current forms of work deny such opportunities. However, not all workers want these opportunities, and indeed some may regard them as threatening. The problem is that neither old nor new forms of work organisation include machinery to permit the expression of individual differences.

Effects on supervisors and management

There are a number of unintended consequences that may affect the long-run viability of a project concerned with new forms of work organisation. One of these consequences relates to first-line supervision. Such projects require a total re-structuring of the organisation. The objective is to change the character of work not only for the blue-collar workers but also at all other levels of the organisation. Most projects are designed to increase the personnel's control over its work environment. This generally takes the form of passing certain responsibilities to the workforce. Proponents of new forms of work organisation believe that the change in control does not merely take responsibility from one segment of the organisation and give it to another but rather increases the whole influence structure; production workers take over activities performed by management and management's role expands into new areas. Actually the re-structuring of work puts a heavy strain on the first-line supervisor. Most new forms of work organisation require first-line supervisors to stop performing much of their traditional role, and often to perform new tasks (e.g. planning) that go beyond their existing skills. Thus the simple fact of change creates a high level of perceived role ambiguity for the supervisor. The resulting stress may affect the supervisor's performance and acceptance of a work re-structuring experiment. In most cases it has been unanticipated. Management or the external consultants rely on training and counselling to meet this stress, but those measures are not highly developed in this field.

The changes brought about through experiments with new forms of work organisation have cumulative repercussions throughout the whole organisation. Often the experiments are initiated at the highest level of the organisation and most attention is paid to implementation at the lowest level, the roles of middle and upper management being sometimes ignored. Nevertheless, job roles at those higher levels are changing too, and require certain activities to be given up and new skills acquired. The implications of role ambiguity for middle management are the same as those identified for the first-line supervisor: stress can affect performance and acceptance of the experiment. There is some evidence that when middle management becomes alienated from an experiment, its viability will be threatened. A vital point to bear in mind would therefore seem to be that when a comprehensive organisational change is made, action must be taken at different levels of the organisation simultaneously; most of the current experiments seem to be focused on one level at a time.

The personnel function

Experiments with new forms of work organisation have posed an unintended challenge to the personnel function. A special set of skills, that are often not found in most personnel or industrial relations departments, are needed to introduce an experiment successfully in either a new or an existing plant. This absence of skills raises questions about the effectiveness of these departments, and has led to some dismissals, which in turn may lead members of such departments to feel threatened and to resist change.

Even in a new plant, where the basic personnel functions (e.g. selection and training) may be necessary, the process by which these functions are performed is different if a new form of work organisation is being tried out. For example, in the Topeka plant the personnel procedures and administration were primarily introduced and established by the supervisors of the new plant. In existing plants, the basic issues for the personnel department concern the processes of introducing change rather than the traditional practices of selection, training, appraisal, etc. Most personnel or industrial relations departments do not have the resources or technical skills to administer a major organisational change. Even in organisations that have organisational development specialists, the character of most of the experiments with new forms of work organisation is sufficiently different to pose a challenge to current organisational development practices. Also, the fact that in many respects the union must be integrated in the change effort as a joint partner poses problems that have not been tackled by most personnel or industrial relations departments.

It is not surprising, then, that in most cases external consultants have been used to introduce experiments with new forms of work organisation. The short-run problem seems to be how to train someone within the organisation (not necessarily from the personnel department) to work with the external consultant. The role of the insider will be to sustain the change effort after the external consultant leaves. In the long run the problem is to train a number of people in the organisation, both inside and outside the personnel department, to develop skills congruent with those required for the experiments.

Role of trade unions and their leaders

By and large the impetus for work re-structuring has come either from an outside party (a consultant) or from top management. With only a few significant exceptions, experiments with new forms of work organisation have not been made in response to union demands. Some trade unions have chosen to ignore the existence of work re-structuring projects in their own workplaces. That is, they have consented to projects but then withheld approval or disapproval of them. Where unions have participated in projects concerning new forms of work organisation, they naturally did so because they saw these projects as means of attaining their own objectives. Union involvement in the Rushton project, for example, was based on the belief that the project would contribute to better safety—a major objective of the United Mine Workers of America. Contrary to what some have feared, no union officials have lost their positions as a result of work re-structuring projects. However, a number of other, mainly unexpected consequences of the projects have emerged affecting union leaders, relations among members, and relations between unions and their local branches.

In most of these projects a labour-management committee is the principal means of integrating union and management efforts. The committee generally operates outside the traditional collective bargaining arrangements. Members of the committee have reported that through frequent meetings they have developed a better understanding of each other. That consequence should facilitate traditional labour-management negotiations. On the other hand the frequent association between management and union officers outside the traditional collective bargaining arrangements can raise feelings of distrust on the part of ordinary members of a union towards their leaders. This, in turn, weakens the leaders' commitment to the programmes as they try to re-establish their credibility.

In many of the projects concerning new forms of work organisation, the change is introduced within a particular department or work area in a given plant. This course of action has two implications for the internal functioning of the local union branch. First, the pilot project is different from the other operations of the plant. There may be differences in pay for the same work, or differences in the work activities. These differences are likely to generate (and have generated) feelings of inequity which lead to conflict among union members. A second unexpected consequence is that a new potential power structure is created within the local union branch. As work groups are given more control over their environment, there is a possibility that they will attempt to exercise greater control in the sphere of union activities. This will especially be true if the new work groups become cohesive. In the Rushton project some of the experimental groups voted en masse at union meetings, whereas in the past most of the men had not attended the meetings at all. Irrespective of whether this emerging power structure is good or bad, it constitutes a possible challenge to the existing power structure, and thus a potential source of conflict.

Most of the activities in the work re-structuring projects have occurred at the local level, while the authority for trade union participation in the experiments has generally come from the national executives of the unions concerned. As experiments proceed at the local level under a sheltered agreement, new forms of labour-management relations are developed. In this situation an interesting political dilemma occurs. On the one hand, at the local level, union and management have a mandate to innovate. On the other hand, and especially if the new labour-management arrangements are thought to go far beyond what could be incorporated in a future national collective agreement, the national organisation may view the local project as only experimental and temporary. In the long run the local project is unlikely to survive without legitimisation. This situation can result in conflict between the local union branch and the national organisation if the local branch wants the project to continue.

Another unexpected consequence is that political activities at the level of the national union organisation can affect the viability of the local project quite independently of the success of the project. It is unlikely that the entire power structure of any nation-wide union will uniformly support a programme of new forms of work organisation: there are ideological as well as practical reasons for unions to oppose such a programme. Therefore changes in the power structure at the national level might lead to a withdrawal of support for an experiment; such an act would generally terminate the programme since most experiments are based on mutual interest in participation.

Continuity

Clearly, acceptance of a new form of work organisation is not of interest primarily because of its novelty. Once it has been introduced, the next question is whether the new structure will continue in being. So far, many of the projects that have been started are continuing. Although some of them have changed course, there seems to be a spirit and thrust to them that survives even fairly major setbacks. In many other experiments, on the other hand, there is a problem in that once the external change agent leaves the organisation or the novelty of the project subsides there is a tendency to revert to old ways. Continuity is also of great theoretical importance for any programme of organisational change since it raises the question of when to evaluate the outcome of an experiment. If new structures tend to decline over time then one must be careful in defining the time period of an organisational experiment. Very little is known about institutionalisation: there have been no systematic investigations into why certain structures persist and others do not. Postulations of "lack of commitment" or "novelty" are inadequate explanations since it is still not known, for example, why commitment to new forms of work organisation declined. Unless more can be learnt about why structures persist (or do not persist) over time, experiments with new forms of work organisation are likely to have only negligible effects.

Diffusion

The current set of work re-structuring projects in the United States are important in their own right, but they are important also in terms of stimulating further projects. More attention should be directed to the process of diffusion. At the national level a variety of centres are trying to diffuse ideas relevant to experiments with new forms of work organisation. These centres are in competition with each other for the same resources, and their own survival gives cause for much concern. Important questions are whether these centres operating at the national level are adequate to stimulate organisations and unions to participate in experiments with new forms of work organisation, and whether the Government should play a more active role. Another problem is how to design a project so that results in one organisation will have an effect on other organisations. So far, there has been only limited evidence that the success of a project in one firm will promote participation in similar projects by other firms. The Rushton project, for example, has become very well known because it was reported through various mass media. Yet no other coal mine has experimented with new forms of work organisation. An alternative approach is being tried in Jamestown, New York: there a number of firms in different industries have been working together in a labour-management committee to improve the economic viability of the town as well as in making experiments with new forms of work organisation in their respective firms. The participation of a number of firms has the advantages of reinforcing the validity of labour-management co-operation in such experiments, increasing the credibility of the principles on which they are based and encouraging other firms to participate. However, there is as yet no convincing evidence of the success of this approach.

Within individual firms most projects involve relatively few individuals: the experiments are usually made in small plants, offices or departments, and little attention is given to how to spread what is learned to other units. The reason for this state of affairs seems to be that most individuals connected with work re-structuring projects in the United States do not feel able to deal with systems larger than their own. In essence, they view work re-structuring as an art that cannot be reduced to formulae of general application and requires their personal attention; consequently the experiment must generally be on a limited scale because of the amount of personal attention it requires, and each experiment calls for a new approach. In general, very little thought is given to how diffusion will take place and very few steps are taken to ensure it.

Prospects

There are thus a great many unanswered questions and unsolved problems with respect to projects concerning new forms of work organisation in the United States. Some of these probably never will be adequately dealt with (e.g. the problem of individual differences), while others are tractable and probably will be (e.g. the future of the personnel function of management). It is not essential that all of these problems should be solved, and indeed there is every reason to believe that projects will spread even though not all the problems are solved. For one thing, the management systems that are being superseded have their problems as well. Furthermore, some of the projects are producing significant results, and this is a stimulant to diffusion. Finally, the values which underlie most of the projects are widely accepted in the United States, and as a result there is in many quarters a basically favourable stance toward them. Thus it can be predicted that the next few years will see a further growth in projects concerning new forms of work organisation in this country.

Notes

[1] *Business Conditions Digest* (Washington, US Government Printing Office), various issues.

[2] Agreement reached in March 1973, whereby the United Steelworkers of America and the ten largest steel companies in the United States agreed not to resort to strikes or lockouts at the national level during negotiations for a new national contract for the basic steel industry. See *Social and Labour Bulletin* (Geneva, ILO), No. 1/74, p. 27, and No. 2/77, pp. 141-142.

[3] See Irving Bluestone: "Creating a new world of work", in *International Labour Review,* Jan.-Feb. 1977, pp. 5-8.

[4] A description of all these bodies is to be found in National Center for Productivity and Quality of Working Life: *Productivity and quality of working life centers,* Conference report and directory (Washington, 1976). Further information is contained in Louis E. Davis: "Enhancing the quality of working life: Developments in the United States", in *International Labour Review,* July-Aug. 1977, pp. 53-65.

[5] Public Law 94-136.

[6] Now the American Quality of Work Center.

[7] See pp. 159-162.

[8] See note 3 above.

[9] See pp. 147-152.

[10] Further details will be found in P. Goodman: *Rushton Quality of Work Project: Interim report,* submitted to the Institute for Social Research and the National Quality of Work Center (Pittsburgh, Pennsylvania, Carnegie-Mellon University, Graduate School of Industrial Administration, 1975-76).

[11] B. Moore: *A plant-wide productivity plan in action: Three years of experience with the Scanlon Plan,* Report to the National Center for Productivity and Quality of Working Life (Washington, 1975).

[12] See E. Glaser: *Productivity gains through work life improvement* (New York, Harcourt-Brace-Jovanovich, 1976).